LEGENDARY LOCALS

OF

HUNTINGTON BEACH

CALIFORNIA

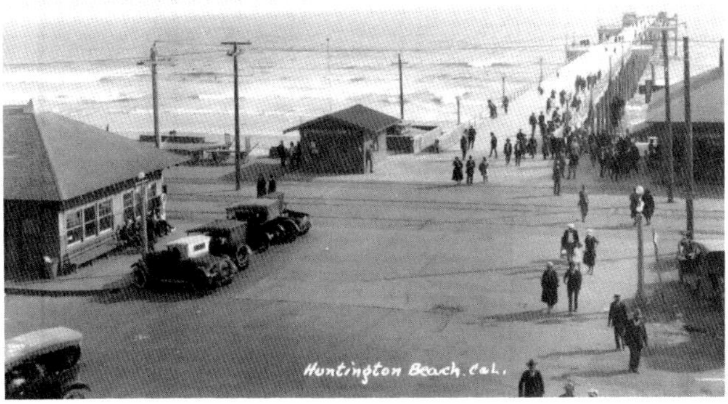

I0805759

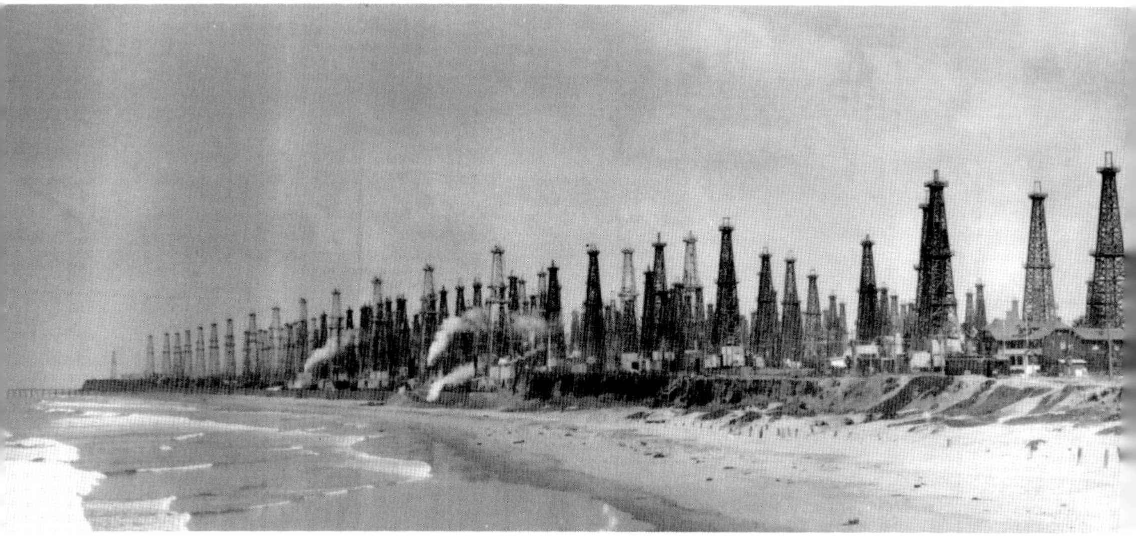

Oil

After oil was discovered in Huntington Beach in 1920, the city became a boomtown almost overnight. Though production has waned over the years, there is still plenty of oil being pumped in Huntington Beach, as well as just offshore. (Author's collection.)

Page 1: **By the Pier**

Downtown Huntington Beach is pictured in the early 1920s. (Courtesy Orange County [OC] Archives.)

LEGENDARY LOCALS

OF

HUNTINGTON BEACH

CALIFORNIA

CHRIS EPTING

LEGENDARY LOCALS

ISBN 978-1-4671-0186-8

Legendary Locals is an imprint of Arcadia Publishing
Charleston, South Carolina

Printed in the United States of America

Library of Congress Control Number: 2014944079

For all general information, please contact Arcadia Publishing:
Telephone 843-853-2070
Fax 843-853-0044
E-mail sales@arcadiapublishing.com
For customer service and orders:
Toll-Free 1-888-313-2665

Visit us on the Internet at www.arcadiapublishing.com

Dedication
This book is dedicated to the residents of Huntington Beach, both past and present.

On the Front Cover: Clockwise from top left:
The Salt Water Plunge (courtesy OC Archives), George Freeth (author's collection; see page 62), city leaders (courtesy OC Archives), Helen Harris (photograph by author; see page 32), Ed Manning (author's collection; see page 18), Southern California Veterans Association (courtesy OC Archives), Art Nerio (photograph by author; see page 122), Duke Kahanamoku (courtesy OC Archives; see page 63), Henry Huntington (author's collection; see page 17).

On the Back Cover: From left to right:
Golden Bear (Courtesy OC Archives; see page 42), Historic Methodist Auditorium (Courtesy OC Archives, see page 12).

CONTENTS

ACKNOWLEDGMENTS

There are many people over the years who helped teach me about this amazing city. In particular, I would like to thank Duane and David Wentworth, their mom, the late Alicia Wentworth, Chris Jepson, Jerry Person, and, last but not least, Cindy Cross, who provided invaluable support on the surfing chapter.

All images are from the author's collection unless otherwise noted.

INTRODUCTION

The birth of the place that came to be called Huntington Beach occurred more than 100 years ago. On what was originally a 30,000-acre Spanish land grant, the Stearns Rancho Company ran cattle and horses and raised barley. Around 1890, the city was called Shell Beach, becoming Pacific City in 1901, when P.A. Stanton formed a local syndicate and bought 40 acres along the beach. Stanton's goal was to create a town on the Pacific Coast to rival Atlantic City on the East Coast. The actual name of the city today goes back to 1904, when Pacific City became Huntington Beach in honor of H.E. Huntington, who brought the Pacific Electric Railway to the area.

On February 17, 1909, the City of Huntington Beach was officially incorporated. From that time, its history begins to truly take shape. It remained a sleepy seaside town until the famous oil boom in the 1920s. Almost every major oil company began production in the rich field below. Wells sprang up overnight; in less than a month, the town grew from 1,500 to 5,000 people. During the years that followed, Huntington Beach was known primarily for oil production and agriculture. Local farms grew lima beans, sugar beets, chili peppers, tomatoes, and similar truck-farming crops in the fertile soil. Expansions began in 1957, when annexations were made from large property holdings and many farmers asked for admittance to the city because of its sound tax base. From 1957 to 1960, Huntington Beach experienced its most rapid growth, increasing to 25 square miles through annexations.

In 1956, construction started on the huge Edison generating plant, and in 1963, the Douglas Aircraft Systems Center opened. This brought major industry to the city, employing nearly 8,000 people. During the 1960s, Huntington Beach became identified as Surf City when the popular Jan and Dean song of that name climbed the charts, bringing the fantasy of the beach lifestyle to the nation. Today, with the city hosting the International Surfing Museum and the US Open of Surfing, as well as many other contests and some of the best year-round recreational surfing, it continues to hold the title of Surf City, USA. But it is more than just the actual surfing that makes the place so special. It is the free-spirited attitude and independence of a place that always has (and seemingly always will) danced to its own drummer.

There are many ways to spend time in Huntington Beach. Museums, parks, shopping, and, yes, the beaches, contribute to an environment that is as ideal as it gets. Factor in some of the best weather in the United States, and it is no wonder that the city continues to grow at unprecedented rates, along with the growing influx of tourists. But, what to do first?

Apart from the popular beaches, it is worth noting that Huntington Beach is also a haven for nature lovers. The newly refurbished Shipley Nature Center is a lush, 18-acre natural area located smack-dab in the middle of scenic Central Park. In the nature center, opened in 1974, local wildlife thrives among native plants and trees. Butterflies, birds, snakes, and turtles—they are all found here, along with many interactive displays. The center includes 4,000 feet of well-maintained trails that wander through myriad habitats, including oak woodlands, Torrey pines, meadows, and Blackbird Pond, a freshwater wetland with mature willows and sycamores. The center's mission statement reads: "The Friends of Shipley Nature Center is a non-profit organization formed to manage the nature center as an ecological sanctuary for California native plants and wildlife and to provide environmental education in an urban setting in partnership with the City of Huntington Beach and the local community, and with the wider world." There are more than 70 parks in Huntington Beach, including the famed Bolsa Chica Ecological Reserve, a 300-acre coastal sanctuary for wildlife and migratory birds. A boardwalk bridge located on Pacific Coast Highway (PCH) crosses over a newly constructed tidal inlet, where a pretty, 1.5-mile loop trail can be found. The walk provides incredible wildlife viewing, and birders from all over the world flock here to take photographs and enjoy the majestic array of feathered friends.

This place is called "Surf City, USA" for a reason, and at the International Surfing Museum, it all becomes clear. This shrine, located just off Main Street, boasts surfing memorabilia, exhibits featuring surfing films and music, and, of course, relics related to the great Duke Kahanamoku, the famed Olympic swimmer who made surfing popular in the 1920s. But there are other historic sites that also help define the city. The Newland House is a restored 1898 home of Huntington Beach pioneers W.T. and Mary Newland. The picturesque Victorian farmhouse, located at 19822 Beach Boulevard, offers interesting, docent-led tours.

Some of the best surfing, swimming, and fishing in California can be found along the beaches in Surf City, USA. Huntington City Beach flanks Pacific Coast Highway between Beach Boulevard and Seapoint Street. Within this area is the famous Huntington Beach Pier, located where Main Street converges with Pacific Coast Highway. It is perhaps the most famous landmark in Huntington Beach. Here, restaurants, shops, hotels, bars, and more are all within earshot of the ocean, making every day seem like a vacation.

Huntington State Beach extends two miles from Beach Boulevard south to the Santa Ana River on the Newport Beach boundary. Here, as with the other beaches in Huntington Beach, there is a bicycle trail, fire rings for those enchanting bonfires at dusk, concessions, and places to rent bikes, boogie boards and other gear.

Want to treat your dog to a day at the beach? The popular Huntington Beach Dog Beach sits along Pacific Coast Highway, between Seapoint Street and Golden West Street. The beach has plenty of metered parking. One of the most popular dog beaches in the United States, it is maintained by a volunteer staff that even provides cleanup bags free of charge. Heading north toward Seal Beach is Bolsa Chica State Beach, which boasts RV camping with full hookups and pay showers. Bolsa Chica, formerly known as "Tin Can Beach," is a popular fishing spot for corbina, perch, sand shark, and more. Plus the Bolsa Chica Ecological Reserve is right across Pacific Coast Highway from Bolsa Chica.

Whether a visitor craves the action and energy of the beaches located near downtown or the more serene, pristine beauty of Bolsa Chica, the city's beaches offer something for everyone. This ocean paradise, a one-time dirt road along the sea, still lures the traveler, still holds magic, and still delivers on the promise of the California Dream.

That is the place. Now get ready to meet some of its people.

CHAPTER ONE

Historic Players

Incorporated in 1909, Huntington Beach remained a sleepy seaside town until the famous oil boom in the 1920s. Almost every major oil company began producing oil from the rich field below. Wells sprang up overnight, and in less than a month, the town grew from 1,500 to 5,000 people.

During the years that followed, Huntington Beach was known primarily for its oil production and as an agricultural area. Local farms grew lima beans, sugar beets, chili peppers, tomatoes, and similar truck-farming crops in the fertile soil.

Expansions began in 1957, when annexations were made from large property holdings, and many farmers asked for admittance to the city because of its sound tax base. From 1957 to 1960, Huntington Beach experienced its most rapid growth, increasing in size to 25 square miles through annexations.

In 1956, construction started on the huge Edison generating plant. In 1963, the Douglas Aircraft Systems Center opened. This brought major industry to the city, employing nearly 8,000 people.

During the 1960s, Huntington Beach became identified as Surf City when the popular Jan and Dean song "Surf City" climbed the charts, bringing the fantasy of the beach lifestyle to the nation. Today, the city hosts the International Surfing Museum and the US Open of Surfing, as well as many other contests and some of the best year-round recreational surfing. Huntington Beach continues to hold the title "Surf City, USA."

What follows is a closer look at some of the people that helped shaped the history of Huntington Beach.

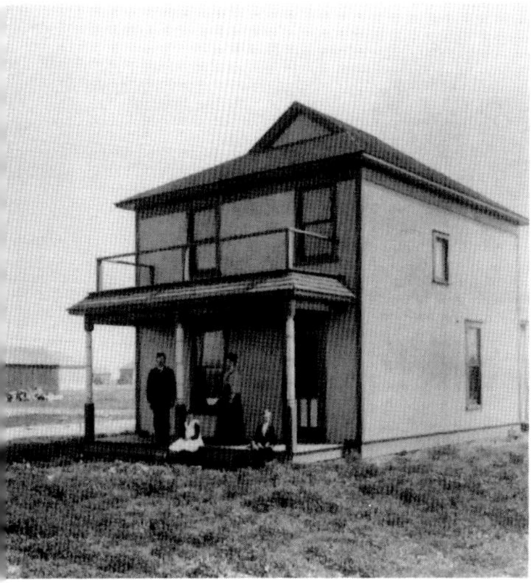

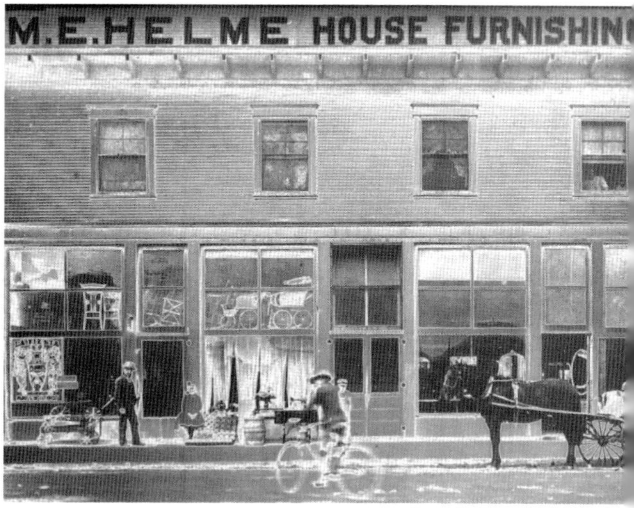

The Helme-Worthy House

One of the best-known homes in downtown Huntington Beach, the Helme-Worthy House (left) is also one of the most historic, as is the adjacent M.E. Helme House Furnishing Company building (right). As described on the approved application to the National Register of Historic Places, "these two buildings retain their integrity of location, setting, design, workmanship, materials, feeling and association with Huntington Beach's early settlement period. Although the residence is simple in style, it is the oldest house in town. Both provide the only visual picture of early Huntington Beach and its settlement period." The application for the M.E. Helme House Furnishing Company describes the structure as "the only surviving commercial building with the original Western falsefront architecture remaining in South and Central Orange County." The house was built in the 1880s and moved to Huntington Beach in the early 1900s. The furnishing company building was erected in 1904. Today, Susie Worthy, the great-granddaughter of Matthew Helme, runs the antiques store at the site and lives in the actual residence, which she and her husband have been restoring for a number of years. Matthew Helme played a vital role in the formation of the incorporated city of Huntington Beach. He owned the first furniture store in the city and served as mayor, too.

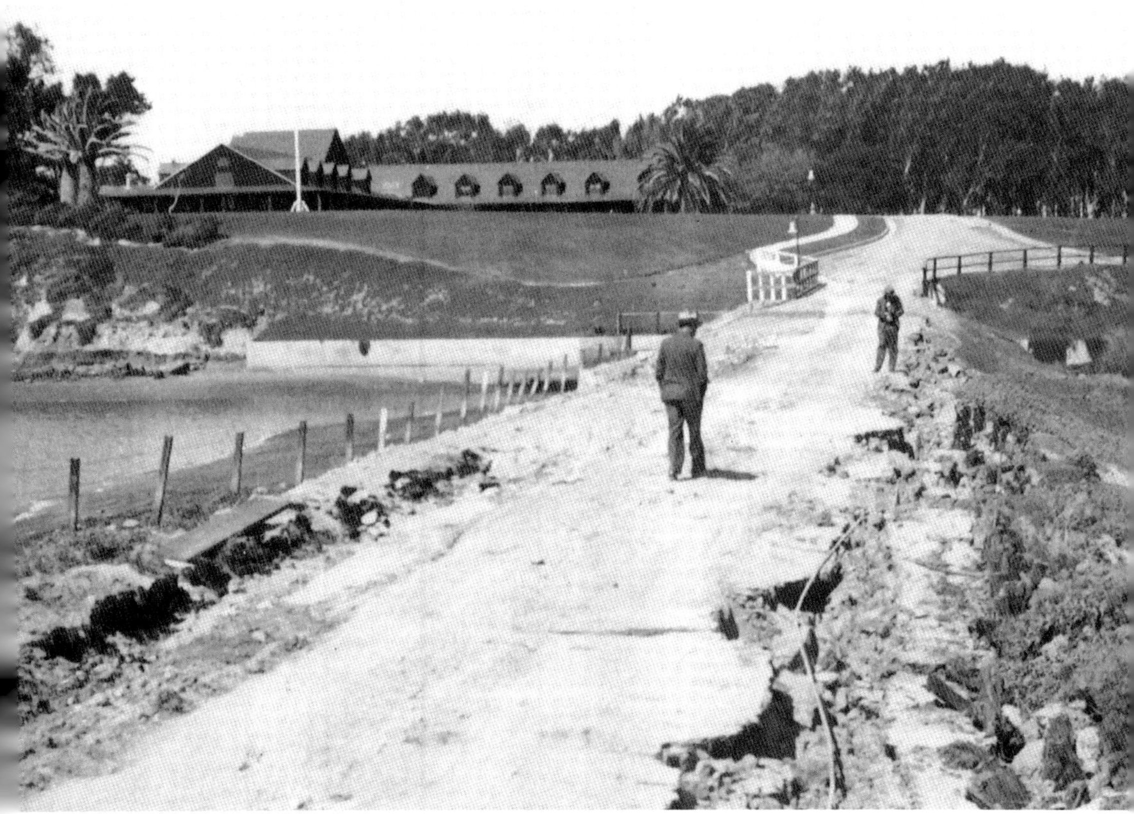

The Gun Club

What do Teddy Roosevelt, King Gustaf of Sweden, the Prince of Wales, and Pope Pius XII have in common (at least as it relates to Huntington Beach)? They all visited the Bolsa Chica Gun Club. Opened around 1900 on property that is now the Bolsa Chica wetlands, the club boasted a beautiful redwood and cedar hunting lodge and many amenities catering to the well-heeled duck hunters of the day. Initially, membership in the club was limited to 40, with an initial fee of $1,000 and annual dues of $60, making it one of the most exclusive clubs in the area. A great source of information about the club is David Carlberg, renowned microbiologist, environmental activist, and author of several books, including the exceptional *Bolsa Chica—Its History from Prehistoric Time to the Present*. Carlberg and his wife, Margaret, have long been active in the Amigos de Bolsa Chica. He also has a keen interest in the history of the gun club, where prominent local men with names like Torrance, Slauson, and Huntington roamed, and where Teddy Roosevelt left his footprints (and, no doubt, a few less ducks).

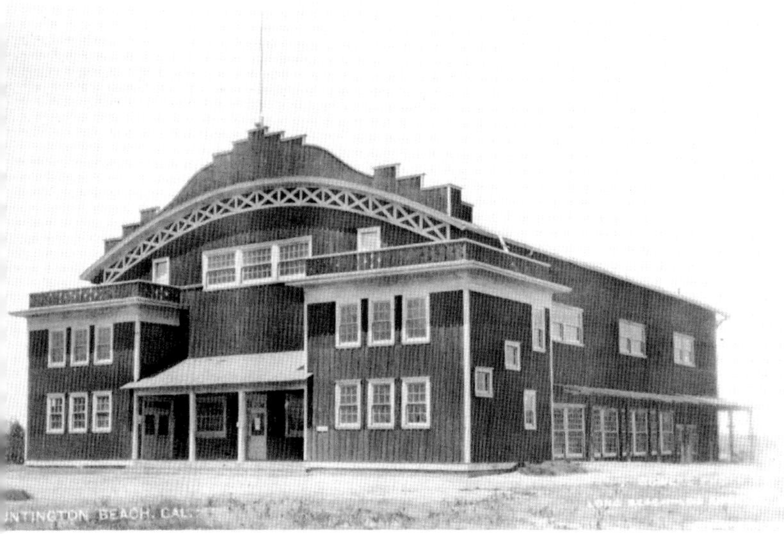

Methodist Auditorium

In 1906, city boosters attracted the Methodist convention away from Long Beach by giving up a large campsite and building a 3,000-seat auditorium for that denomination. For more than 10 years, visitors and residents flocked to the gospel meetings held here each summer, as well as to other conventions, like those of the Grand Army of the Republic. Today, the area is a residential district. (Courtesy OC Archives.)

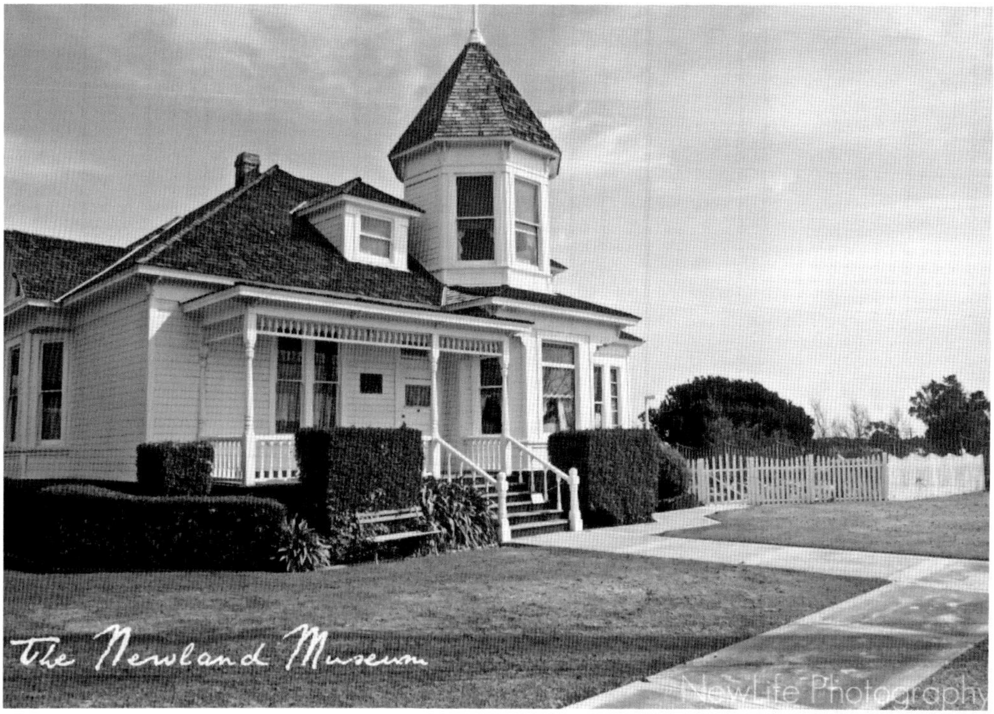

Newland House

Built in 1898 by W.T and Mary Newland near the intersection of Beach Boulevard and Adams Avenue, this beautiful two-story farmhouse has been lovingly restored by the Huntington Beach Historical Society and is now listed in the National Register of Historic Places. William and Mary Newland, two of the most notable pioneers in the area, lived here for 54 years and raised a family here. The original home and ranch at one time extended all the way from Beach Boulevard to Magnolia Street and from Yorktown Avenue south to Atlanta Avenue. This comprised more than 500 acres, and back then, the family planted and harvested sugar beets, celery, chili peppers, and lima beans. Tours of the house are offered. A visit to the site is highly recommended.

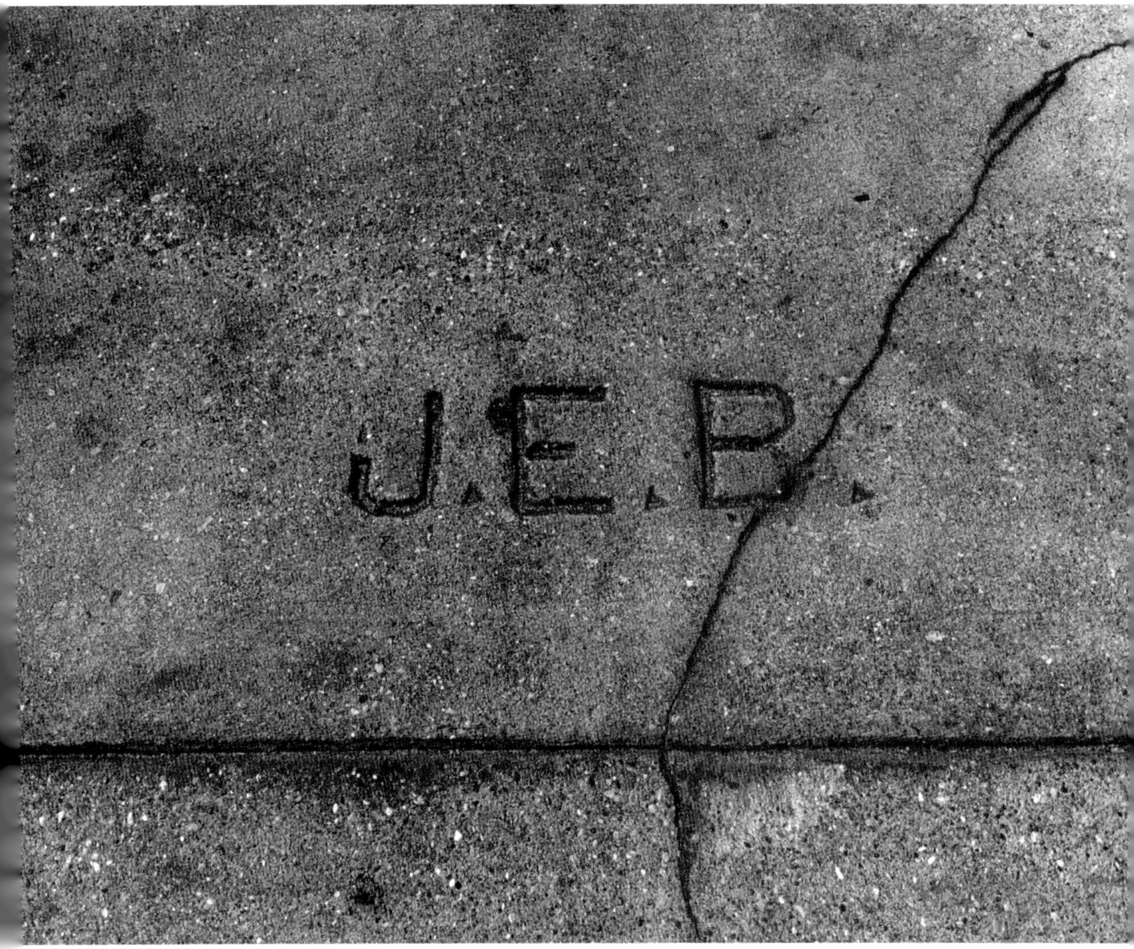

Look Down

Walking around downtown, one notices the initials "J.E.B." imprinted on certain sidewalks. Local cement contractor James E. Brunton inscribed those letters about 100 years ago. He did quite a job, as the letters still look sharp. A native of Kansas, Brunton lived in Huntington Beach for 33 years and was responsible for sidewalks all over Southern California. Wherever one sees those initials, one knows that he was there.

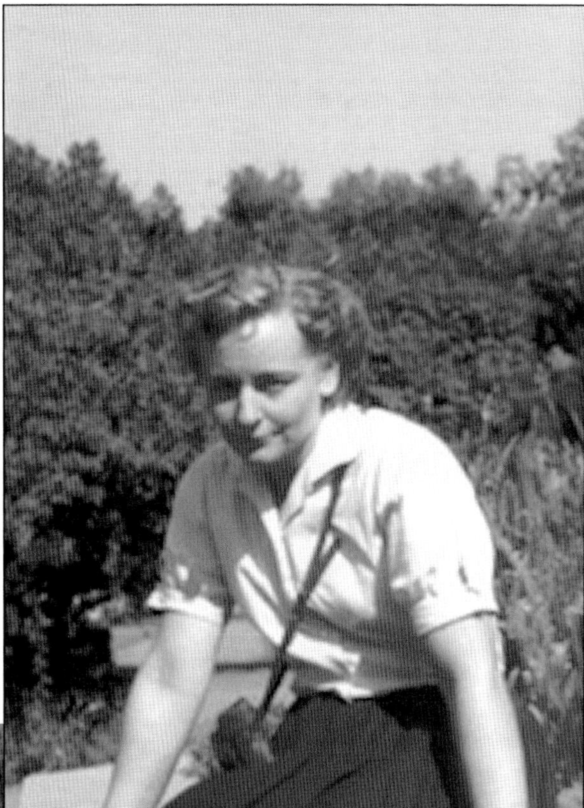

The Historian

As a descendent of three passengers of the *Mayflower*, Alicia Wentworth was born with history in her blood. Born Alicia Mae Becker on December 1, 1926, in Rochester, New York, she took off to California in 1947 with her older sister Melva and her family. Melva, her husband, George Mirch, their three kids, and Alicia hooked up a travel trailer to George's car and followed Route 66 all the way to California. They rented a space at the Municipal Trailer Park in a little town called Huntington Beach and set up camp on the beach for the next year. The first night, Alicia walked out on a beach for the first time in her life, looked at the sunset, and swore that she would never go back to New York. She kept that promise for 45 years. (Both, courtesy Wentworth family.)

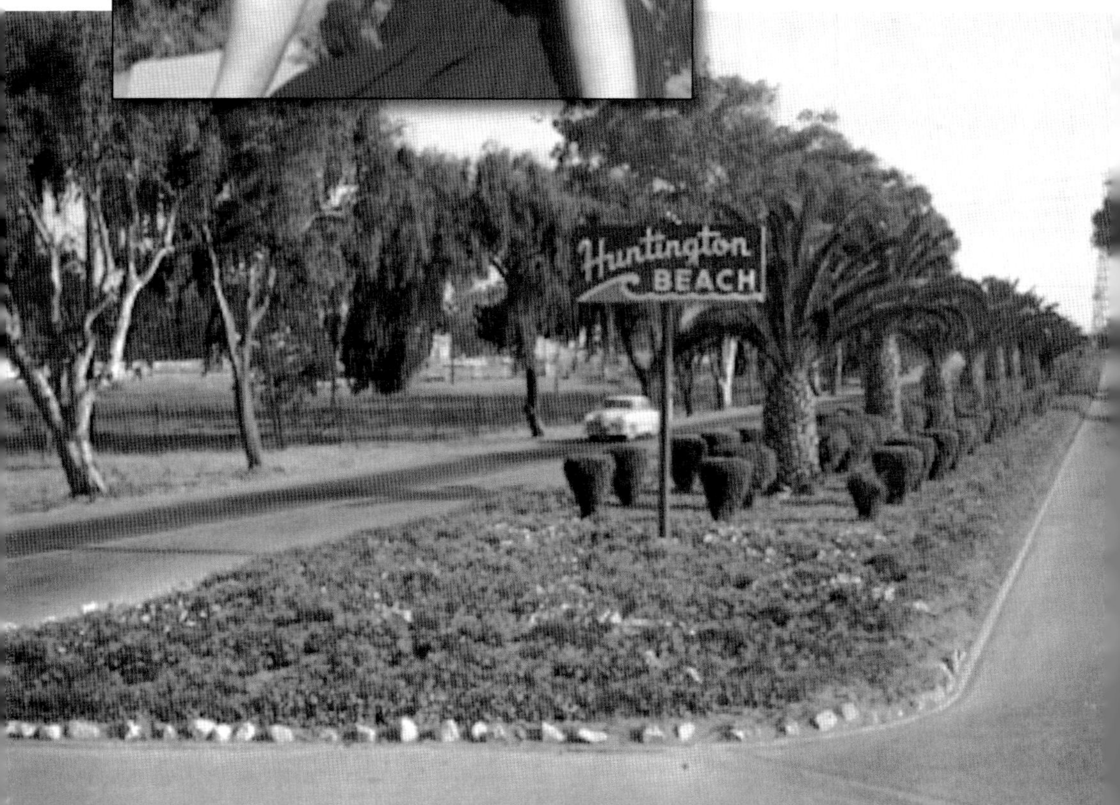

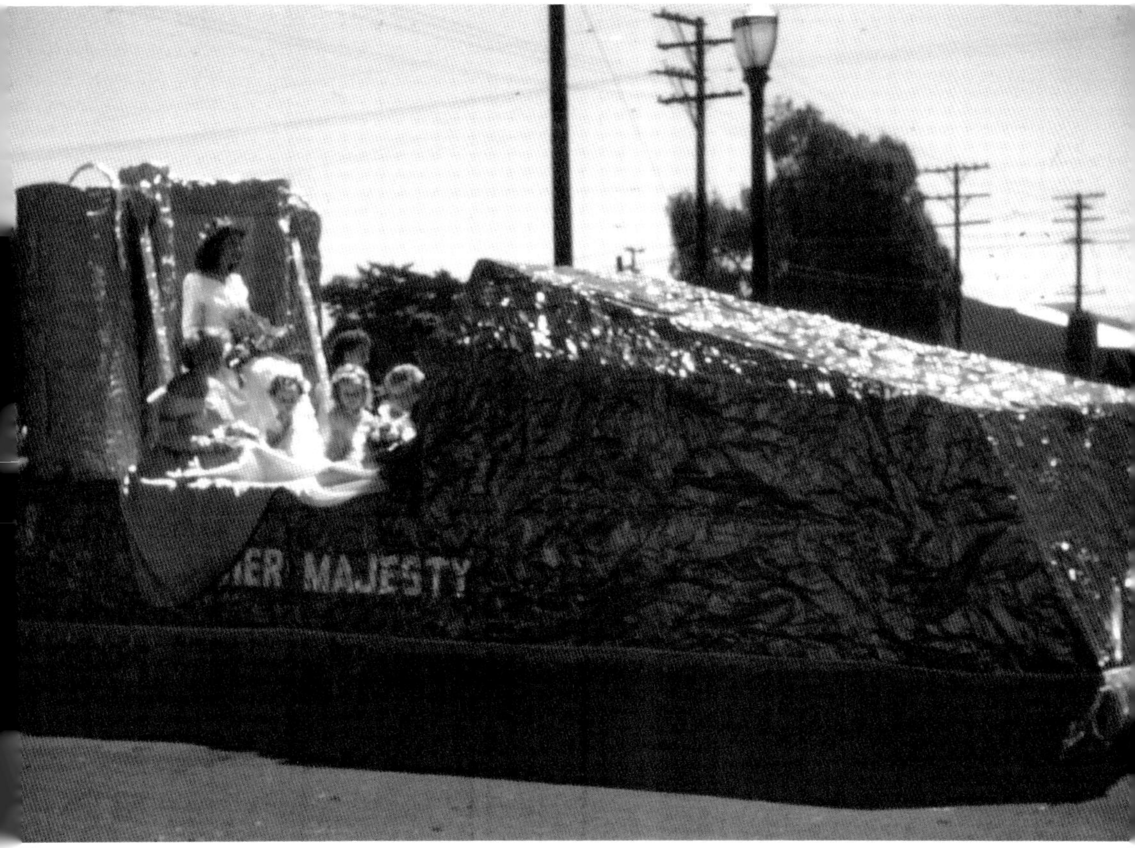

And the Photographer

George got Alicia a job at Kodak in Los Angeles. She would ride the Pacific Electric Red Car to work each day. It cost 10¢ to ride from Huntington Beach to downtown Los Angeles. Shortly after arriving, she met a young maintenance worker at the trailer park named Vernon Wentworth. They were married a year later. Vern was the grandson of Huntington Beach's first mayor, Ed Manning. They would have four children, twins David and Donna, Duane, and Diane. Alicia was rarely without her trusty 35-millimeter camera and constantly documented the childhood of her kids. In the process, she took hundreds of color slides of a growing Huntington Beach. This would become a remarkable Kodachrome history of her beloved town. She found work as a church secretary and as a legal secretary until finding a job as a receptionist in the city clerk's office in 1962, where she worked her way up to deputy city clerk. In 1973, after the death of City Clerk Paul Jones, Alicia Wentworth was appointed by the city council to fill out his term. She won her first election in 1974 and easily won reelections until her retirement in 1988. Upon her retirement, she was appointed city historian by the city council. This was her true calling. Wentworth amassed an impressive collection of historic photographs and documents that she would freely share with anyone who asked. She lectured at public functions, gave presentations to classrooms of school kids, wrote newspaper articles, appeared on local television shows, and even helped a young author, a fellow New York transplant, write a book about the history of Huntington Beach. She still always managed to find time to travel and to be a hands-on mother, grandmother, and great-grandmother. Alicia Wentworth passed away on September 1, 2006, at the age of 79. Her two sons, David and Duane, are on the city's Historic Resources Board and continue to carry the torch of historic preservation in Huntington Beach. Pictured is a float in the Huntington Beach Fourth of July parade around the mid-1950s.

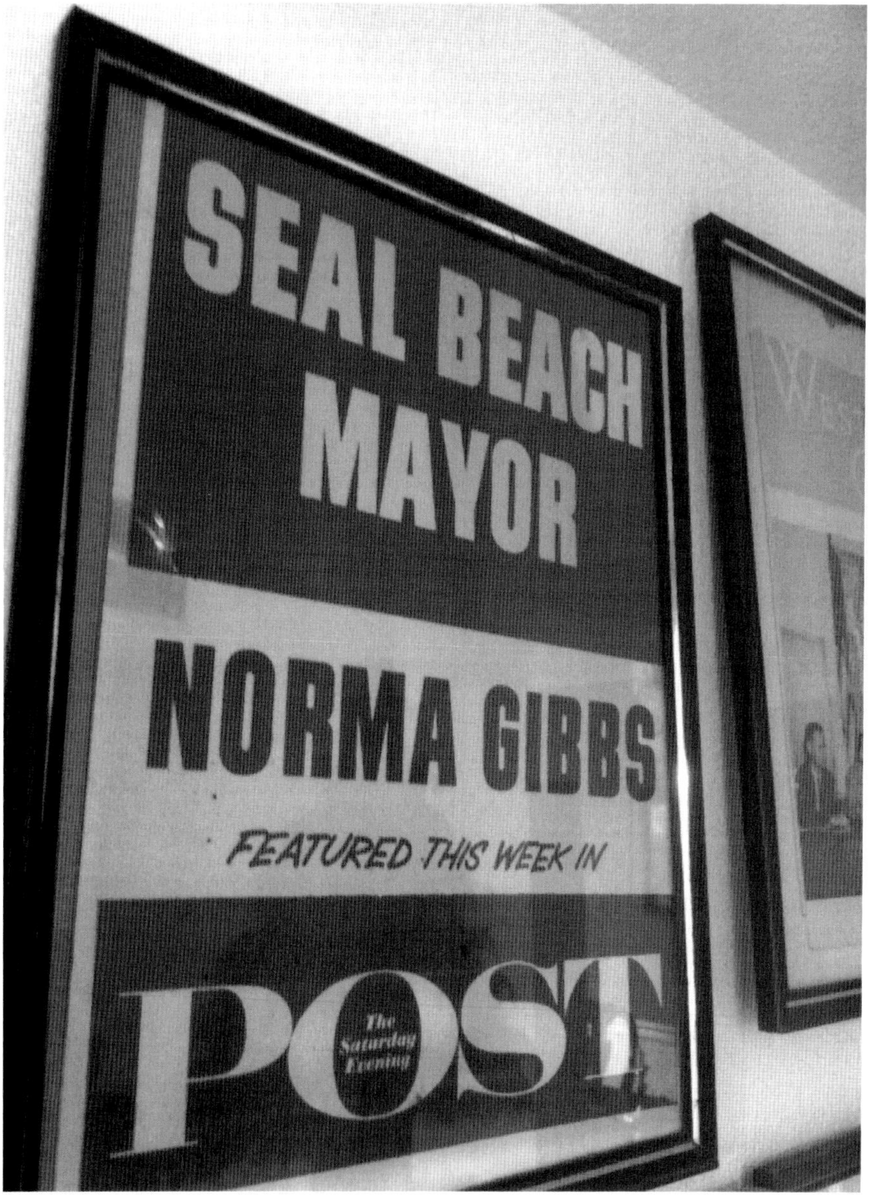

First Lady of Huntington Beach

In discussing Huntington Beach today, Norma Gibbs says how proud she is that the fight for open space was as successful as it was. "We received an award for having the best park system in the country and I'm still proud of that. We still have a wonderful system. Parks are scattered all around the city for everybody to enjoy. When I learned that the city had a goal to reach 200,000 in population, all of a sudden it became extra important to protect and preserve open space. People can't act like they live in mazes. People need open space to thrive." Today, Gibbs remains proud of all the parks, including Gibbs Butterfly Park, named for her in 1995. The walls of the Gibbs home are covered with plaques and tributes. Gibbs has a rich legacy in Huntington Beach, creating and preserving parks, bike paths, the beach, and wetlands. She became the city's first female mayor and founded Interval House, a shelter for victims of domestic violence.

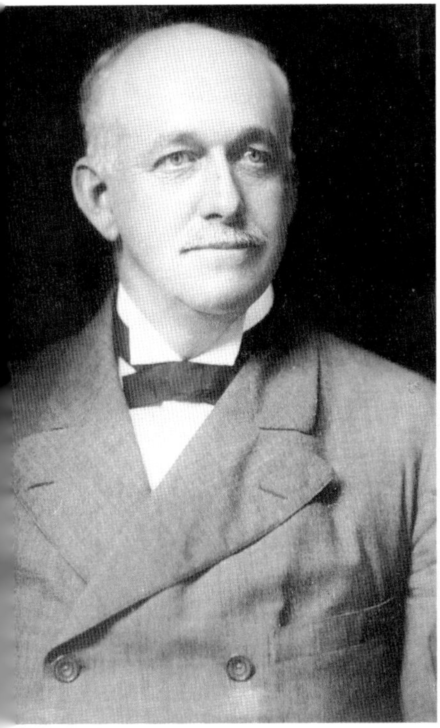

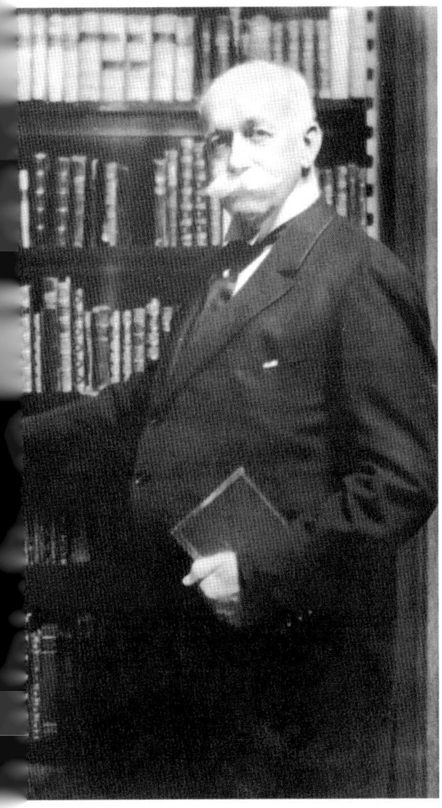

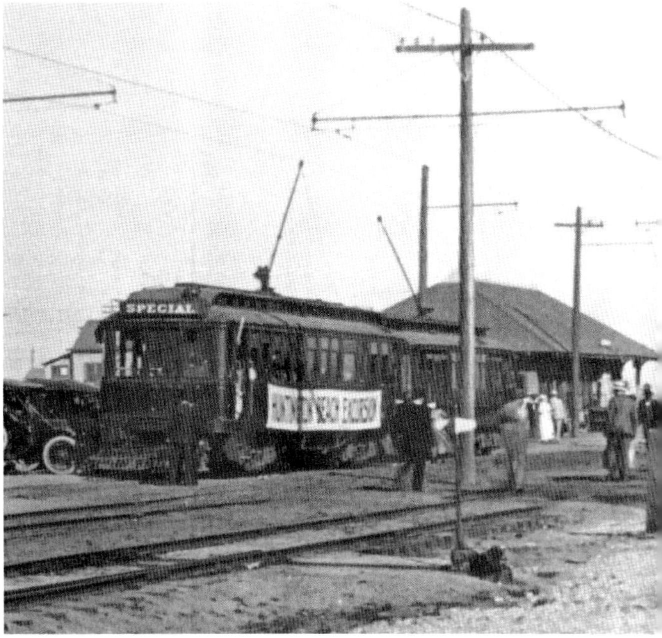

City's Namesake

Henry Huntington formed the Pacific Electric Railroad in 1901. It revolutionized travel throughout Southern California. In 1902, Philip Stanton sold a 40-acre tract he had laid out to Huntington and, within a year, Huntington was running his trains to the beach community. In 1904, Pacific City became known as Huntington Beach, honoring the man who brought Pacific Electric Railroad to the coast. A train station located by the pier and Main Street became the hub of the community. The famed railroad magnate died in 1927 and left a prominent legacy, including the Huntington Library, art collections, and a botanical garden on his former estate in Pasadena. He was also associated with hospitals, schools, hotels, and parks. But, certainly, one of his most lasting legacies is the beach city that still bears his name.

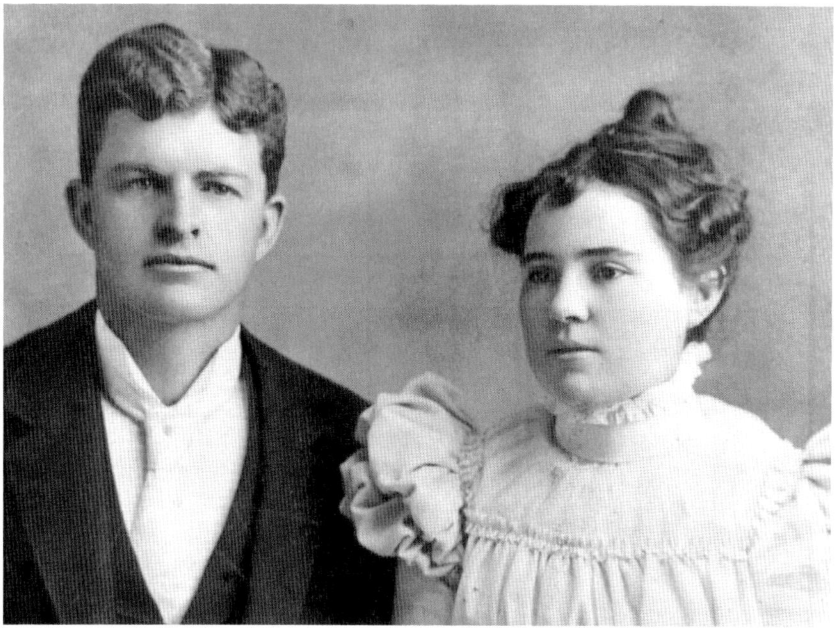

First Mayor

Ed Manning, a plumber, was the city's first mayor. He and his wife, Carrie, lived at 701 Delaware Street, where they raised three daughters. Born in Illinois on March 20, 1872, Manning came to California when he was 20 and never looked back. He settled in at a small beach town that was then called Pacific City and opened his plumbing business. He also became a civic leader. After his first tenure as mayor, Manning served once again starting in 1920, just after the oil boom had started. He died at home on December 20, 1942. Today, he is remembered at Manning Park on Delaware Street.

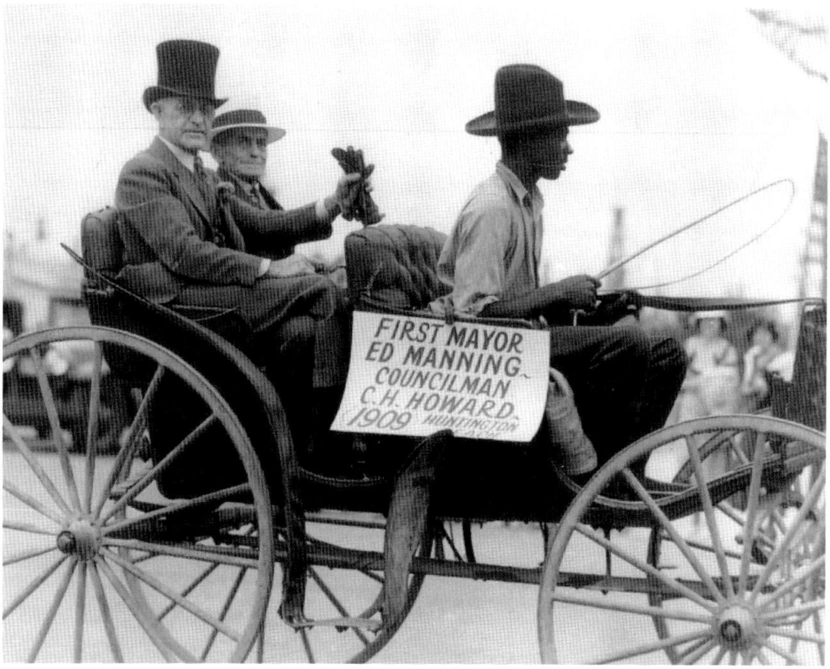

CHAPTER TWO

Military and Police

Today, the Huntington Beach Police Department comprises 237 sworn police officers, including patrol officers, detectives, narcotic officers, a Directed Enforcement Team, Neighborhood Enhancement Team, a SWAT unit, beach detail, and aero bureau. They are responsible for protecting over 200,000 residents and 11 million visitors to Huntington Beach every year. All 32 square miles of the city and 8.5 miles of beaches are patrolled by the police department, using cars, quads, motorcycles, and helicopters.

The Huntington Beach Fire Department also plays an integral part in keeping the city safe. Since the city was founded more than 100 years ago, both departments have grown in size and scope. But, to many residents, they still seem almost impossibly understaffed, especially when summer hits and millions of visitors roll in.

In addition to the great law enforcement officers and fire department staff, the city is also lucky to have many veterans call Huntington Beach home. As with most chapters in this book, the subjects of this chapter could easily make up another book. The veterans, in particular, make up a fascinating part of the Huntington Beach population. For the most part, they are quiet and humble. Getting them to share their stories is a feat in itself. But once they begin talking, and once they begin sharing their experiences, one is struck with just how special these soldiers really are.

Presented here are soldiers with compelling and unforgettable stories to share. The window is closing on service members who fought in World War II. But some of them are still around, and it is indeed an honor to include them in this collection.

Female Flyer (BELOW AND OPPOSITE PAGE)
Vi Cowden was a 35-year Huntington Beach resident that described herself as a former "little girl on the prairie." Originally from South Dakota, she had dreamed of flying for as long as she could remember. "I'd watch the hawks fly above the fields," she smiles, "and think, my God, if I could just do that."

In 1942, a local barnstormer taught Cowden to fly, and the rest is history. World War II was declared, and she wanted to serve her country. There was no program for female fliers, so she contacted Washington to see what she could do to help. Soon, a program for female pilots opened, and Cowden was on board.

Trained in Texas for the Air Force, she soon was picking up planes at the factory and taking them to training fields or places of embarkation—whatever helped the cause. She said she would have loved to fly combat missions, but she was not allowed. The men came home after the war and wanted their jobs back, so Cowden and the other female fliers were deactivated.

"We didn't get our benefits for 33 years," she says. "But we survived, and now feel we encouraged a lot of young women to take up flying. One-thousand, seventy-four of us made it through the training back then, and today many of us stay in touch."

Cowden's favorite plane to fly was the P-51, the fastest plane at the time. She is seen posing in a P-51 in the photograph on the opposite page. "I was the first woman to deliver a P-51 to the Tuskegee Airmen," she said. "It went 445 miles per hour. One time when I took off, I thought, the quicker you got up, the better chance you had to survive. So I blast off once and a guy on the radio calls and says, 'Identify yourself.' I do, and he says, 'No woman can fly like that!'" Cowden passed away in 2011 at the age of 94.

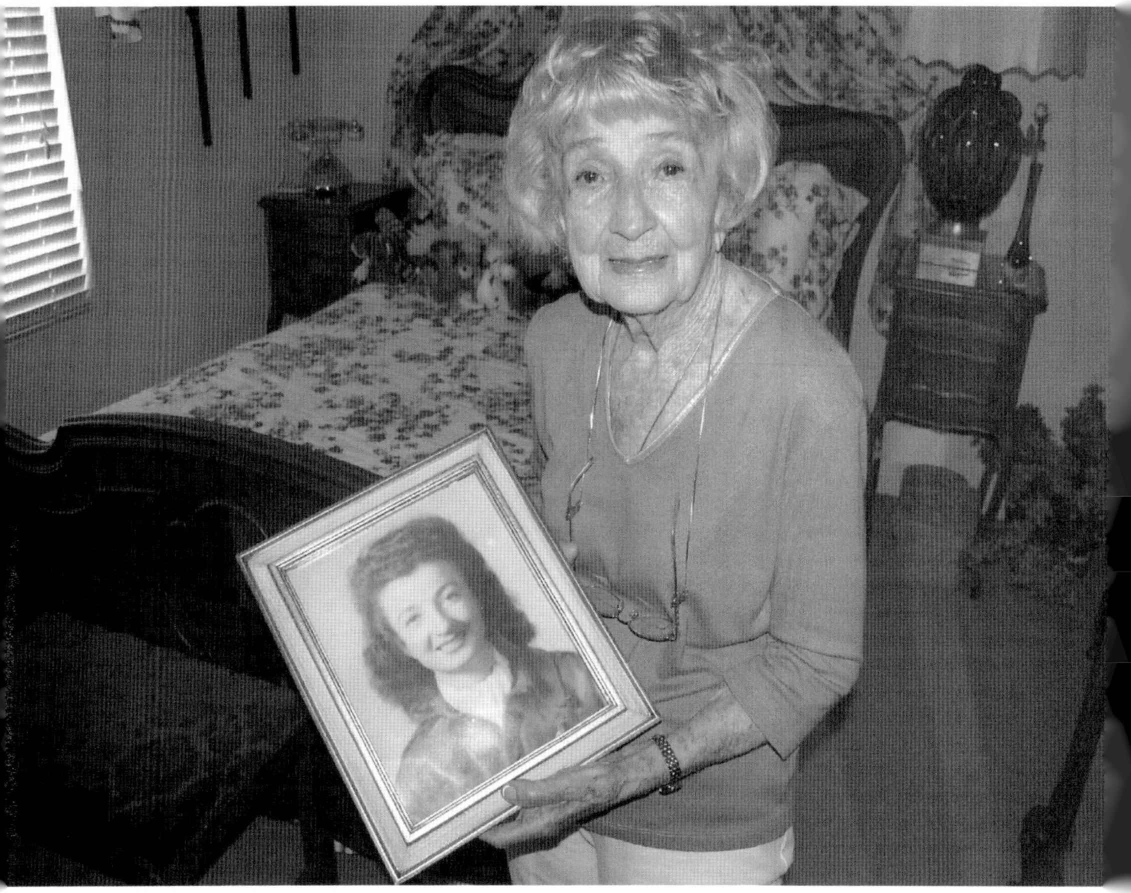

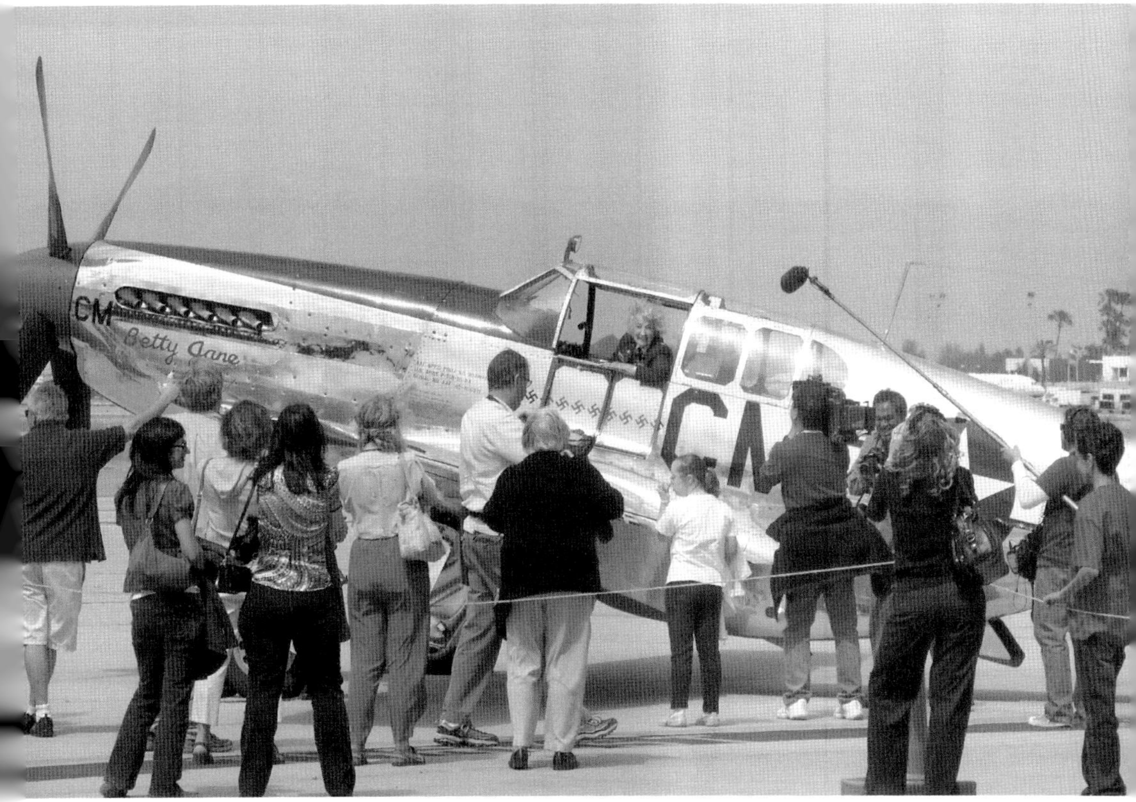
CM
Betty Jane

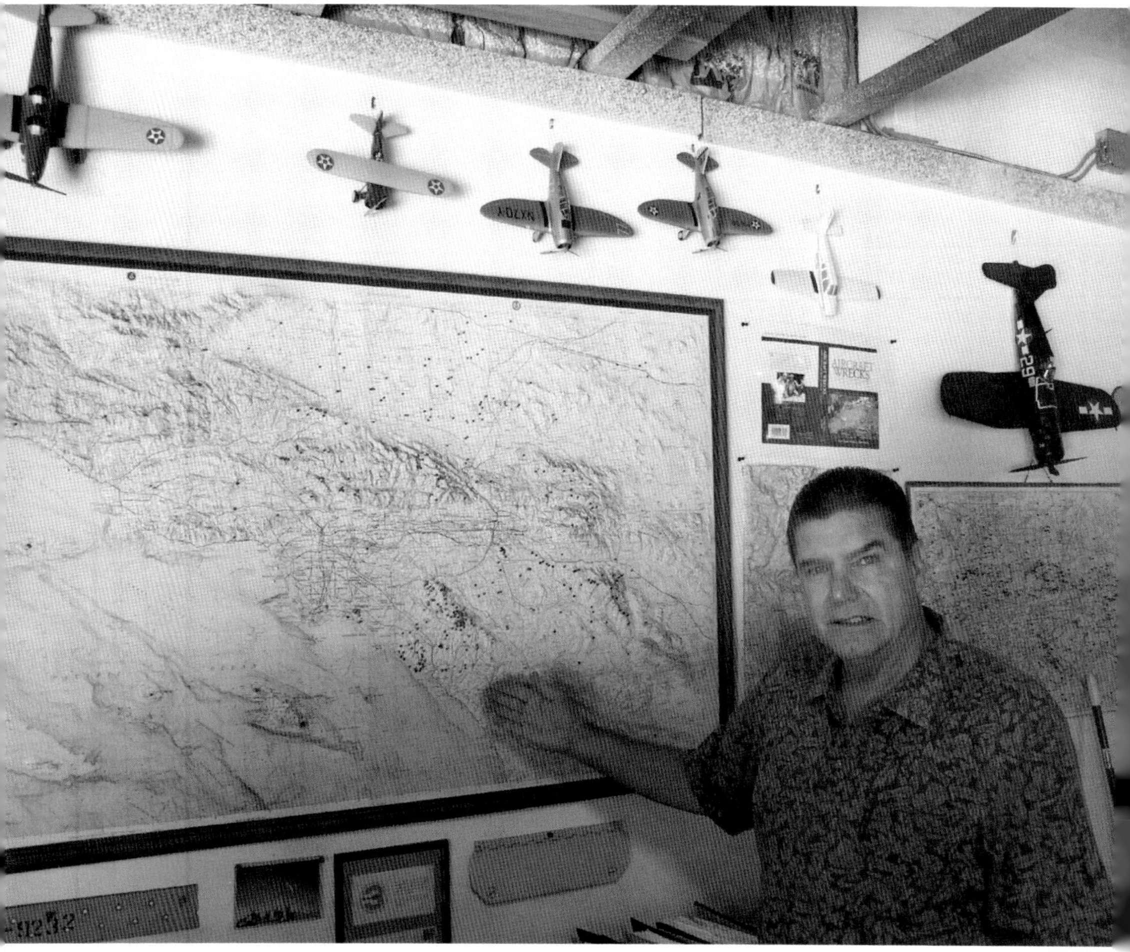

Plane Finder (ABOVE AND OPPOSITE PAGE)
Pat Macha, a longtime Huntington Beach resident who moved to Mission Viejo a couple of years ago, has been locating downed aircraft in remote regions for more than 40 years; the pictures opposite were taken in May 2008 in the Santa Ana Mountains near El Toro. He has trudged to more than 800 sites all over the world, looking primarily for military wrecks. Since the early 1980s, he has also made it his mission to deliver the next of kin to many of these sites so that they can make private peace where loved ones gave their lives. "I wasn't in the service," the retired high school teacher said recently. "But I had many family members who were. Maybe this is my way of serving my country." As to why Macha does it, he shrugs and says, "I'm just here as a grateful citizen of the republic." He adds, "This is the least I can do to help others pay their respects."

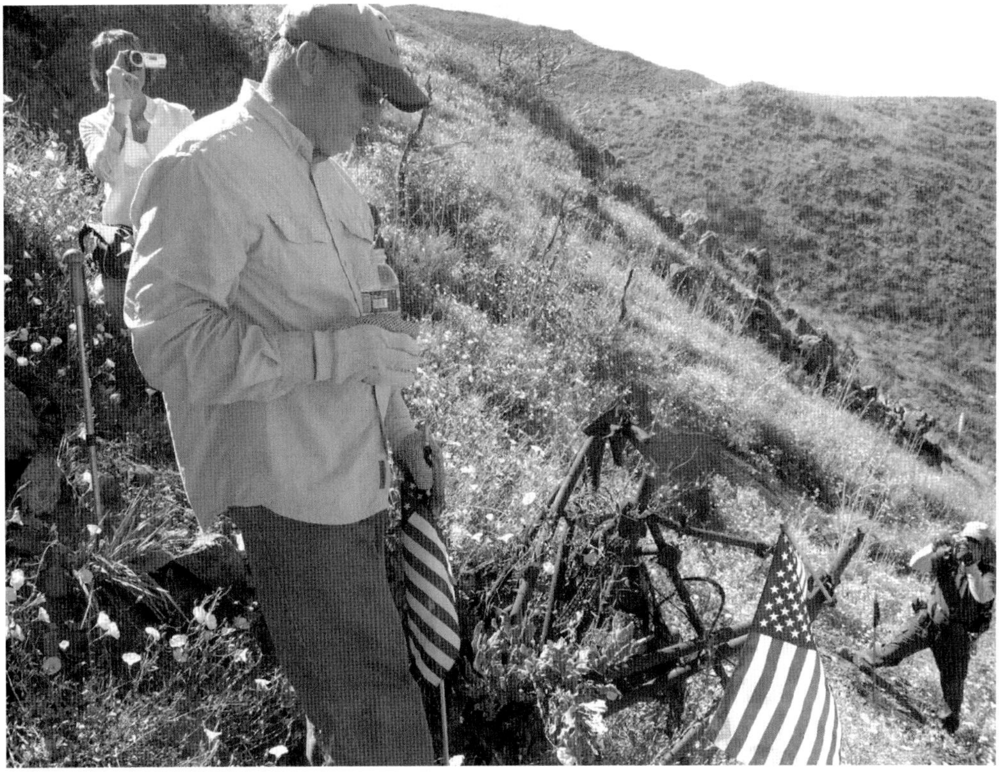

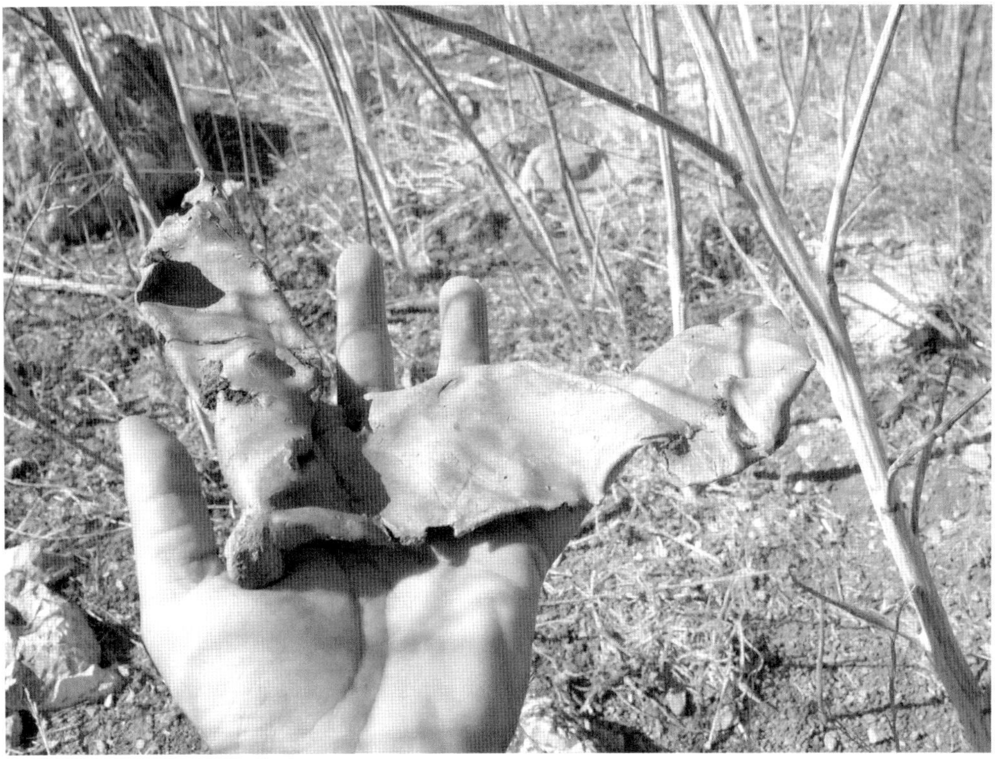

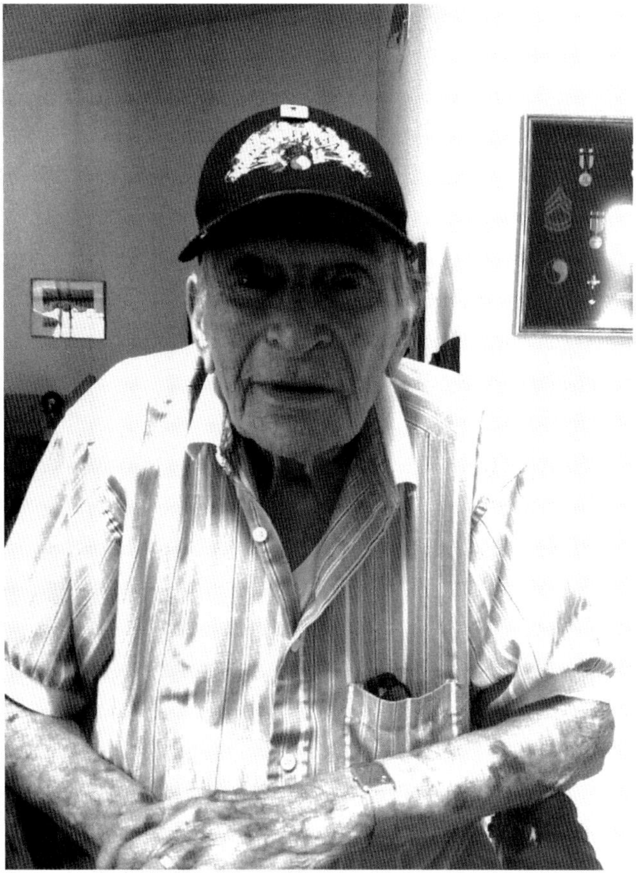

Two Purple Hearts

"They like me because I never complain. I never talk about my medication or my health or my doctors. Instead, I'll tell jokes and talk about life. That's what makes me happy."

Aaron Smith is talking about the daily call he gets from his senior center, asking him to "Make sure I'm still alive." The fact that he is 97 years old may seem to warrant a daily check-in call for himself, but time spent with Smith makes it clear why he is on the giving end of these visits, not the receiving end. In a comfortable retirement community in Huntington Beach, Smith lives with his 16-year-old female dachshund, Tiger. "We're just about the same age," he jokes. Tiger was a gift from Smith's daughter Barbara during a difficult time, when he was nursing his beloved wife, Vivian, near the end of her life. They had wed when Pearl Harbor broke out and were married for 58 years. Smith has lived in Huntington Beach for 29 years. He was born in Russia in 1917, the year of the revolution. When he was four and a half years old, his family was smuggled into Romania, and they eventually made it to Brooklyn.

In his early 20s, at the onset of World War II, Smith's life, like that of many other young people, was altered forever. "I was drafted in March 1943, and by June 1943, I was overseas." In a frame on a wall in his residence are two Purple Hearts, along with several other commendations. In his soft Yiddish accent, Smith is philosophical about his war experiences. "I can't ever go back to that site at Normandy where I was first wounded because of what I associate with it. But as hard as those times were, I always tried to be positive, to not fear death and to look at the bright side of things. I found humor wherever I could." Reflecting on his life, Smith says, "I was lucky enough to grow up during some of the most interesting times in history. You can't imagine, being a little boy and running outside with your friends when a plane would fly overhead because it was such a new thing to see. I never expected to live this long, and even though my body is not in great shape, my mind is still very sharp and for that I'm very thankful."

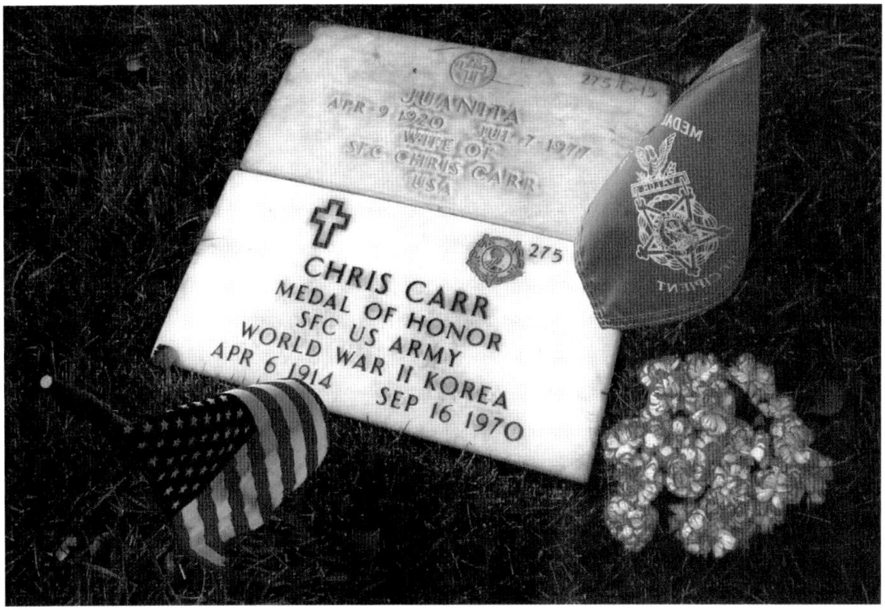

Medal of Honor

Chris Carr (born Karaberis) was an Army soldier who received the US military's highest decoration, the Medal of Honor, for his actions in World War II. On October 1, 1944, while serving as a sergeant in Company L, 337th Infantry Regiment, 85th Infantry Division, near Nola, Italy, Carr single-handedly attacked and captured five German machine-gun emplacements. He was awarded the Medal of Honor one year later. Carr went on to reach the rank of sergeant, first class. He served in the Korean War before retiring from the Army. He died at the young age of 56 and is buried at Los Angeles National Cemetery in Los Angeles, California. His Medal of Honor citation reads:

> Leading a squad of Company L, he gallantly cleared the way for his company's approach along a ridge toward its objective, the Casoni di Remagna. When his platoon was pinned down by heavy fire from enemy mortars, machineguns, machine pistols, and rifles, he climbed in advance of his squad on a maneuver around the left flank to locate and eliminate the enemy gun positions. Undeterred by deadly fire that ricocheted off the barren rocky hillside, he crept to the rear of the first machinegun and charged, firing his sub-machinegun. In this surprise attack he captured 8 prisoners and turned them over to his squad before striking out alone for a second machinegun. Discovered in his advance and subjected to direct fire from the hostile weapon, he leaped to his feet and ran forward, weaving and crouching, pouring automatic fire into the emplacement that killed 4 of its defenders and forced the surrender of a lone survivor. He again moved forward through heavy fire to attack a third machinegun. When close to the emplacement, he closed with a nerve-shattering shout and burst of fire. Paralyzed by his whirlwind attack, all 4 gunners immediately surrendered. Once more advancing aggressively in the face of a thoroughly alerted enemy, he approached a point of high ground occupied by 2 machine guns which were firing on his company on the slope below. Charging the first of these weapons, he killed 4 of the crew and captured 3 more. The 6 defenders of the adjacent position, cowed by the savagery of his assault, immediately gave up. By his 1-man attack, heroically and voluntarily undertaken in the face of tremendous risks, Sgt. Karaberis captured 5 enemy machinegun positions, killed 8 Germans, took 22 prisoners, cleared the ridge leading to his company's objective, and drove a deep wedge into the enemy line, making it possible for his battalion to occupy important, commanding ground.

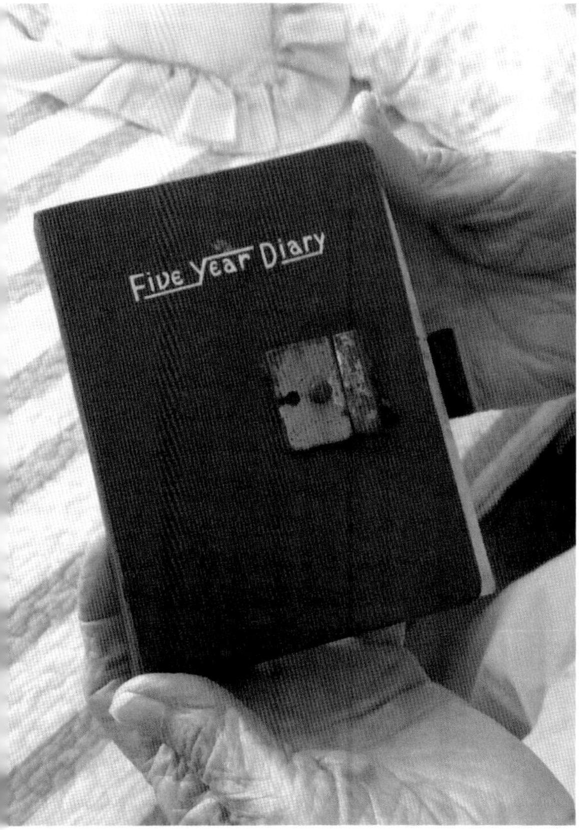

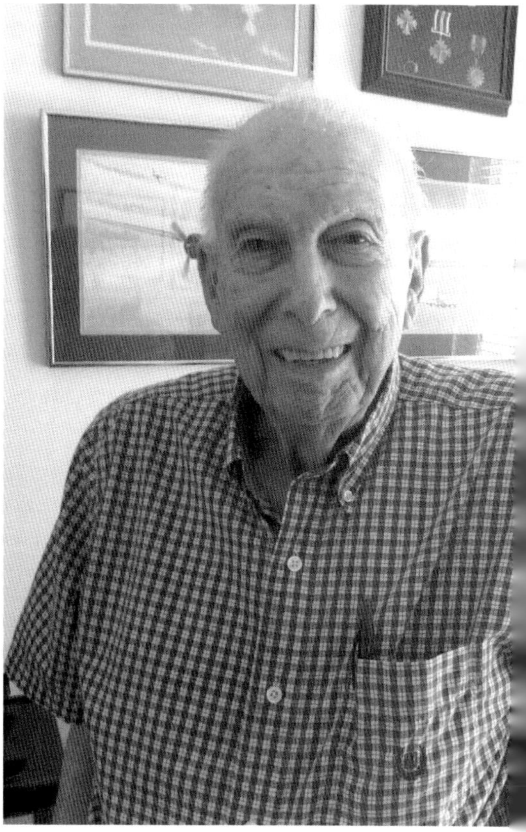

32 Missions (ABOVE AND OPPOSITE PAGE)
Dave Hanst joined the 91st Bomb Group in May 1944, and his crew was assigned to a B-17G (opposite page), which they named "Hikin' For Home." The enlisted men on the crew found a painting, done by an artist named Elvgren, in a magazine, believed to be *Esquire*. The entire crew decided that was the picture they wanted, and they gave it to Tony Starcer, who was one of the nose artists for the 91st. He painted the young lady on the side of the plane, along with a sign that listed each crewmember's home state. Lieutenant Hanst flew 32 combat missions in 72 days, primarily against German transportation and oil refineries. Hanst carefully documented each of those 32 combat missions in a small diary (above, left) that he still has today. Worn and weathered, it is a stunning wartime artifact. A sample entry reads, "Wednesday, June 7, 1944. Started out on this one late in the afternoon. On the bomb run we got some pretty close flak bursts. Dropped our eggs right on the runway. Back over the English coast after dark, landed at almost midnight in pouring rain with a low ceiling." Besides flying "Hikin' for Home," he also flew "Wabash Cannonball," "Wee Willie," "Boston Bombshell," and a couple other 322nd Squadron planes. After he completed his 35 missions, Hanst returned to the United States, where he began flying for the Military Air Transportation branch of the Air Transport Command (ATC). After leaving the Air Force, he began a 35-year career flying for United Airlines. As of this writing, Dave Hanst lives in Huntington Beach, which he has called home for almost 50 years. He is 95 years old and is still a sharp and adroit storyteller.

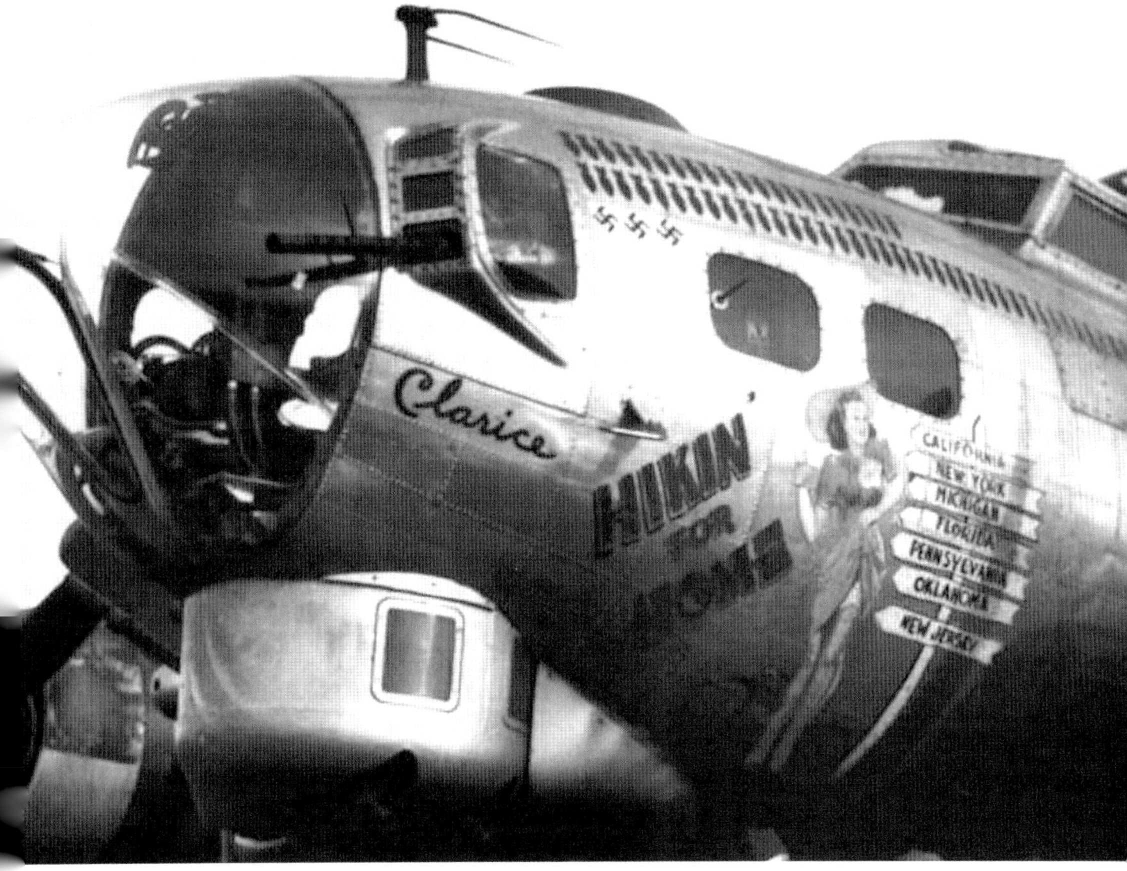
Clarice
HIKIN
FOR
CALIFORNIA
NEW YORK
MICHIGAN
FLORIDA
PENNSYLVANIA
OKLAHOMA
NEW JERSEY

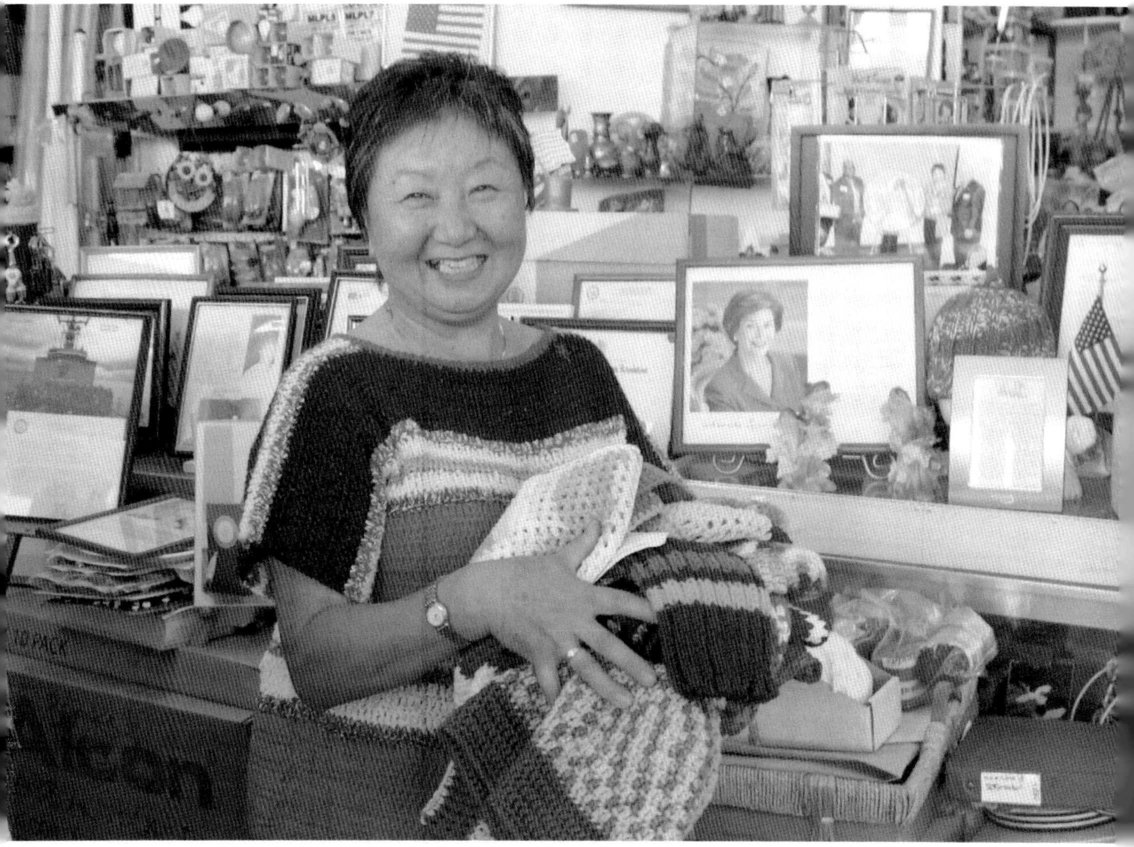

Helping the Troops

In a yarn shop on Hamilton Avenue near Bushard Street in Huntington Beach, great things are happening. A hint of this is seen upon approaching the shop and seeing, out front on a blue plastic table, photographs of soldiers and a red, white, and blue beanie cap. Welcome to Miki's California Yarn Sales, at 9452 Hamilton Avenue. It is run by Japanese immigrant Miki Sessler. She and her husband, Bertram, opened the yarn shop 43 years ago and worked tirelessly to make it a success. He died 10 years ago, and that loss threw Sessler into an emotional tailspin. She and Bertram had been inseparable, and a year or so after his passing, she got an idea. "I looked outside, the sun was shining, a bird was at the feeder, and I realized how beautiful life still was," she said. "My husband had served his country proudly, and so I decided it was time to do something to honor not just him but all of the other men and women that serve and sacrifice for the United States of America." Thinking that beanies would always be a practical item for soldiers, she set a goal for herself: to eventually have one million beanies made and delivered to servicemen and servicewomen around the world. Thus, Operation Beanies for Service Members was born on Thanksgiving 2004. Sessler designed a pattern for beanies, made about 50 of them herself, and then printed out 200 fliers for interested customers. To date, the program is responsible for making and shipping more than 107,000 beanies around the world. It is an astounding labor of love that boasts more than 2,500 "Beanie Angels," as Sessler calls the volunteers who make the caps and send them to the shop.

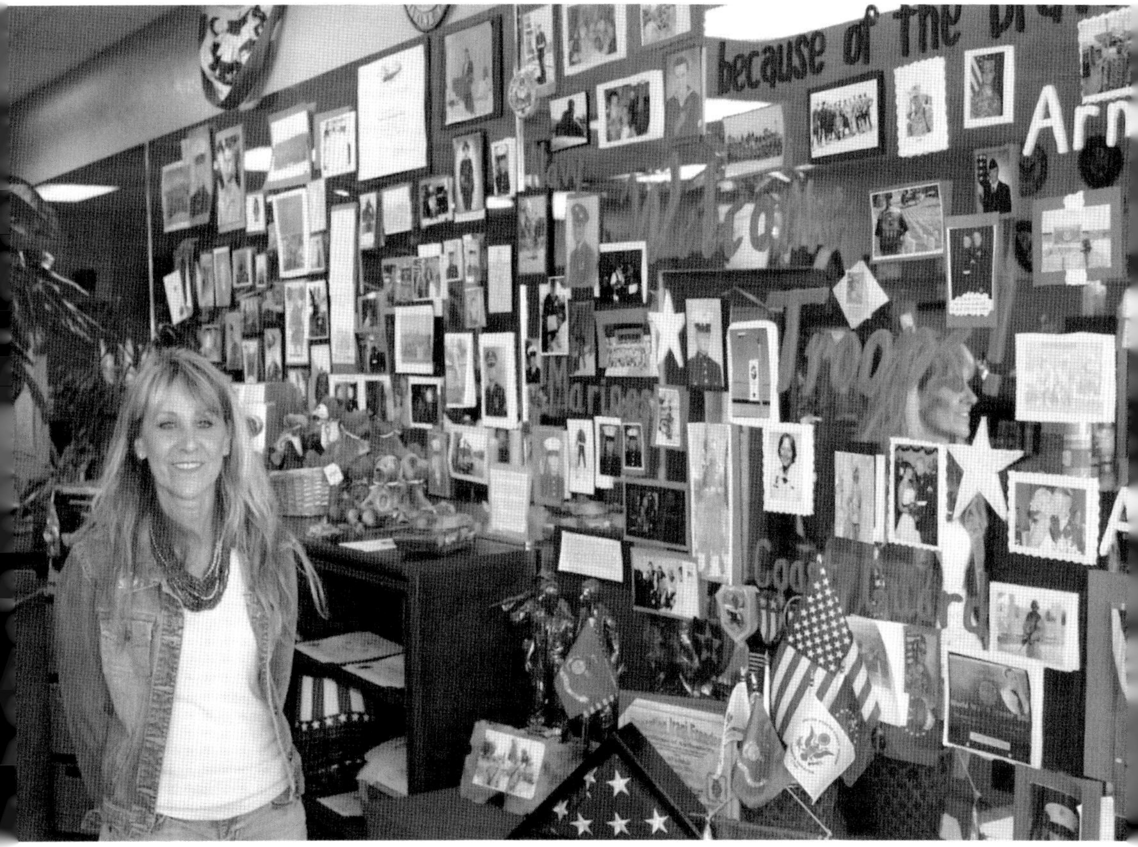

A "Country" Girl

"Don't include me in the picture. This isn't about me—it's about them." This quote says all there is to know about Denise Burelli, who, with her husband, Anthony, runs the Beauty Supply Zone & Salon near the intersection of Bolsa Chica Street and Heil Avenue. By "them," Denise Burelli means the dozens of images of men and women serving in the US military that are taped to the mirror in the salon. This makeshift shrine honors those who serve the nation. There are also American flags, statues, figurines, and a red, white, and blue banner that reads, simply, "Freedom." Inspired several years ago by a Marine Corps fundraiser, Burelli staged a "cut-a-thon" at the shop, donating all proceeds from a day of haircuts to the Marines. After that event, something dawned on her. "I started feeling that today, many of us had started to take for granted the sacrifices made by the men and women in our armed forces," she said. "We take for granted the freedom and liberty they fight to defend and protect, and we forget that our country is at war—so I just wanted to think of ways to remind people of how important it is to always thank our troops when you see them."

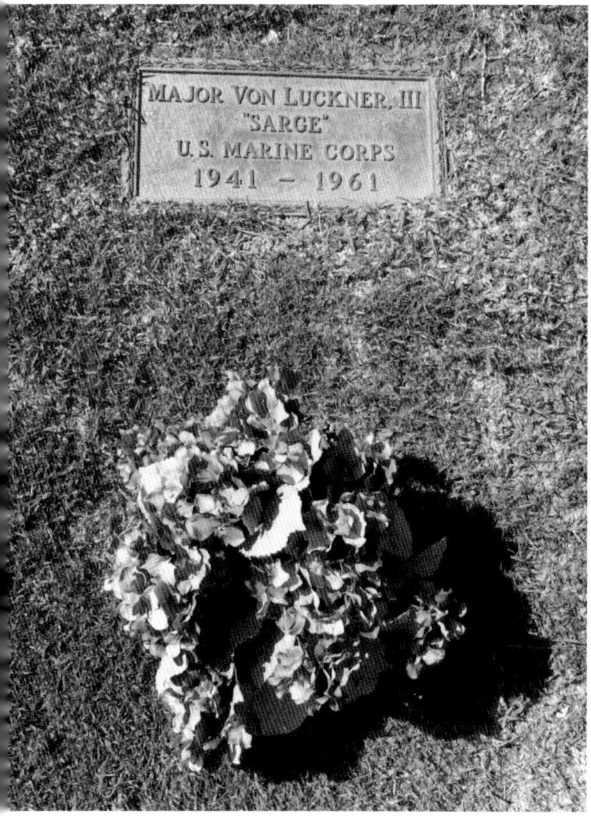

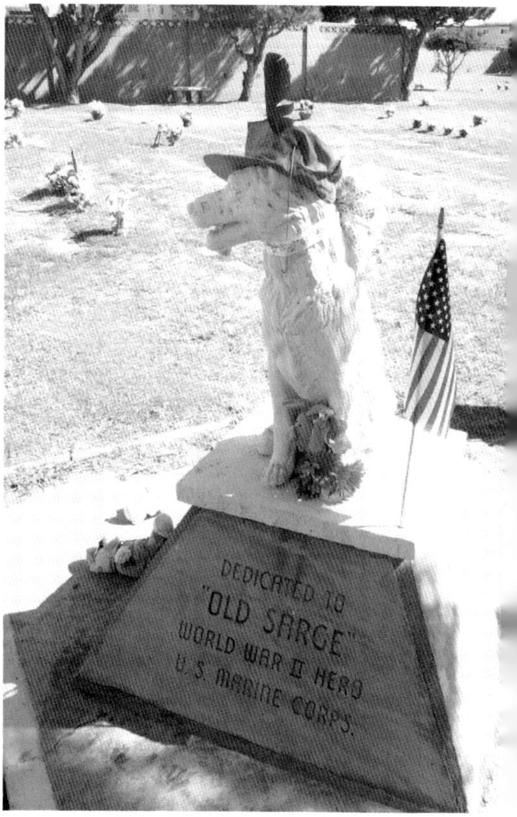

Sarge (ABOVE AND OPPOSITE PAGE)
Sea Breeze, at Beach Boulevard and Yorktown Avenue, was opened on three spacious acres in 1961 and today is the only pet cemetery in Orange County. Today, it is run by Alan and Brenda Weaver (the original owners were on Alan's side of the family). Brenda detailed one recent morning some of the history and logistics of the peaceful little place created to help celebrate the memory of a family pet.

For instance, she said how, in tracing the history of the in-ground markers from oldest to most recent, the pet names change with the times. Spot, Fluffy, and Snowball gradually give way to Britney, Amanda, and Tyler. Brenda showed this author where some of John Wayne's family pets are laid to rest, along with the dogs of Richard and Karen Carpenter, and, of course, Sarge, the tough Marine Corps battle dog of World War II. Sarge (Major Von Luckner III) even has a shrine inside that includes his flag, Purple Heart and Silver Star medals, and a telegram from Gov. Edmund "Pat" Brown offering his sorrow and praise in light of the dog's passing. The sturdy 20-year-old pooch saved nine wounded men by dragging them to safety during battles and even wore a silver plate in his head, a souvenir of a wartime injury in the South Pacific. Sarge is laid to rest directly in front of the main building, and a decorated statue of him sits at attention to the left.

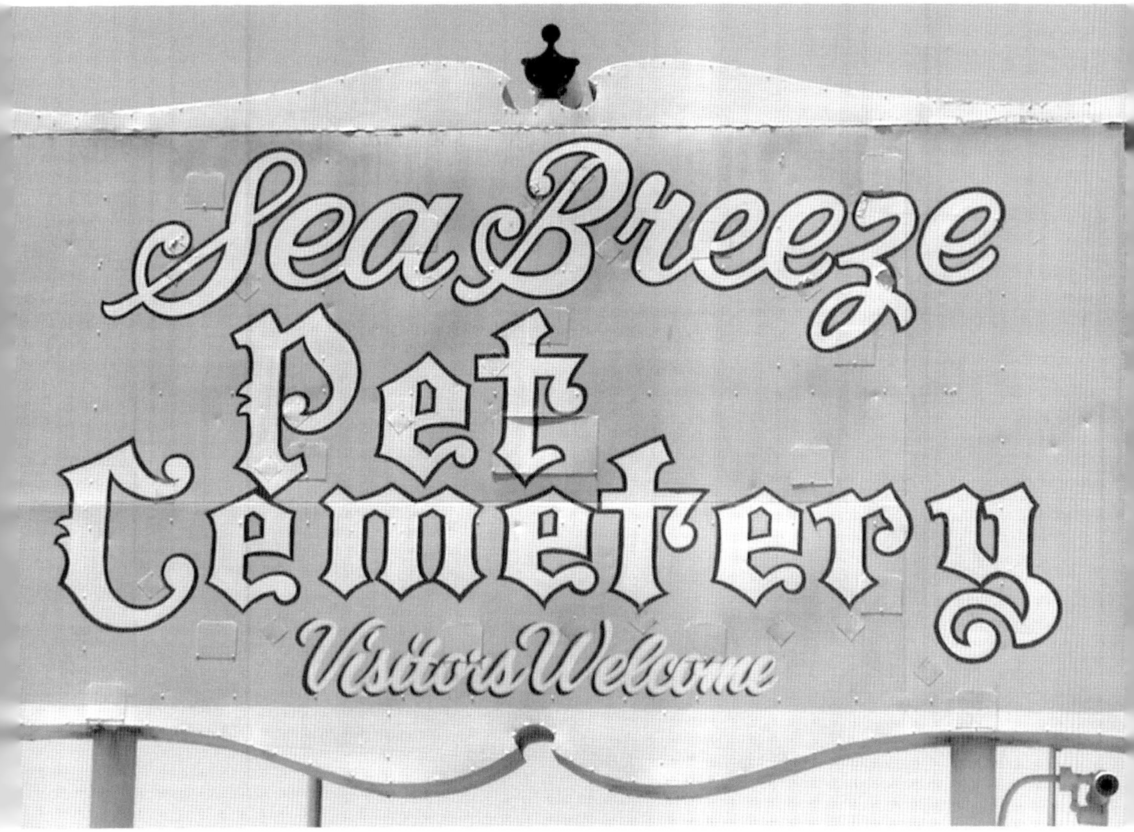
Sea Breeze
Pet
Cemetery
Visitors Welcome

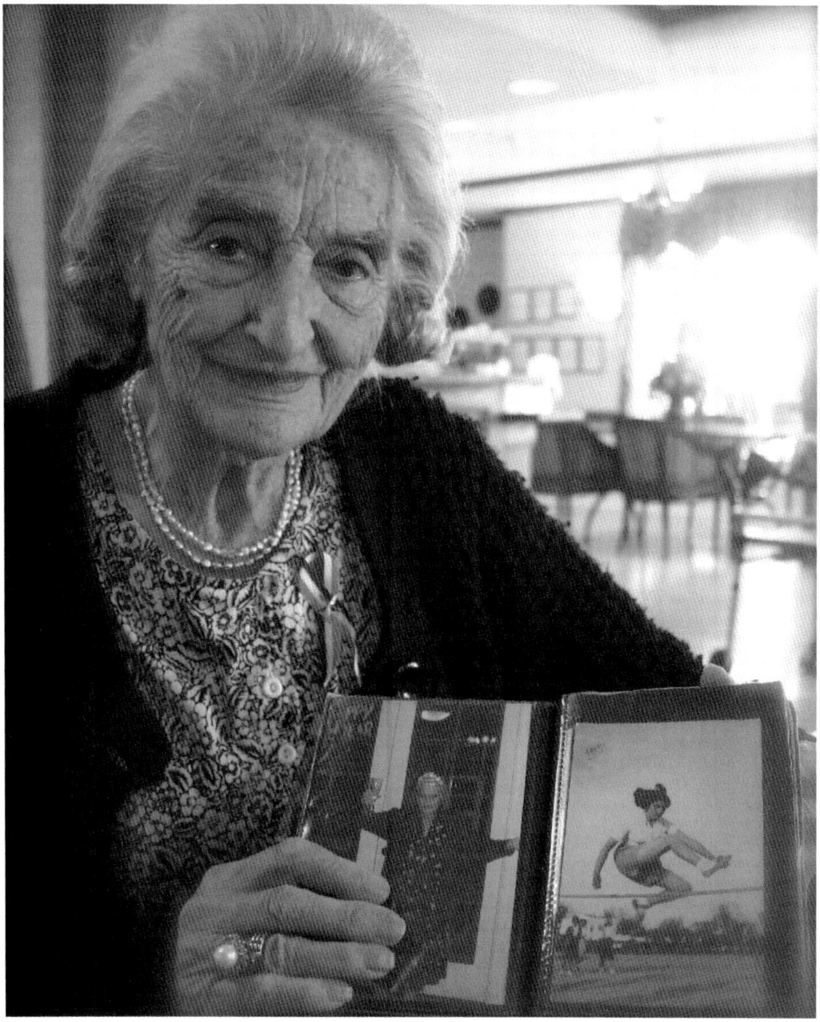

A Veteran

Helen Harris was a gifted athlete, winning medals for Greece in several track events. The striking, raven-haired young woman was gifted in another area, too: language. She became fluent in five languages (Greek, Polish, German, English, and French), which made her invaluable as a translator. Leaning over to speak in a whisper, Harris told the author about an incident that happened during the war. "I was in Germany," she said, "and I was introduced to Adolph Hitler. Very strange moment. He told me I spoke perfect German and he asked me how this was so, given that I was from Greece. I explained to him that I had a German nanny when I was young, and that I picked it up from her." Her eyes open wide and she shrugs as if to say, "What was I to do?" "He saw me in Poland once as well," she continued. "And remembered me. Came right over to say hello." Also an expert in accounting, for 27 years Harris worked at Bank of America in California. Her old-world demeanor and experiences seem exotic today, because they are. But she has in common with many other seniors at Sunrise the fact of having made a difference during wartime. George Washington said, "The willingness with which our young people are likely to serve in any war, no matter how justified, shall be directly proportional to how they perceive the Veterans of earlier wars were treated and appreciated by their nation." All of the veterans at Sunrise, and those throughout Huntington Beach, are appreciated for all that they have done for their city and their country.

Police Dogs

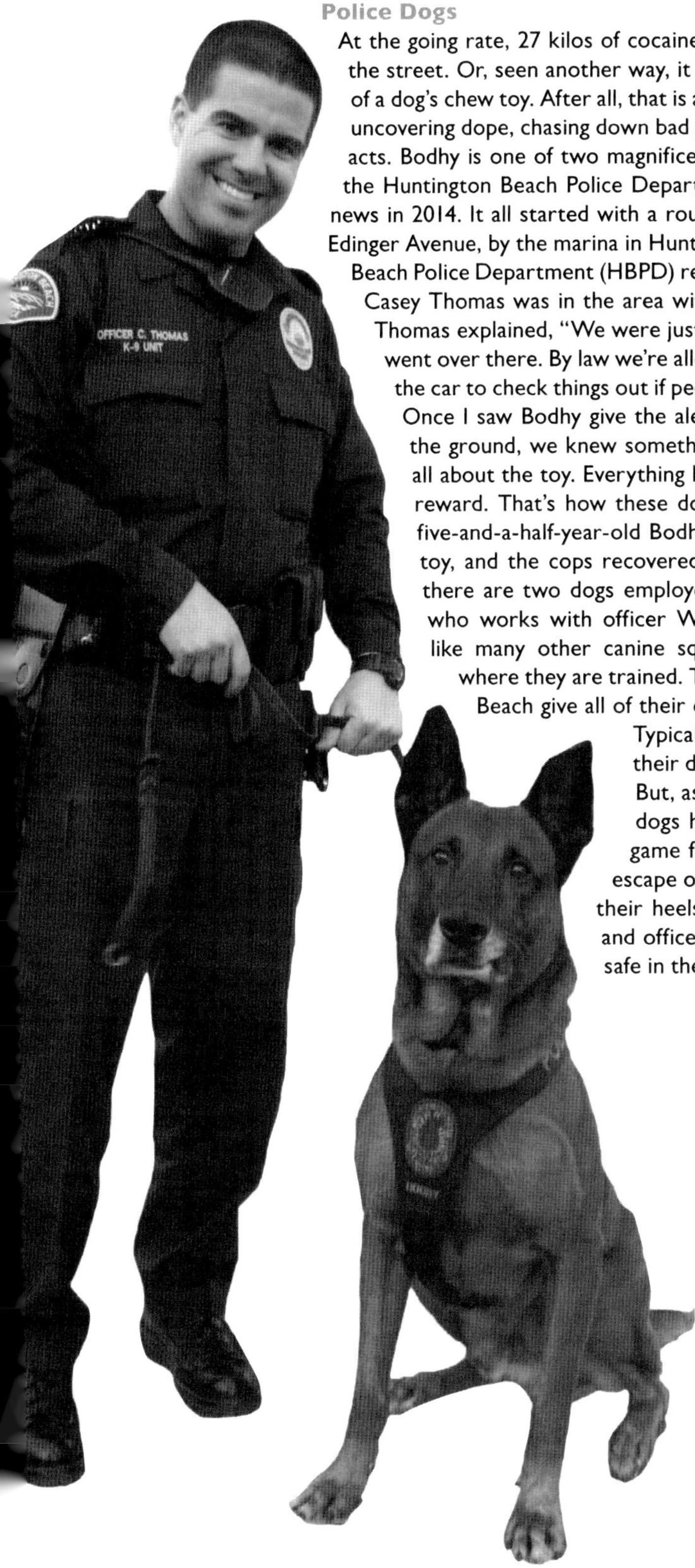

At the going rate, 27 kilos of cocaine will fetch about $1.3 million on the street. Or, seen another way, it may be worth about the amount of a dog's chew toy. After all, that is all Bodhy ever wants in return for uncovering dope, chasing down bad guys, or performing other heroic acts. Bodhy is one of two magnificent Belgian Malinois shepherds in the Huntington Beach Police Department K-9 division. He made big news in 2014. It all started with a routine traffic stop near the end of Edinger Avenue, by the marina in Huntington Harbour. The Huntington Beach Police Department (HBPD) requested a backup car, and officer Casey Thomas was in the area with his partner, Bodhy. As officer Thomas explained, "We were just in the area coincidentally so we went over there. By law we're allowed to have the dog run around the car to check things out if people are being rightfully detained. Once I saw Bodhy give the alert, which he does by scratching the ground, we knew something might be up. For Bodhy, it is all about the toy. Everything he does is just about getting that reward. That's how these dogs are trained." Moments later, five-and-a-half-year-old Bodhy got the reward, a simple rope toy, and the cops recovered 27 kilos of cocaine. Currently, there are two dogs employed by HBPD, Bodhy and Marco, who works with officer Wade Wilson. Bodhy and Marco, like many other canine squad dogs, come from Holland, where they are trained. This is why officers in Huntington Beach give all of their commands to the dogs in Dutch. Typically, the dogs work at night, so their days are spent resting up at home. But, as the officers described, once the dogs hit the street, their put on their game faces. Pity the perp who tries to escape on foot with one of these dogs on their heels. And, perhaps, envy the family and officers who keep the dogs warm and safe in their homes.

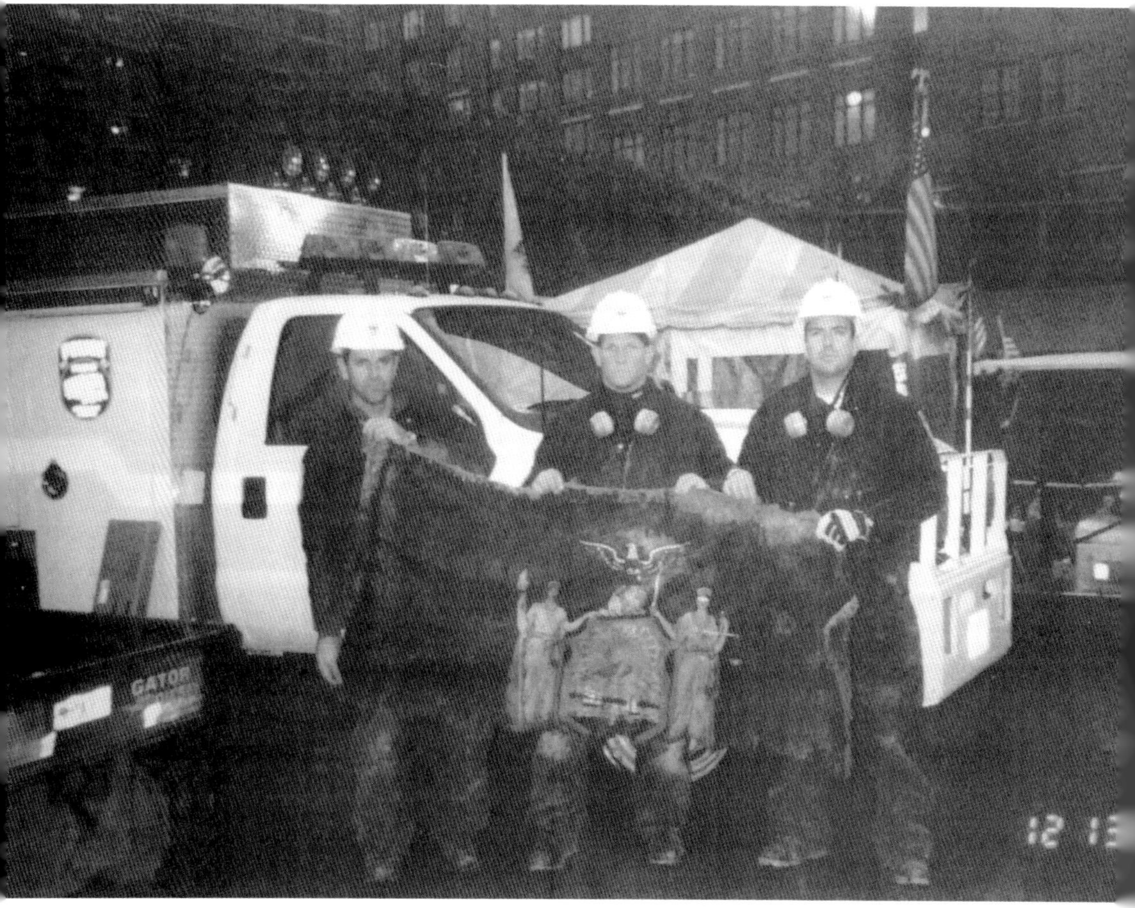

HBPD and 9/11

For a number of Huntington Beach police officers, September 11 will always include thoughts of friendships that were forged in the aftermath of the attacks on the World Trade Center, when a new brotherhood was formed. Motor Officer Bobby Frahm, who has been with the Huntington Beach Police Department since 1992, explained how his life changed in 2001. "After the event, the Huntington Beach Police Officers Assn. wanted to do something to help the departments back East that lost so many officers," he said. "So we started selling T-shirts to raise some funds. The department got really involved in helping to get the word out, and then the community responded and it really took off. In just a few months, we actually raised $90,000. In December of 2001, about 12 of us flew back to New York to present the money, which was split equally between NYPD, the Fire Department and the Port Authority." In April 2002, Frahm and several other HBPD officers went back to Ground Zero to help work at the site. "At that point, we were looking for lots of personal effects," Frahm said. Tommy Kennedy, a Port Authority sergeant, told the author his bond with the HBPD officers was like a gift that emerged from the tragedy. "Bobby Frahm and those guys are not 'like' my brothers—they are my brothers."

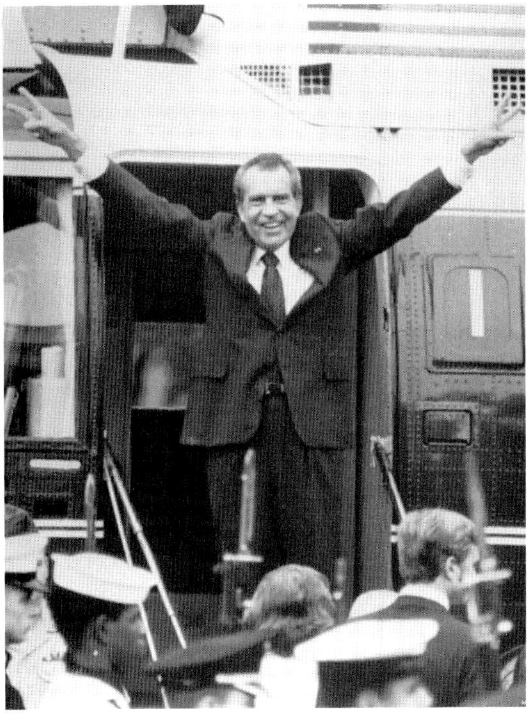

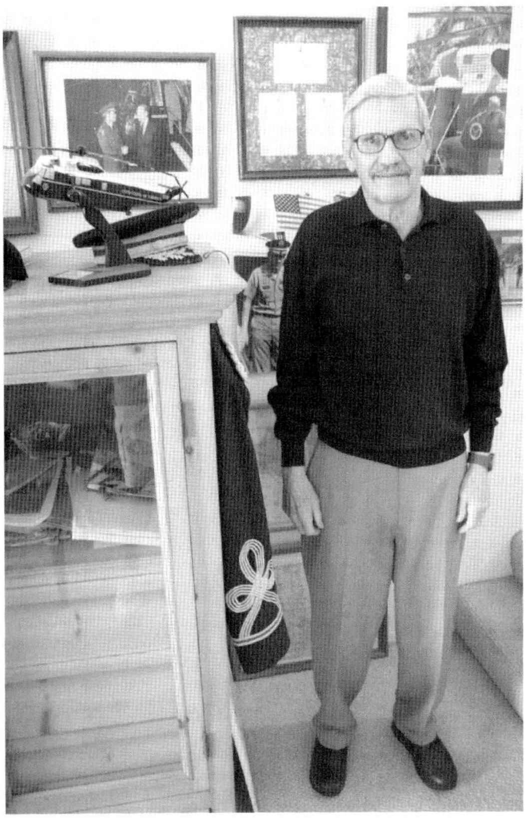

Presidential Pilot

Lt. Col. Gene Boyer (below), a decorated war hero who flew MASH missions during the Korean War and was shot down in Vietnam, is also a master storyteller. Fortunately, he wove his rich, cinematic life into a wonderful book, *Inside the President's Helicopter: Reflections of a White House Senior Pilot.* Boyer's life, in one sense, can be measured in numbers. He had 6,900 hours of helicopter flight time, 368 combat hours, 580 "code one" presidential missions, 451 Richard M. Nixon flights, and 55 flights with at least one foreign head of state on board. He conducted two forced landings but zero crashes. Boyer flew in 49 states and 17 countries. He flew five US presidents, as well as Gen. William Westmoreland, Henry Kissinger, Anwar Sadat, Hosni Mubarak, King Hussein, Charles de Gaulle, Robert Kennedy, Nguyen Van Thieu, Leonid Brezhnev, John Steinbeck, Bob Hope, and John Wayne. Boyer was also the first pilot to fly a sitting president and first lady into a combat zone, and he recruited the first three African American pilots to fly for the White House, one of which was his copilot the day Nixon resigned (above).

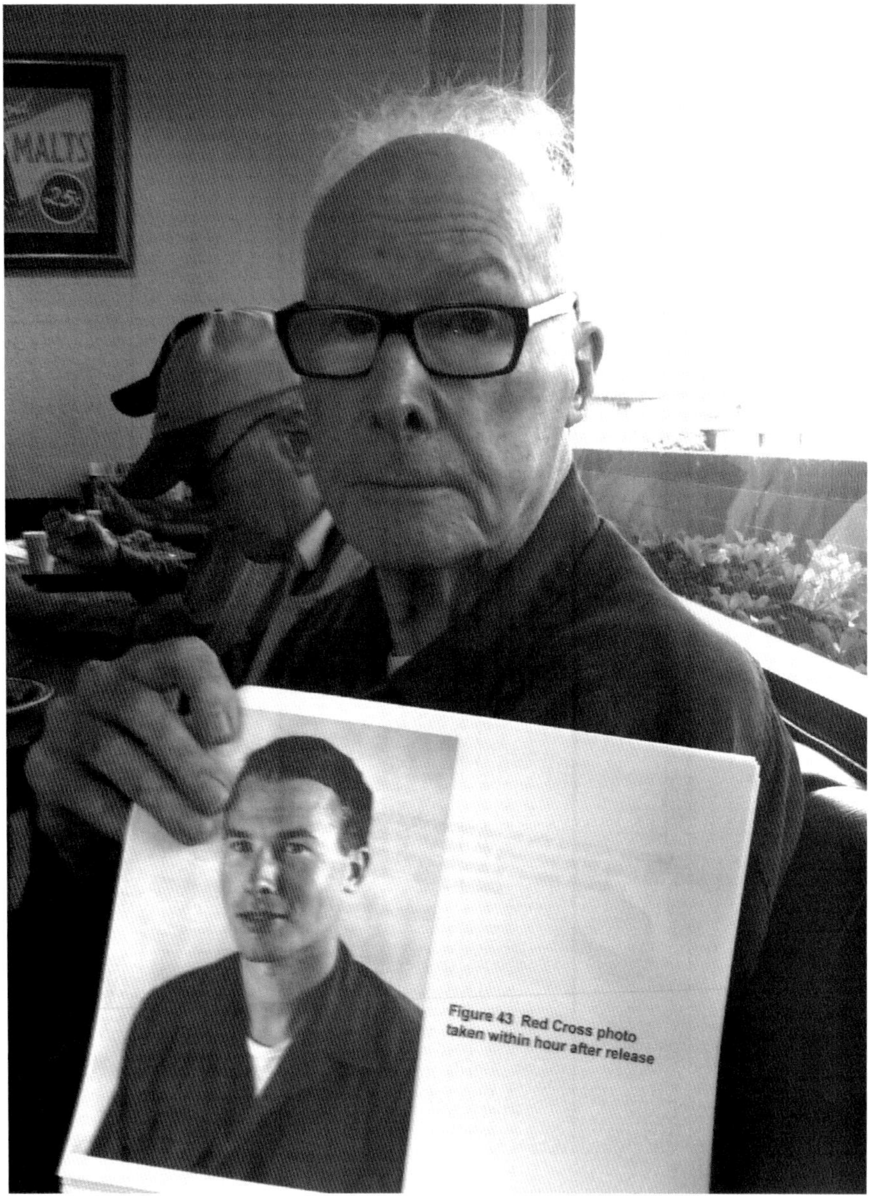

POW

Lloyd Roberts, an infantryman in the US Army, 2nd Division, 23rd Regiment, was captured in central Korea near the 38th parallel. "The Chinese attacked and surrounded us that night," he said softly. "We lost about 150 vehicles during the fight, and many of us just scattered off into the hills. But they caught me and a lot of other guys." He adds, "The Chinese wouldn't mistreat us; they would just let us die from neglect. They might make us get out there and hike 15 to 20 miles a night and then when guys got sick, they were just left to die. They just didn't give a damn about us." Yet Roberts survived. After returning from Korea in August 1953 (he weighed just 80 pounds upon release), Roberts met his wife-to-be and enrolled at the University of Minnesota to study physics. He graduated in 1962 with a bachelor of science degree and accepted a job in Huntington Beach at Douglas Aircraft as a systems engineer. He retired in 1990.

CHAPTER THREE

Music and the Arts

Over the years, Huntington Beach has produced a number of notable performers, writers, artists, and other creative professionals. But for every famous artist, there are 1,000 more that may never garner widespread attention. But those unsung artists are still here. Like many beach cities, Huntington Beach is a haven for photographers, painters, musicians, and many other creative dreamers and doers who are inspired by the surf and sand.

Interestingly, Huntington Beach was also one of Orange County's centers for the punk rock movement of the late 1970s and to the present day. As described in this chapter, many bands born in Surf City have gone on to electrify and inspire listeners all over the world. And there are plenty of other bands that, while not becoming famous beyond Orange County, still maintain a presence here, playing countless house parties and bars all over Huntington Beach and neighboring cities.

Huntington Beach will forever inspire the community's creators; for that reason, the city will also always function like a magnet for those in search of their muse.

A busy playhouse in Huntington Beach puts on a number of shows each year. Although there are not as many as there used to be, a number of venues still exist where bands play live. As long as there is an empty garage or an upstairs attic or a bit of wall space, there will be opportunities in the city for those that express themselves through the arts.

As of this writing, a local band called Avenged Sevenfold recently released its second consecutive number-one album. Who knows what other bands are forming at this moment that, in several years, may also be conquering stages around the world? Perhaps the next edition of this book will include the next wave.

Maverick

The popular actor Jack Kelly (right) is probably most famous for the role of Bart Maverick in the television series *Maverick*, which ran on ABC from 1957 to 1962. Kelly had multiple costars on the show, beginning with James Garner (left) as Bret Maverick, then Roger Moore as Beau Maverick and Robert Colbert as Brent Maverick. In the 1970s, Kelly acted less, becoming more involved in local politics and real estate after moving to Huntington Beach in 1971. During the 1980s and early 1990s, he was elected a Huntington Beach councilman and eventually became mayor. His mayoral campaign slogan was "Let Maverick solve your problems." Kelly suffered a heart attack in April 1992 and died of a stroke at a Huntington Beach hospital in November of that year.

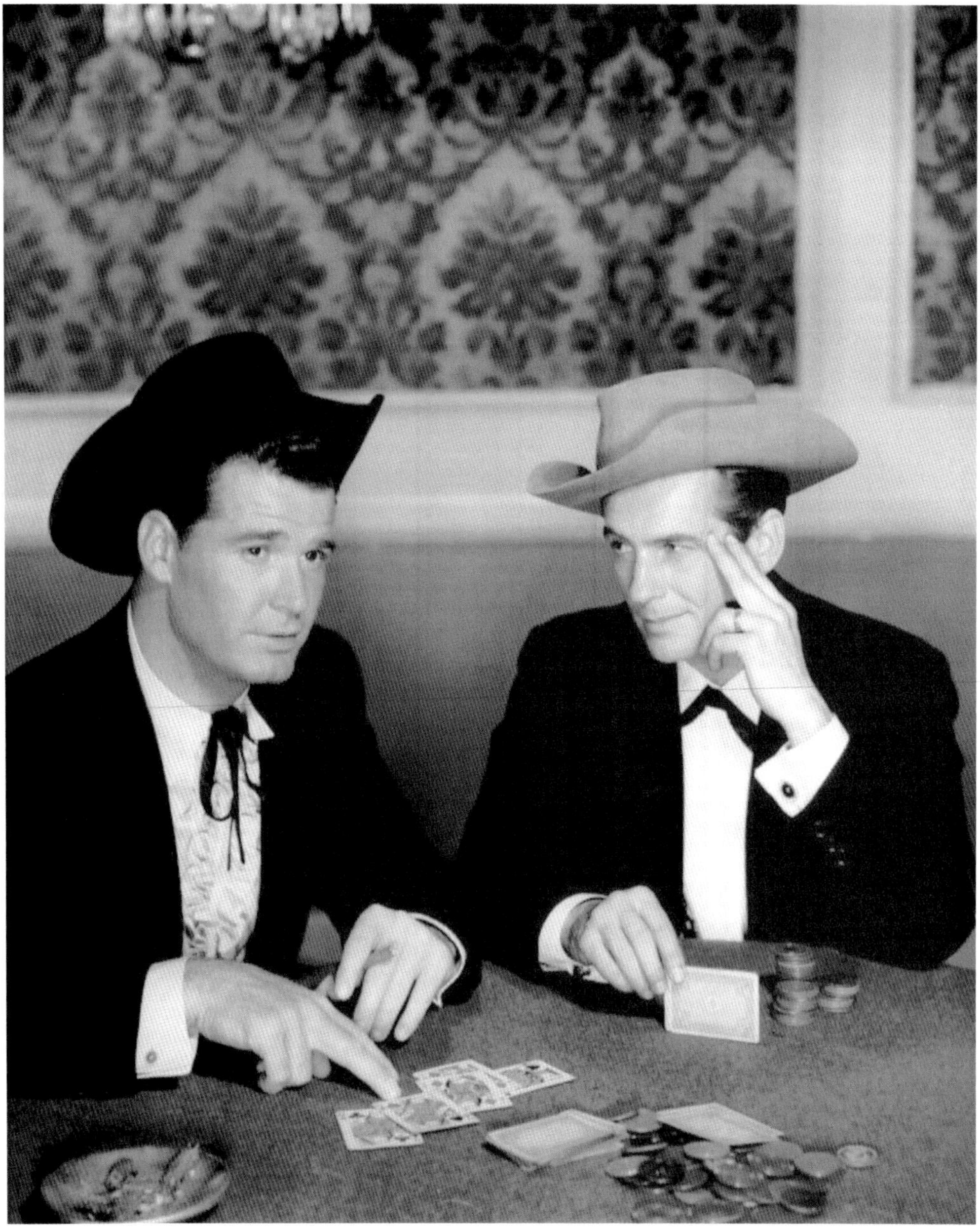

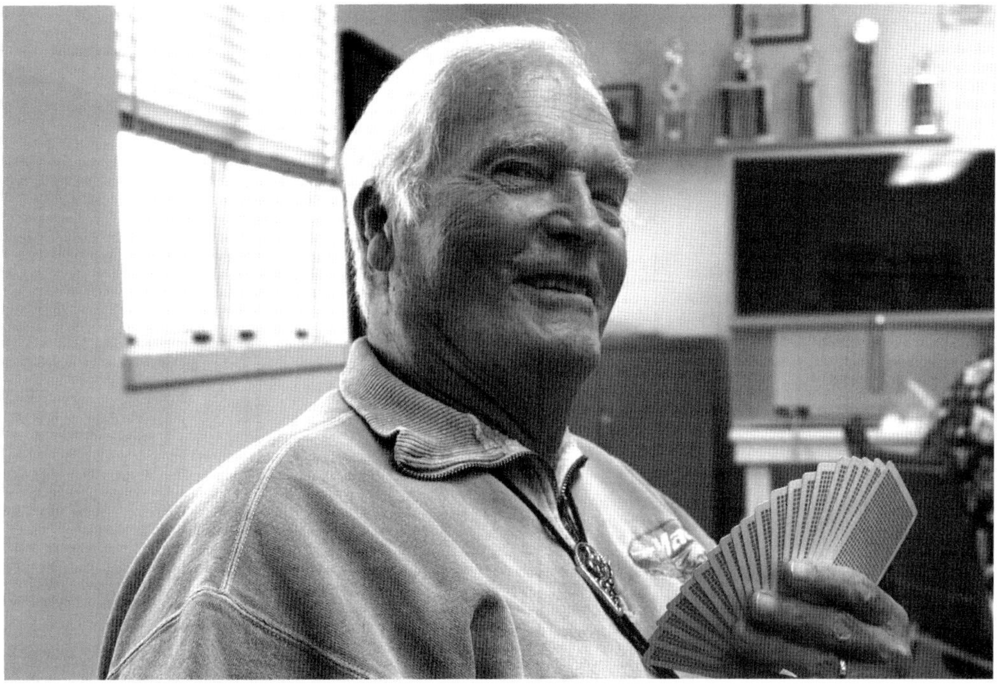

Rugged Star

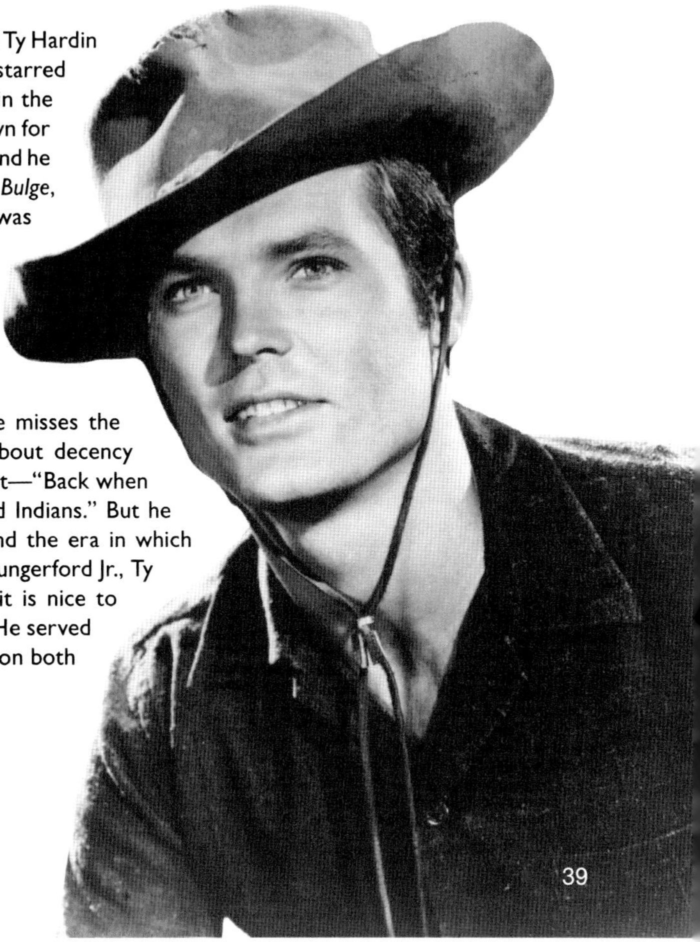

At the local senior center, an actor named Ty Hardin plays cards a couple of times a week. He starred in many Westerns and television shows in the 1950s and 1960s. He is perhaps best known for the television series *Bronco* (1958–1962), and he had roles in the films *PT 109*, *Battle of the Bulge*, and *Custer of the West*. Supposedly, he was the first choice to star in the television series *Batman* but turned down the part because of prior film commitments. In his mid-80s, Hardin, still rugged and handsome, is in terrific shape. He and his wife have lived in Huntington Beach for about six years. Hardin says that he misses the days when Hollywood made pictures about decency and the morals and code of the Old West—"Back when kids still believed in playing cowboys and Indians." But he is also grateful for the career he had and the era in which he got to work. Born Orison Whipple Hungerford Jr., Ty Hardin is a true American classic, and it is nice to know that he resides in this community. He served his country in Korea and served his fans on both the large and small screens.

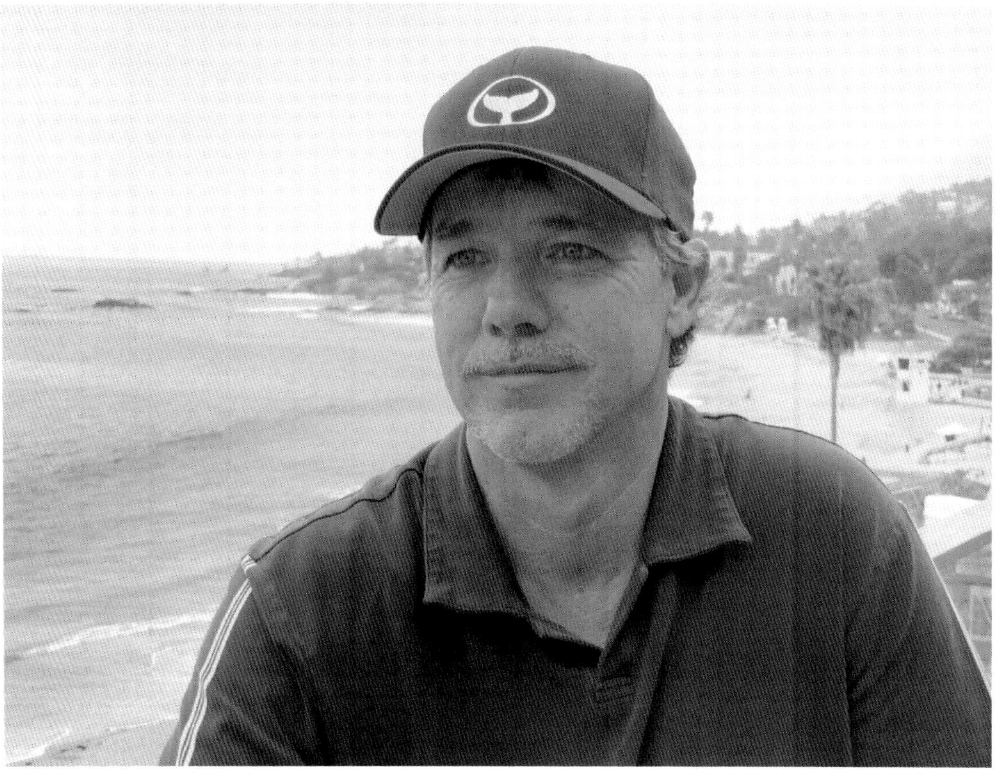

Whale of an Artist

Wyland, a world-famous marine-life artist, knows Huntington Beach well. He lived here for a long time and recently took part in an artistic and charitable program called Surfboards on Parade. He describes the program, and his art in general, as follows:

> It was a great honor to be asked to contribute artwork for Surfboards on Parade. Although I am a Detroit native, I have called southern California my home for almost four decades. Like many, I was drawn to the beautiful beaches, wetlands and a coastal wildlife that make places like Huntington Beach so special. I also had the privilege of contributing a larger-than-life mural to the side of the famous Huntington Beach landmark, the Golden Bear, many years ago. My efforts over the years have focused on promoting art, conservation, and finding numerous ways to give back to our communities. My non-profit Wyland Foundation provides thousands of dollars in grants, scholarships, art supplies to schools, classroom education about the importance of clean waterways and healthy oceans, and our national Mayor's Challenge for Water Conservation. It is gratifying to know that the many invited artists who are participating in the Surfboards on Parade event are playing an important part in supporting some of the most important charities in Orange County. For artists such as myself who believe that art can change the communities we live in for the better, I hope programs like Surfboards on Parade continue to thrive and prosper, just like they do here in Huntington Beach.

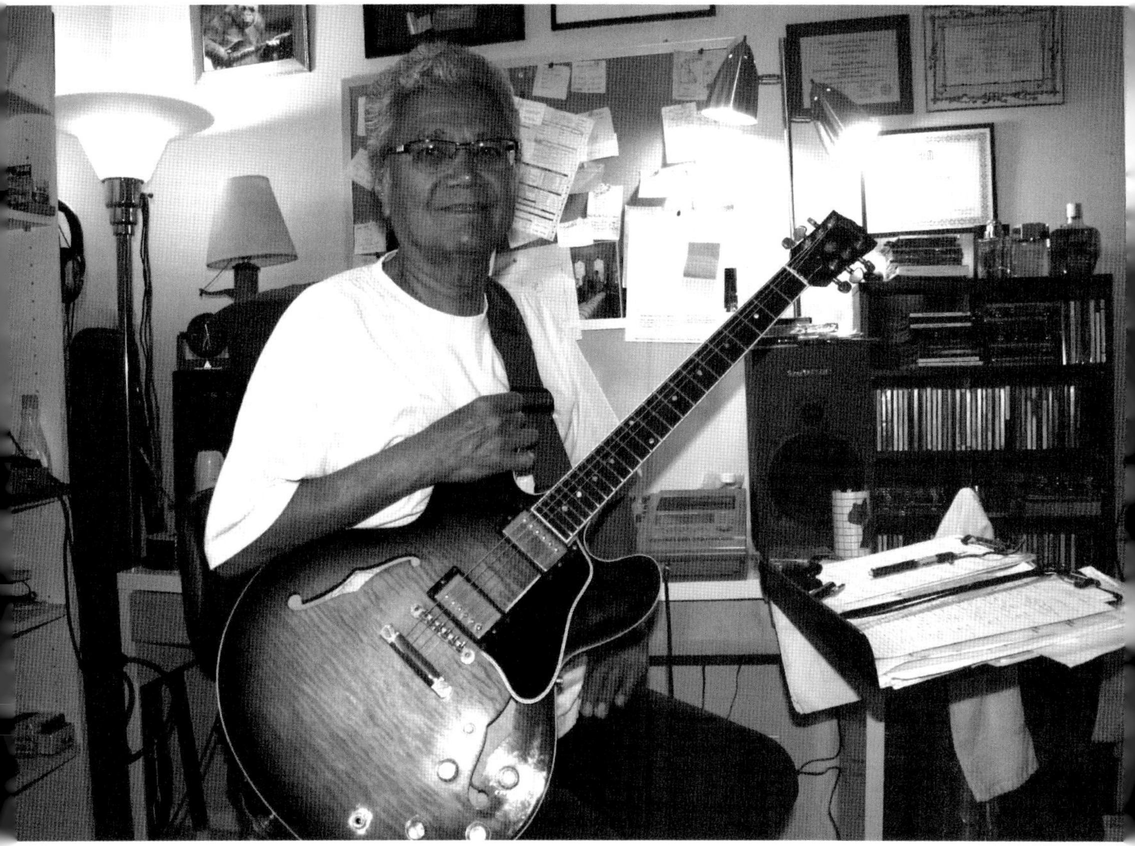

Rock 'n' Roll Hero

It started in Santa Ana in the early 1950s, when Barry Rillera and his brothers put together what is considered to be the very first rock 'n' roll band in Orange County. Known as the Rhythm Rockers, they were influenced by everything they heard around them: music played by their father and songs on the radio, in back rooms, and in dance halls. Wherever it happened to come from, the brothers absorbed the sounds and spun them into their own early brand of rootsy Southern California rock 'n' roll. Blending soul, rhythm and blues, Chicano, Latin, jazz, and more, the Rhythm Rockers were at once the most innovative and flexible band in the county, able to play any kind of party or concert and to always please the crowd.

One night at the old Harmony Park Ballroom in Anaheim, the R&B singer Richard Berry asked Rillera about a song the band was playing entitled "El Loco Cha Cha" by Rene Touzet. Berry, singing with the Rhythm Rockers that night, was writing a song himself. Inspired by the tune's infectious and simple rhythm, Berry finished his tune backstage that night while waiting to go on. He would soon record a version of it, but it was not until another band, the Kingsmen, covered Berry's song that much of the world became aware of "Louie Louie." Rillera and his brothers would soon become part of the Righteous Brothers phenomenon, playing the music behind the blue-eyed soul of Bill Medley and the late Bobby Hatfield. Thankfully, fans can still enjoy Barry Rillera's music in Huntington Beach. He has lived here for many years and regularly performs at local clubs and restaurants.

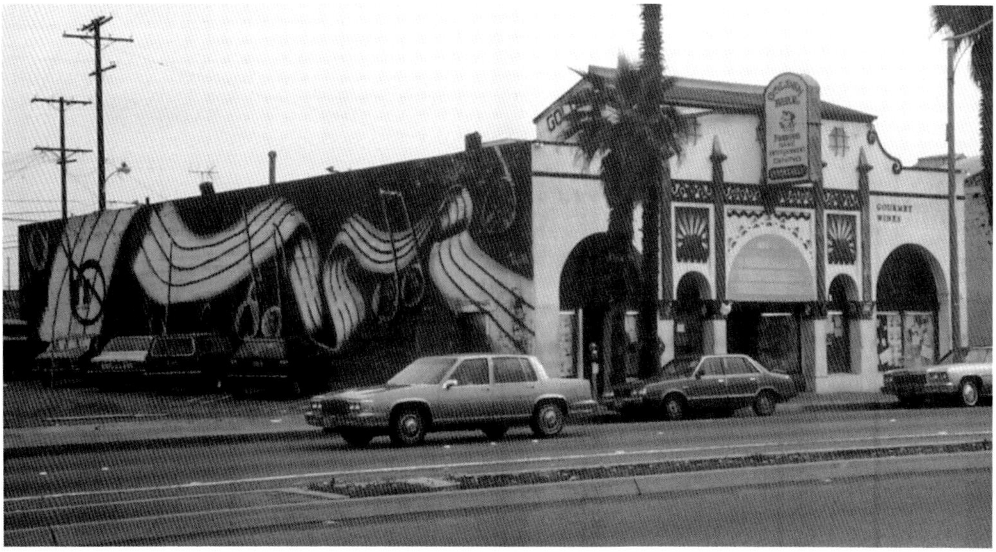

The Golden Bear

Of all the music venues in Orange County, arguably the most beloved, historic, and significant was the Golden Bear in Huntington Beach. The Golden Bear opened at 306 Pacific Coast Highway, just across from the pier, as a restaurant in the 1920s. It was designed by renowned Southern California architect Ernest Ridenour. Movie stars would motor down from Hollywood for dinner after a day at the beach. The original owner, Harry Bakre, retired in 1951. The building was home to various restaurants and then sat vacant for several years after Bakre's death in 1957. Then, in 1963, Delbert Kauffman took over the club and established it as a folk venue. In the mid-1960s, Kauffman brought in a variety of acts that represented the modern folk movement. But running a club proved too much of a financial challenge for Kauffman. By 1966, he was bankrupt. The Golden Bear closed again, but not for long. (Above, courtesy OC Archives.)

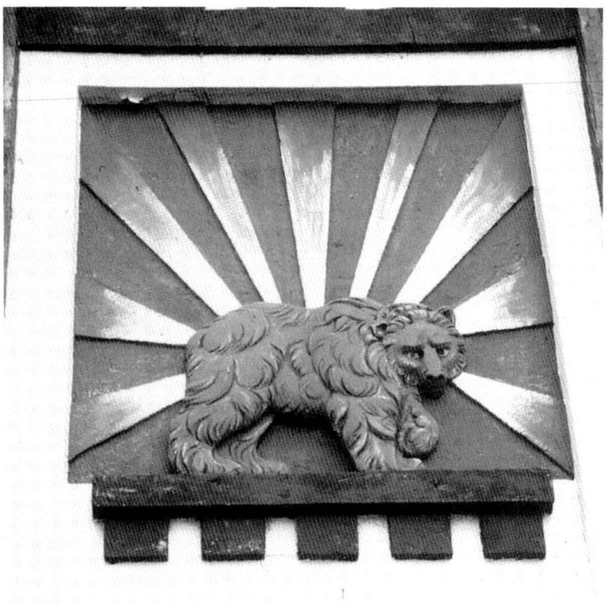

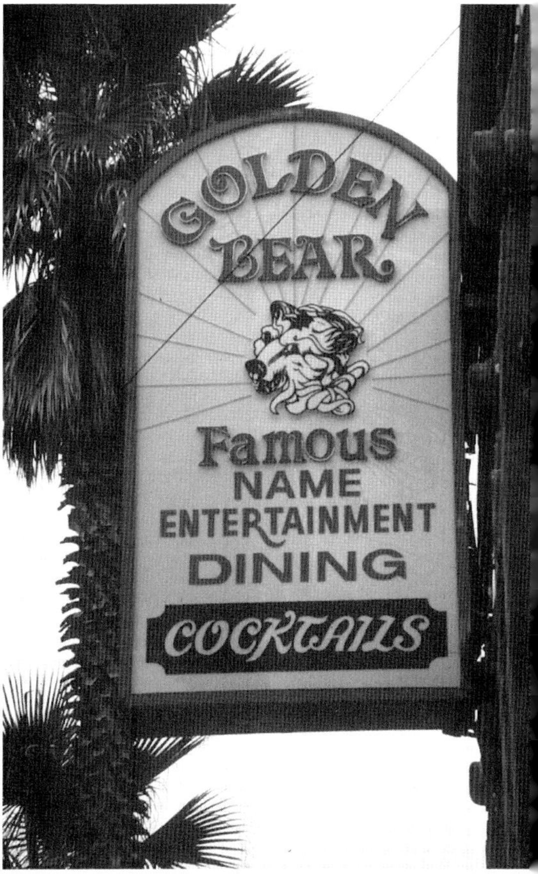

A Second Chance

George Nikas reopened the Golden Bear in 1966 while also opening venues in nearby Seal Beach. With his guidance, the club continued to grow and was soon booking more national acts, including the Flying Burrito Brothers, Richie Havens, and Janis Joplin, who appeared many times. Nikas operated the club until 1974, further establishing it as one of the most popular and acclaimed venues in Southern California. The Golden Bear in Huntington Beach continued to thrive. In 1974, it was purchased by brothers Rick and Chuck Babiracki, along with Rick's wife, Carole. They continued building the legacy of the Bear by booking many of the more relevant and meaningful touring bands of the mid-1970s. Jerry Garcia, Muddy Waters, Patti Smith, the Ramones, Arlo Guthrie, and many others flocked to play there. In 1986, the city was going through a major amount of redevelopment, and the costs involved in retrofitting the brick building for seismic compliance were simply too high for the owners. The final performance at the Golden Bear took place on January 29, 1986, by guitarist Robin Trower. Pictured below are Carole and her friend Dan McCoy, who used to work at the Golden Bear.

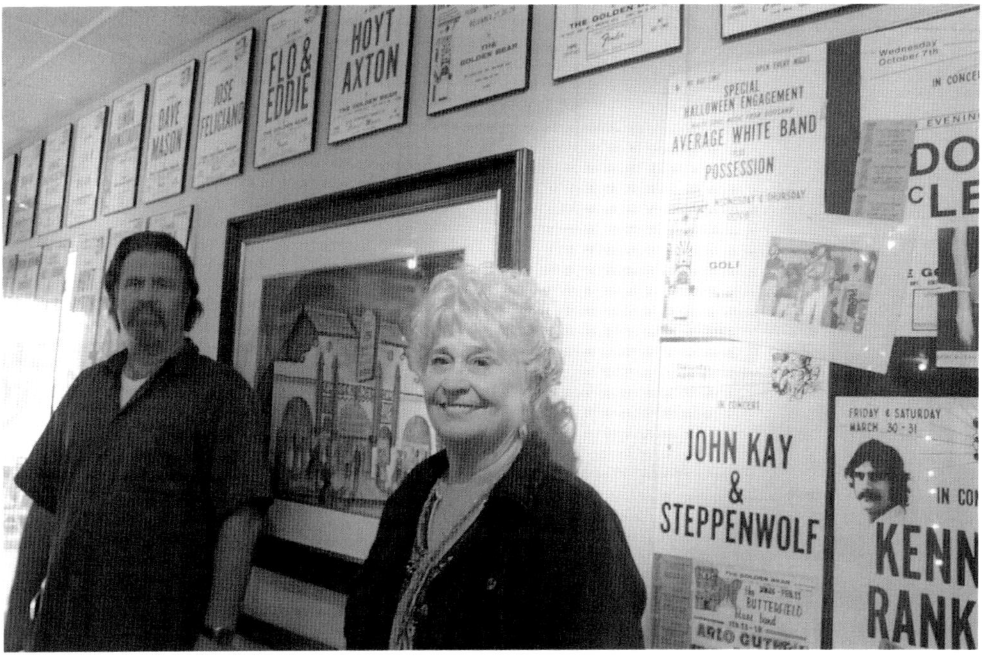

Television Star

Patrick Warburton is famous for many television and film roles. On the small screen, he appeared on *Seinfeld, News Radio, Rules of Engagement*, and many other series. On the big screen, his voice was heard in *The Emperor's New Groove*, among many other productions. In Huntington Beach, Warburton attended St. Simon and Jude School and later went to nearby Servite High School in Anaheim. He studied marine biology at Orange Coast College in Costa Mesa but soon dropped out to pursue modeling and acting.

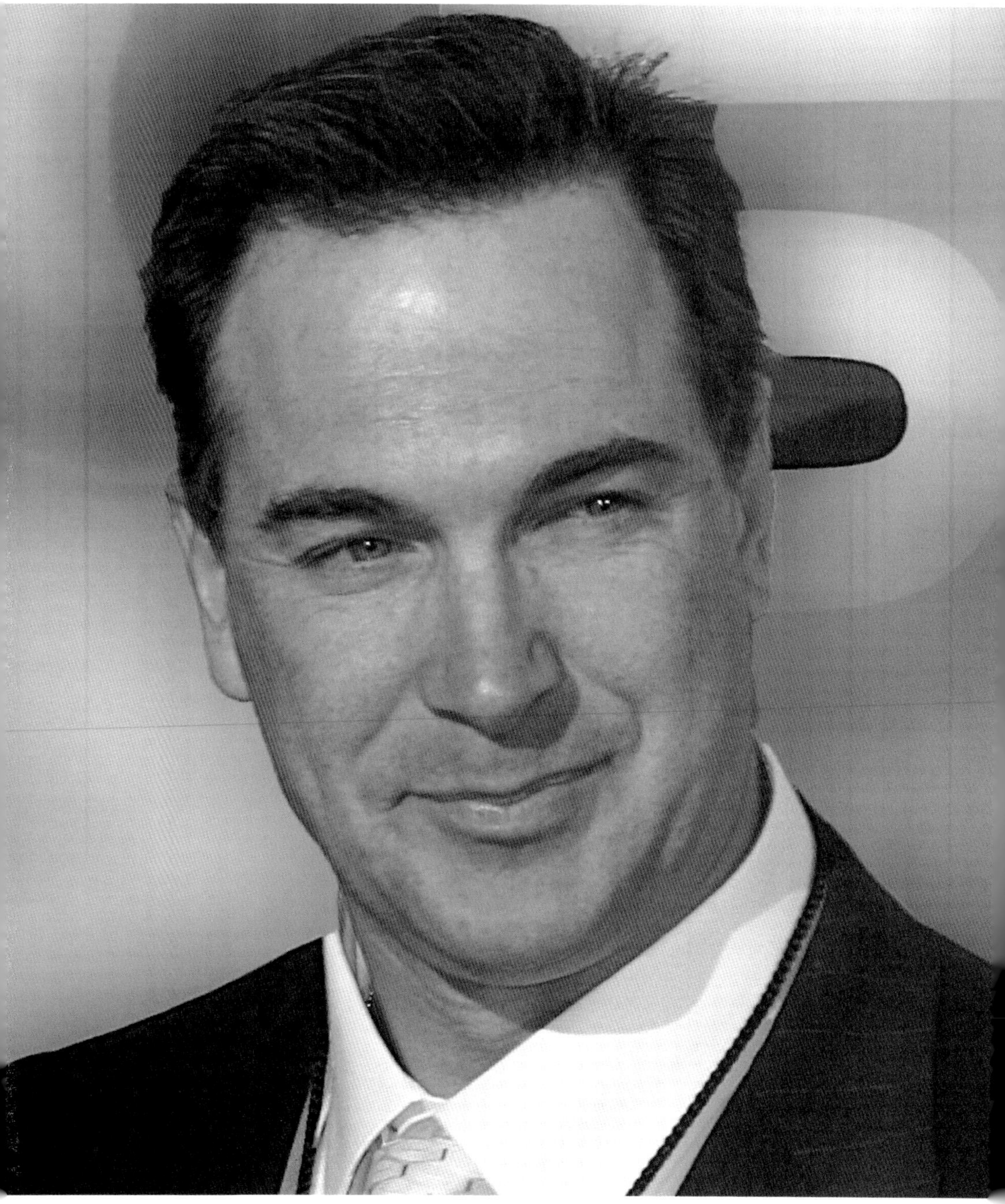

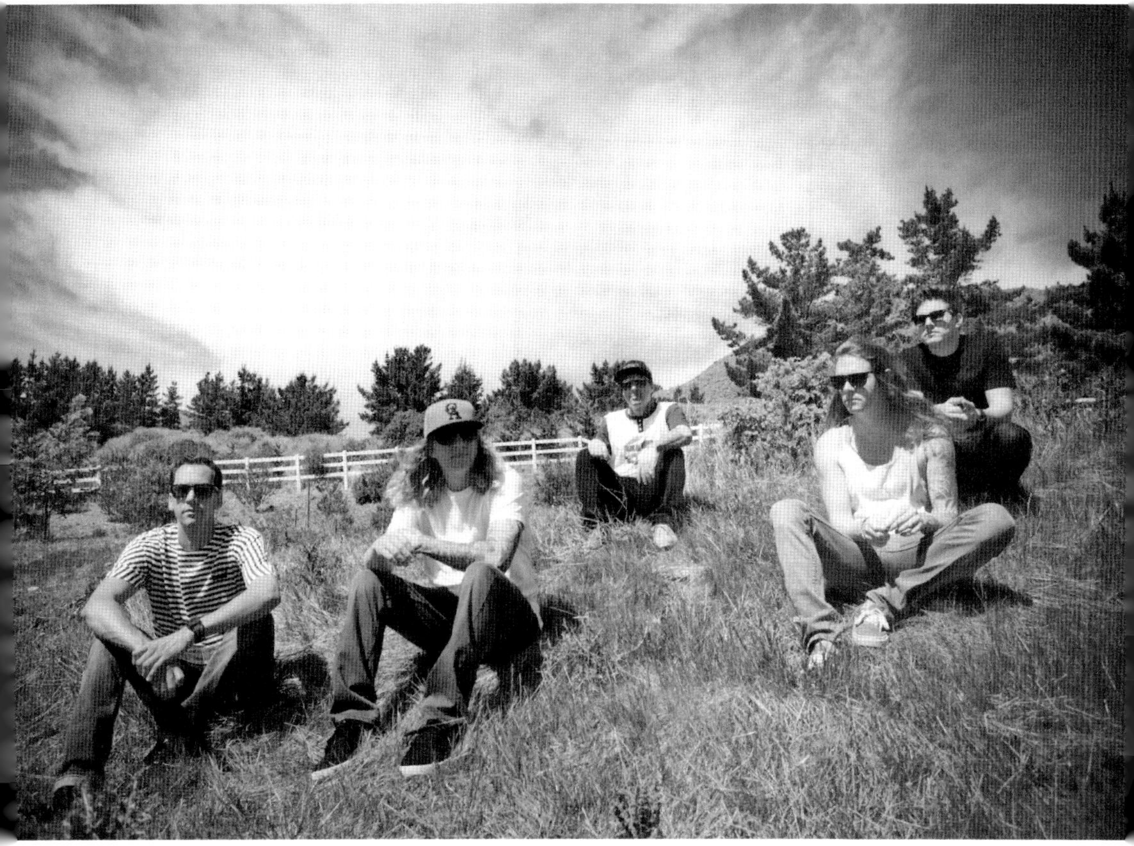

Dirty Heads

Inspired by another Southern California band, Sublime, the Dirty Heads fuse hip-hop, rock, and reggae with a laid-back flavor and lots of beach attitude. The band got together in 2003 in Huntington Beach, when Dustin Bushnell joined forces with his friend, rapper Jared Watson. They soon had a percussionist and began performing as an acoustic trio. The first album, 2008's *Any Port in a Storm*, put the band on the musical map, thanks to a tune called "Lay Me Down," which featured special guest Rome Ramirez of the band Sublime with Rome. The song topped Billboard's Alternative Songs chart before the summer of 2010 and became an instant beach classic. Since then, the Dirty Heads have continued to build upon their success, playing sold-out shows around the world. They released *Cabin by the Sea* in 2012 and *Home–Phantoms of Summer* in 2013, and as of this writing, their latest hit release is the album *Sound of Change*.

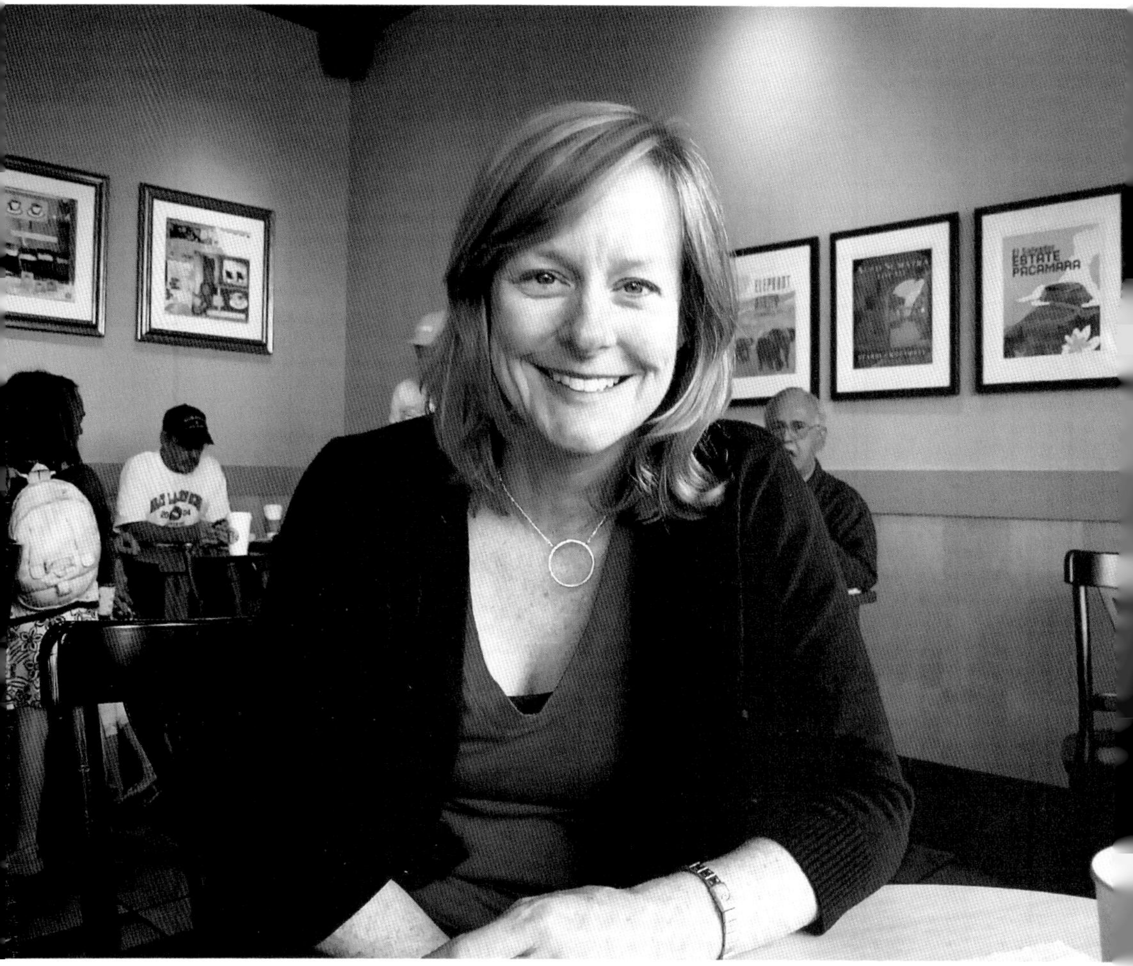

A Walton (ABOVE AND OPPOSITE PAGE)
"I was 10 years old and that was my first audition. Imagine, getting a part on 'The Waltons' your first time out." Imagine. But it happened, and Mary McDonough, sitting in a coffee shop near Bolsa Chica Street and Heil Avenue in Huntington Beach, still appears to be beaming over the experience. The shop is near where she conducts acting classes for young students. Pretty and bright-eyed, the woman millions knew as Erin Walton speaks about an upcoming reunion with the remaining cast members, sort of a floating luncheon that rotates from house to house. She is comfortable telling stories about what it was like entering people's homes for 11 years, portraying a member of one of television's most beloved families. She has also worked as an on-camera host and been in numerous commercials, along with having written and directed. McDonough lives in this neck of the woods now, and she loves the teaching she gets to do. "They're acting classes," she says, "so obviously they're geared to help young people hone their performance skills. But, beyond that, my classes are also designed to help kids deal with things in life. After all, every day we all face challenges that require a certain performance, a certain confidence and belief in oneself, whether it's at school, interviewing for a job, or auditioning for a part." In the photograph on the opposite page, the cast of *The Waltons* included, from left to right, John Walmsley, Ralph Waite, Kami Colter, David W. Harper, Eric Scott, and Mary McDonough.

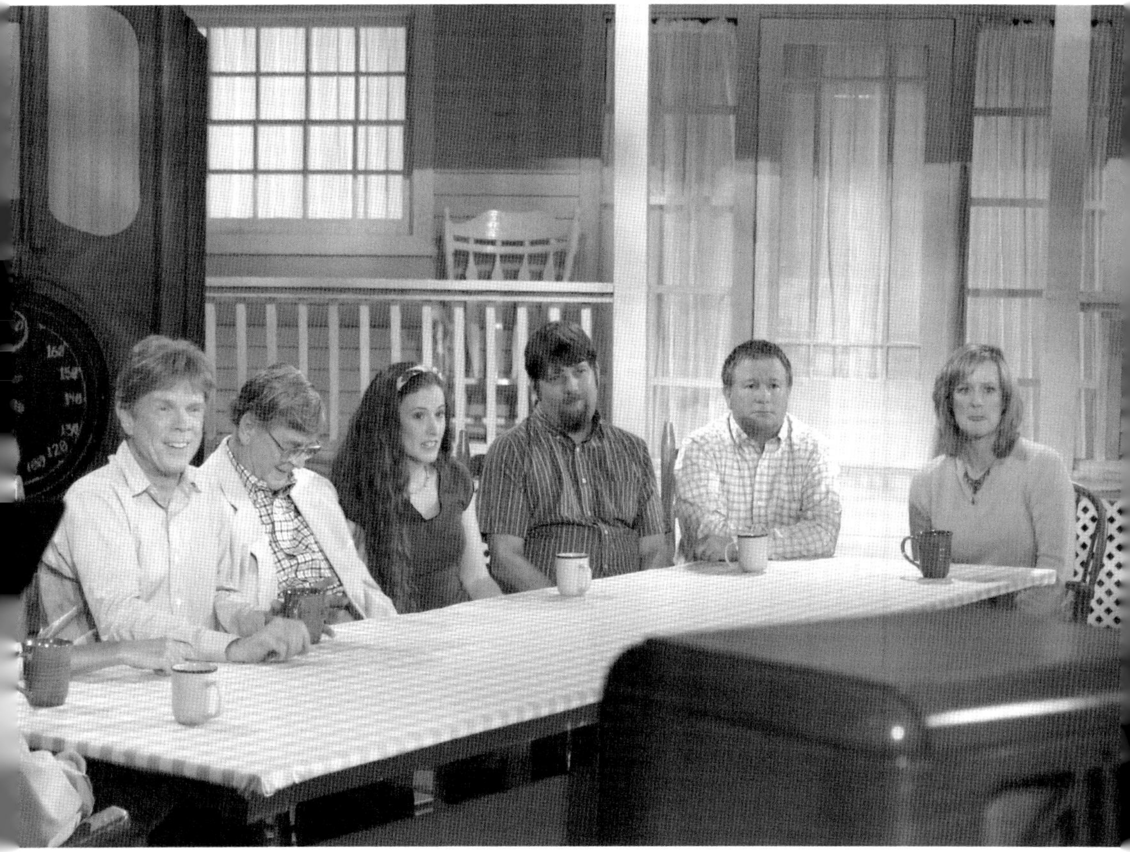

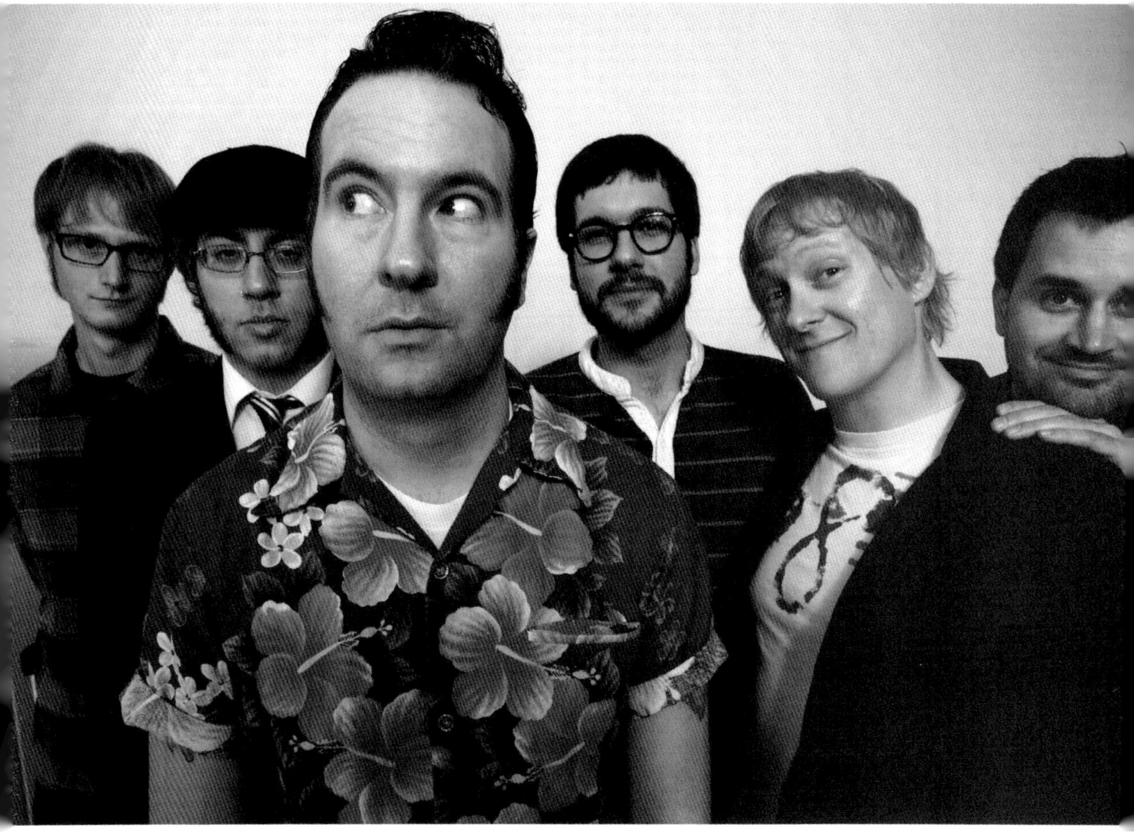

Reel Big Fish

It was on the wave of popularity started by ska-punk bands like No Doubt and Sublime that Huntington Beach's Reel Big Fish found their own fan base. Like their peers, Reel Big Fish delivered high-energy shows, humor, offbeat cover tunes, and a unique form of suburban ska. In the summer of 1997, their single "Sell Out" became a wild MTV and radio favorite, establishing the band as a commercial force. Its appearance in the movie *Baseketball* as the halftime band pushed its brand further, and the band toured all over the world. Over the years, the band has experienced a variety of lineup changes, but it continues to tour and record to this day.

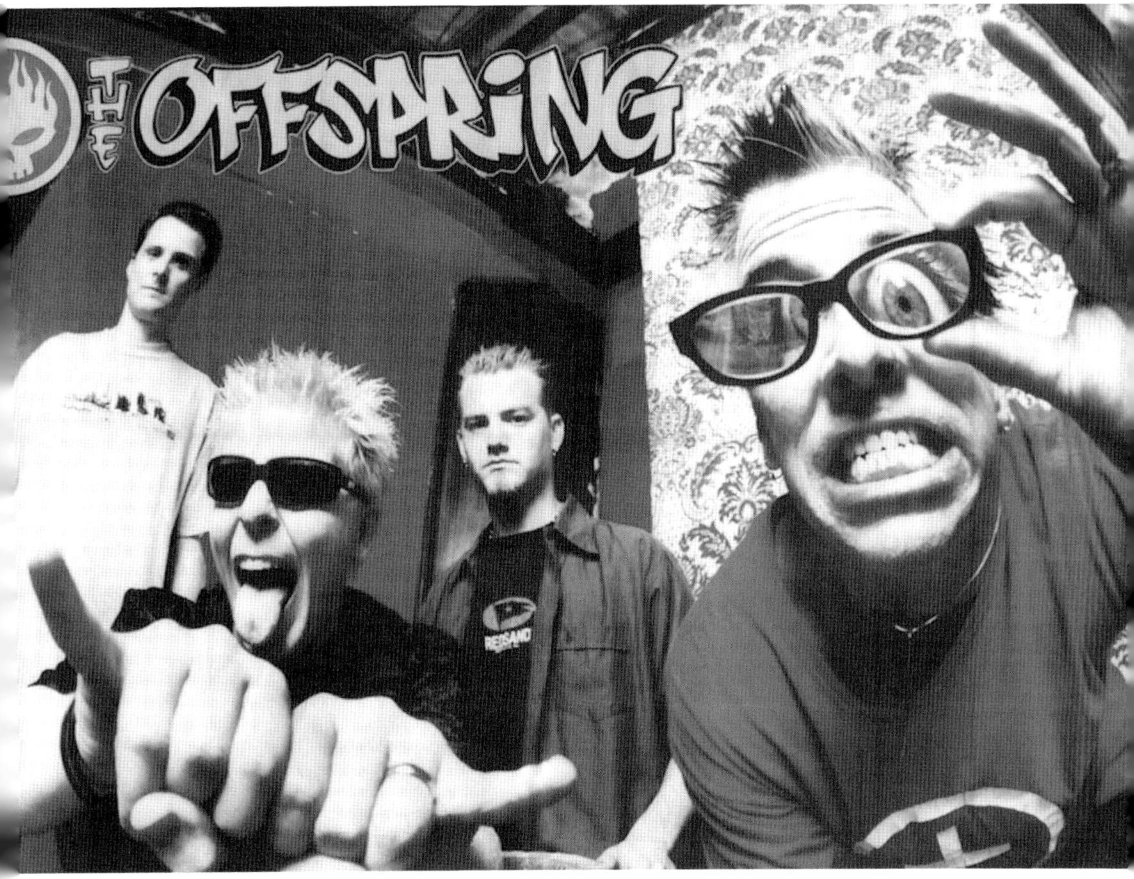

The Offspring

The next wave of new clubs and bands in Orange County was about to emerge. Were it not for a riot at a 1984 Social Distortion show in Irvine, the Offspring might never have happened. The Huntington Beach punk band, including guitarist/singer Bryan "Dexter" Holland and bassist Greg Kriesel, were inspired after that concert. They had already begun tinkering in a garage in Cyprus, but it was the Social Distortion show that led them to form a band called Manic Subsidal. Soon, they added vocalist Doug Thompson and drummer Jim Benton. Thompson would eventually leave, Holland would take over vocals, and Benton would be replaced by James Lilja on the drums. In 1985, Kevin Wasserman came aboard as a second guitarist, and, a year later, they became officially known as the Offspring. The band would not sign a record deal for another couple of years, and it took several albums and tours to truly establish itself. But, by the early 1990s, the Offspring had truly arrived. Its 1994 album *Smash* featured a number of hit singles, including "Come Out and Play," "Self Esteem," and "Gotta Get Away." The release set an all-time record for most albums sold by indie label band, clocking in at 16 million units. There have been some lineup adjustments over the years, but the Offspring has remained one of the big musical success stories to come out of Huntington Beach.

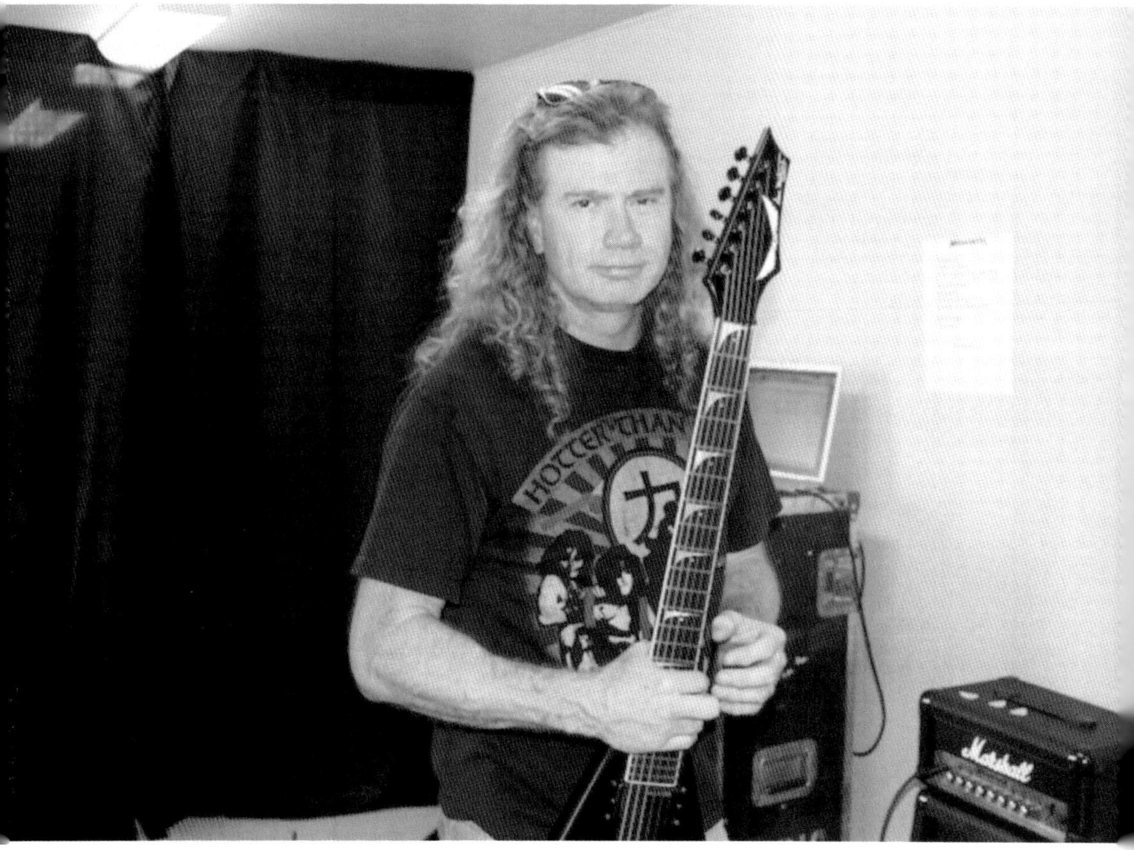

Megadeth
Dave Mustaine is one of the true lions of American heavy metal. An original member of Metallica, he went on to become the founder, lead singer, and lead guitarist of the famed American metal outfit Megadeth. Mustaine, who in the late 1970s attended Marina High School in Huntington Beach, also took his first music lessons in town. Shirley Orlando was owner of Huntington Music at Goldenwest Street and Warner Avenue, where she worked for 26 years. In addition to its being a music store, Orlando used the space to create a haven for area musicians—a place where late-night jam sessions were a common occurrence. And she still remembers the intense teenage guitarist who used to shred in her shop. In Mustaine's compelling 2010 biography, *Mustaine, a Heavy Metal Memoir*, he writes of his years in Huntington Beach, going to high school and working at the nearby Westminster Mall.

Korn

Originally from Bakersfield, Korn relocated to Orange County in 1993 and rented a local studio in Huntington Beach called Underground Chicken Sound. It began playing around Orange County, including regular gigs in Huntington Beach at Club 5902, the original site of Night Moves. While sharing a house in town, the band was spotted by an Epic Records A&R man named Paul Pontious. In Korn, Pontious heard something wildly different and provocative; a darkly ferocious and rhythmic musical concoction that would soon earn the term "nu metal." Led by front man Jonathan Davis, Korn released its initial demo, *Niedermayer's Mind*, in 1993. Though not many copies were printed, the album was influential enough to attract significant attention. In 1994, the band began recording its debut album, and on October 11, this self-titled debut was released on Immortal Records. The band's mainstream breakthrough happened with its third album, *Follow the Leader.* Since starting out in Huntington Beach, Korn has gone on to become one of the most commercially and critically successful bands of its generation. (Courtesy of Charles Epting.)

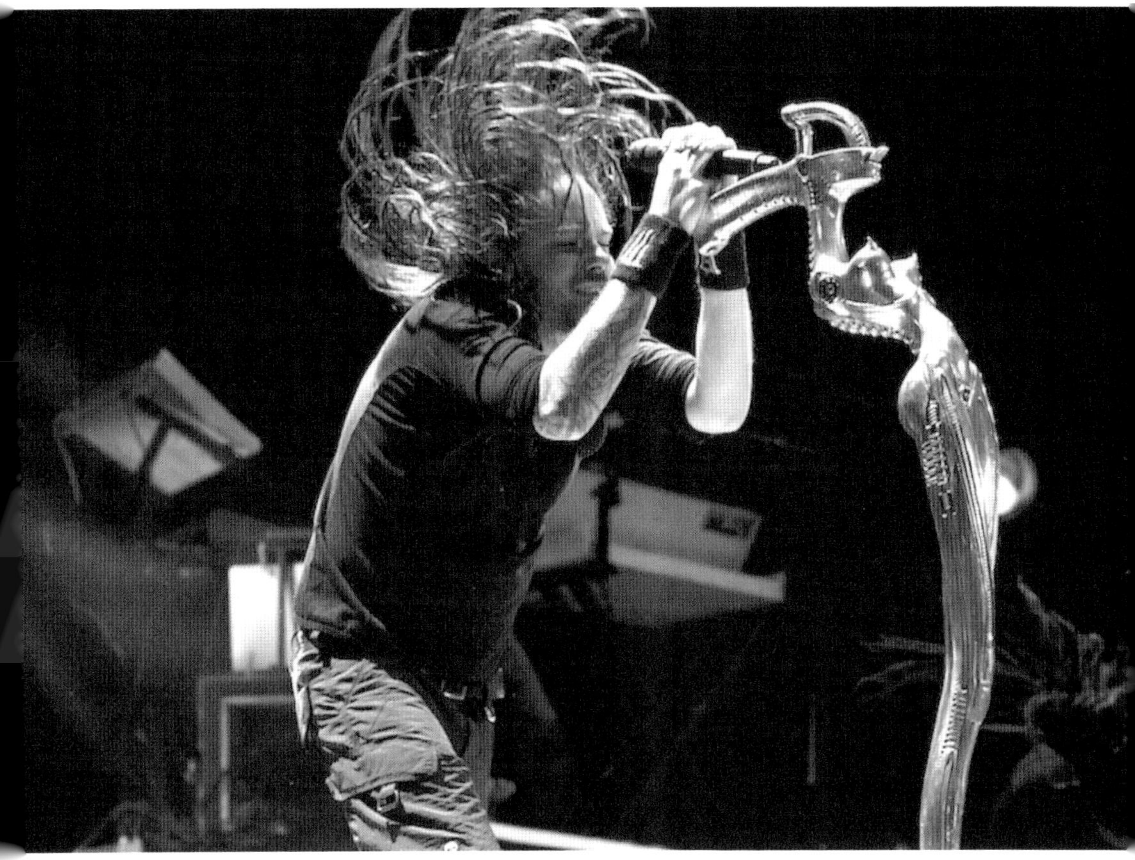

Surf Music Star

For years, he has been one of the most iconic residents of Surf City, one of the men that made the song "Surf City" famous. In the 1960s, Dean Torrence was part of one of the most famous duos in rock 'n' roll history, Jan and Dean. Along with the Beach Boys, the duo helped pioneer the surf-music craze that became so influential in the early 1960s. Torrence's partner, Jan Berry, was severely injured in a 1960s car accident that derailed what was destined to become one of the great pop-music careers. However, the pair managed to keep working until Barry's death in 2004. Torrence's multifaceted career also includes a Grammy Award for designing the best album cover of 1972, for the band Pollution. He has also received a handful of Grammy nominations. In fact, Torrence's career as an art director actually rivals his career as a singer. Today, Torrence still tours with the group he put together, Surf City All-Stars. He has lived in Huntington Beach for a long time with his wife and two daughters and has served as a kind of unofficial city spokesman, especially since Huntington Beach began marketing itself as "Surf City." That song, a number-one hit on both the Billboard and Cashbox music charts in the summer of 1963, still remains a local anthem.

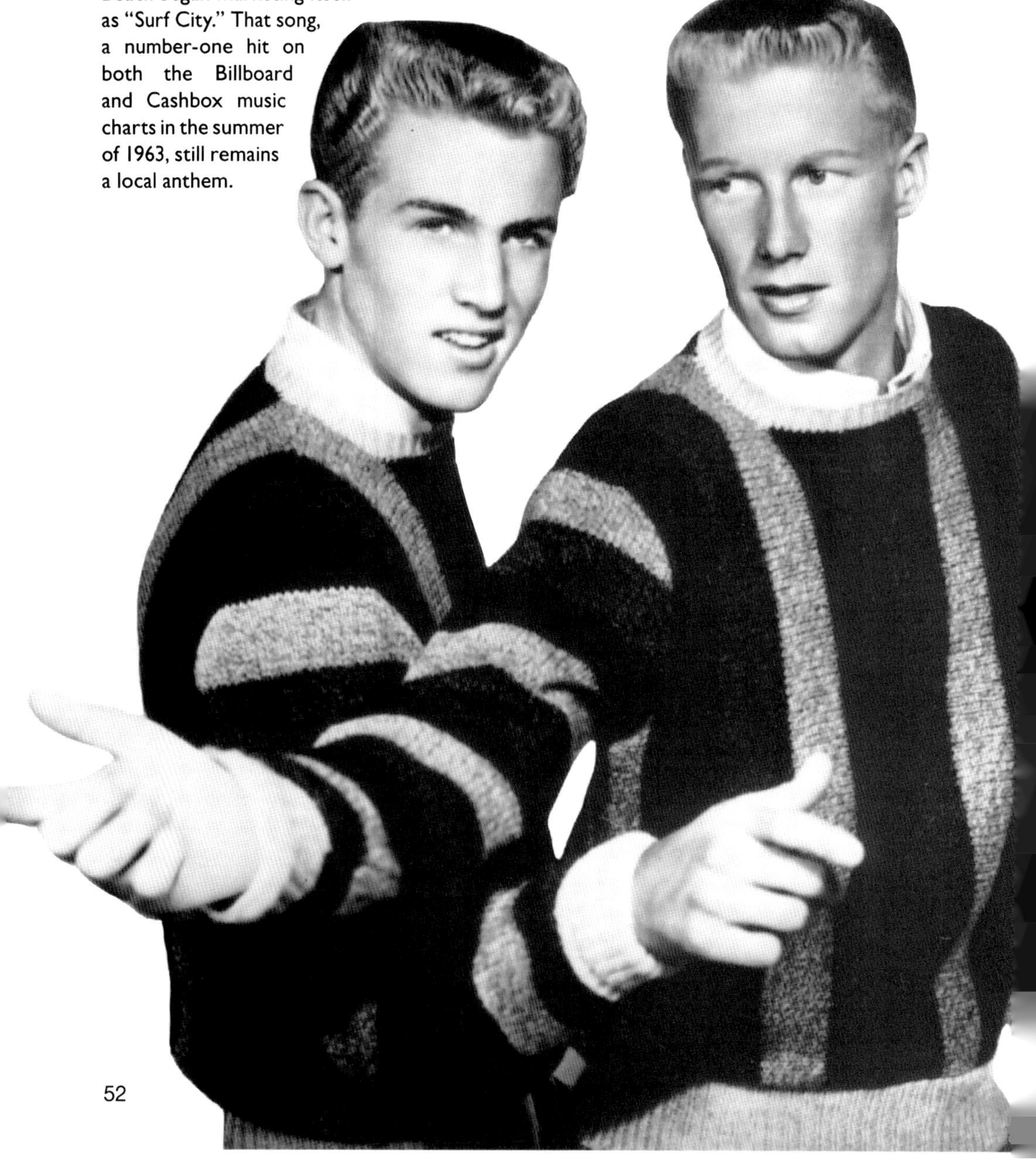

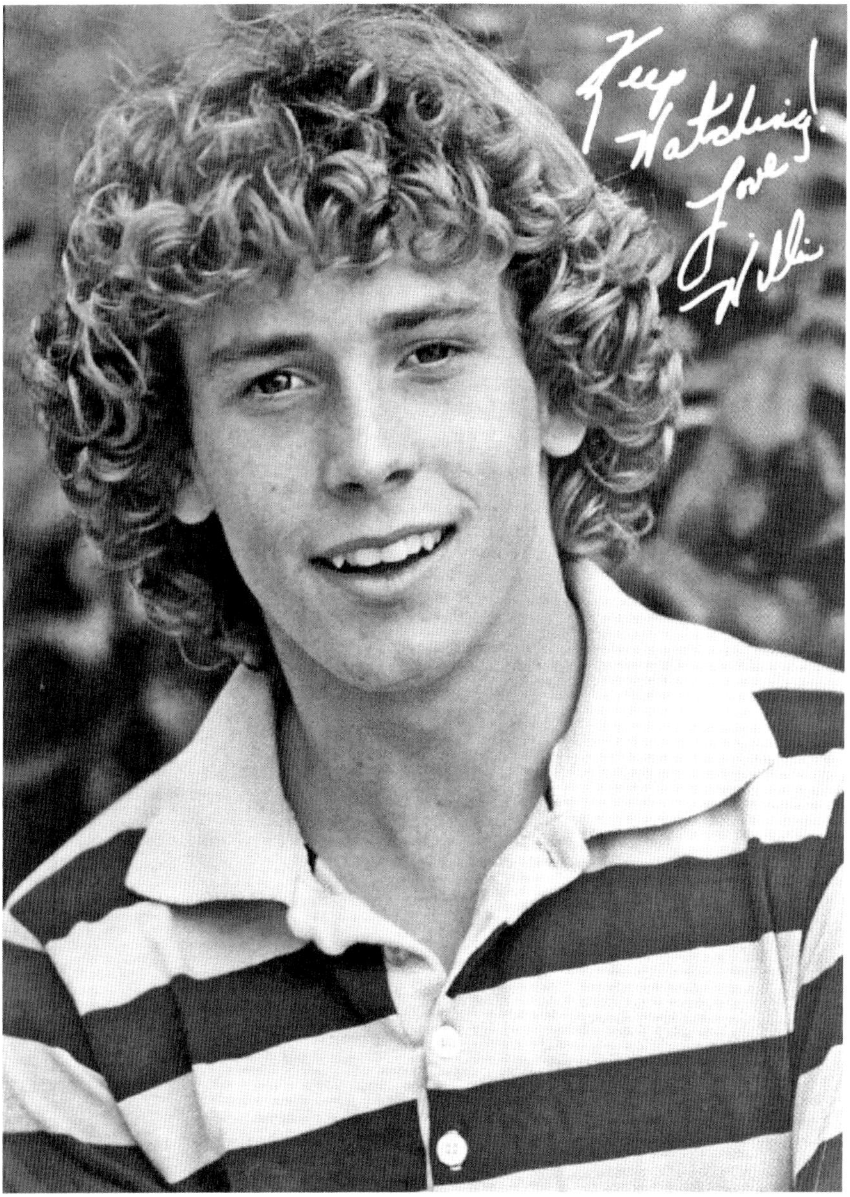

The Actor

Willie Aames was one of the most popular child actors of his time, starting in the late 1960s and appearing on such hit shows as *Gunsmoke*, *Adam-12*, and *The Courtship of Eddie's Father.* In 1971, he was cast as the son of Felix Unger (Tony Randall) on the ABC television series *The Odd Couple*. Many roles followed in the mid-1970s until, in 1976, he won the part that made him famous, Tommy Bradford, in the comedy-drama *Eight Is Enough*. Born Albert William Upton in nearby Newport Beach, Aames attended Edison High School in Huntington Beach, where he also sang in the choir. He continued acting throughout the 1980s, finding even bigger fame on *Charles in Charge* (1984–1990), costarring with Scott Baio. He battled cocaine and depression through this time but, by the early 1990s, had cleaned up his act, become a born-again Christian, and moved to the Midwest, becoming a commercial producer and director. Aames has returned to acting and is recalled fondly by former Edison High School classmates.

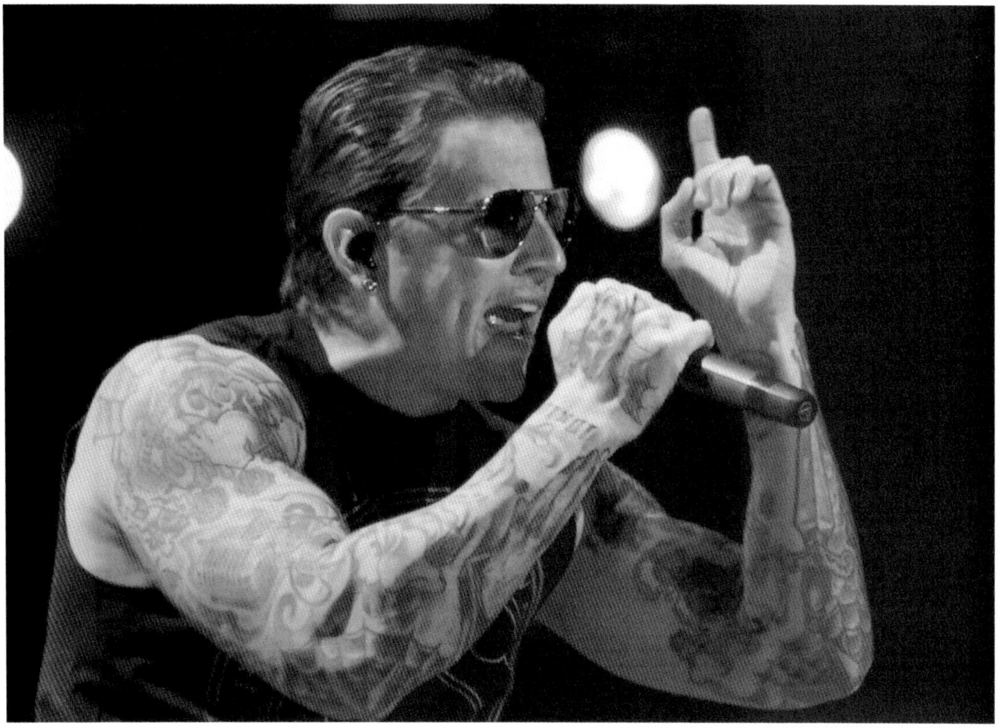

Metal Masters (ABOVE AND OPPOSITE PAGE)
Avenged Sevenfold formed in 1999, with lead vocalist M. Shadows (above), guitarists Zacky Vengeance and Synyster Gates, drummer Jimmy Sullivan, and bassist Matt Wendt (later replaced by Justin Sane). The band cut two demos in 1999 and 2000. After a series of personnel changes, including landing bass player Johnny Christ, the band released its second studio album, *Waking the Fallen* (2003). Now on the Hopeless Records label, the group hit the road on the Vans Warped Tour, among other high-profile tours. Signing with Warner Bros., it next released *City of Evil* in 2005. The album sold 30,000 copies in its first week of release. Avenged Sevenfold played Ozzfest in 2006 and was named best new artist at the MTV Music Awards. The band's dramatic themes and darkly personal lyrics won it a fiercely dedicated and loyal fan base from very early on. Its next release, a 2007 self-titled effort, won it even more fans as it moved further from its death-metal roots and into a more mainstream form of metal that still managed to embrace the emotion and heaviness of earlier efforts. Then, on the heels of a major breakthrough in the form of the band's first number-one album, tragedy struck. On December 28, 2009, Sullivan was found dead at his home in Huntington Beach. Original autopsy results were inconclusive, but, six months later, the cause of death was found to have been intoxication due to combined effects of a variety of prescription drugs. The members originally considered disbanding in the wake of the loss of their musical brother. But in February 2010, they returned to the studio, with Dream Theater drummer Mike Portnoy filling in for Sullivan. Portnoy had been one of Sullivan's idols. After Portnoy reached out to the band to offer his condolences following Sullivan's death, discussions took place that eventually resulted in Portnoy filling in for the fallen drummer. After the album *Nightmare* was released in July 2010, Portnoy went on the road with the band to fill in. By the end of the year, Portnoy left the band, which eventually settled on drummer Arin Illejay as Sullivan's full-time replacement. In 2012, Avenged Sevenfold won the awards for Best Live Band and Most Dedicated Fans at the Revolver Golden Gods Awards. Touring around the world relentlessly, its fan base became stronger and stronger. On August 27, 2013, its album *Hail to the King* was released. It revealed a more classic and mature metal sound for A7X, as the band is also known. The Sullivan family, pictured below opposite, are, from left to right, Jimmy, Joe, Katie, and Kelly, with Barbara in front. (Above and opposite, top, courtesy of Charles Epting; opposite, below, courtesy of the Sullivan family.)

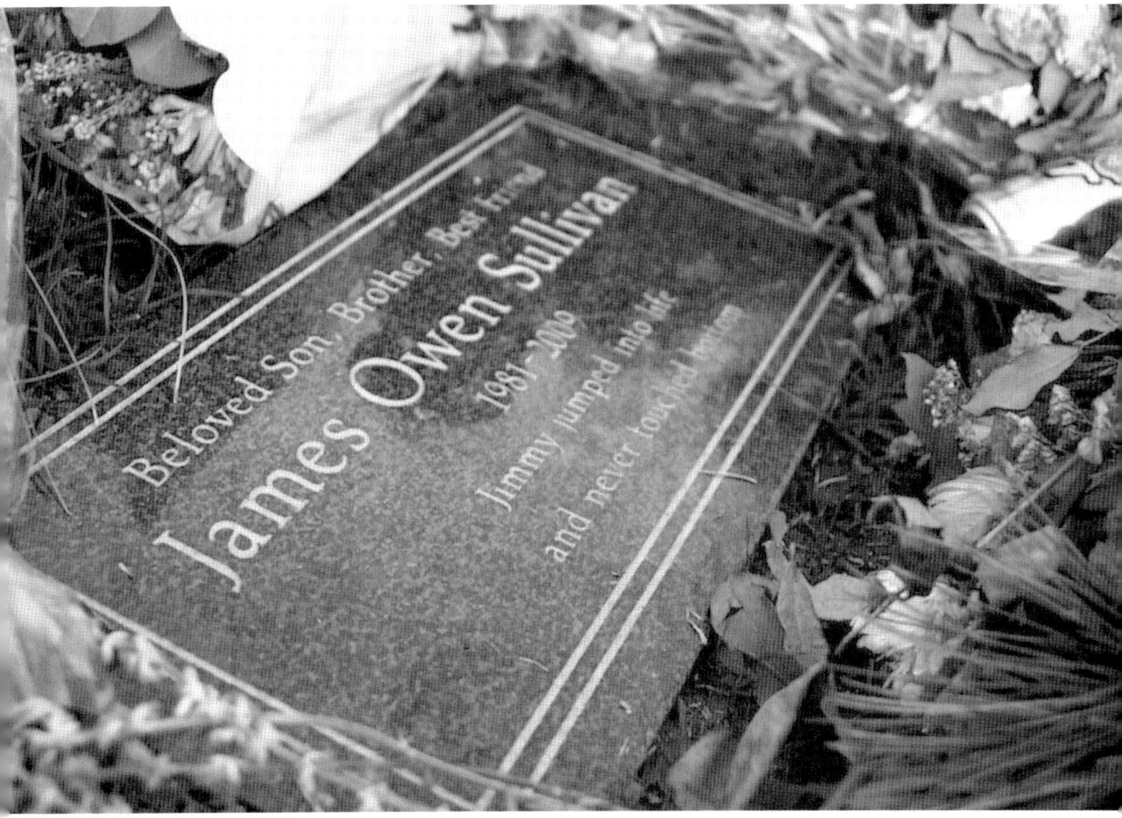
Beloved Son, Brother, Best Friend
James Owen Sullivan
1981–2006
Jimmy jumped into life
and never touched bottom

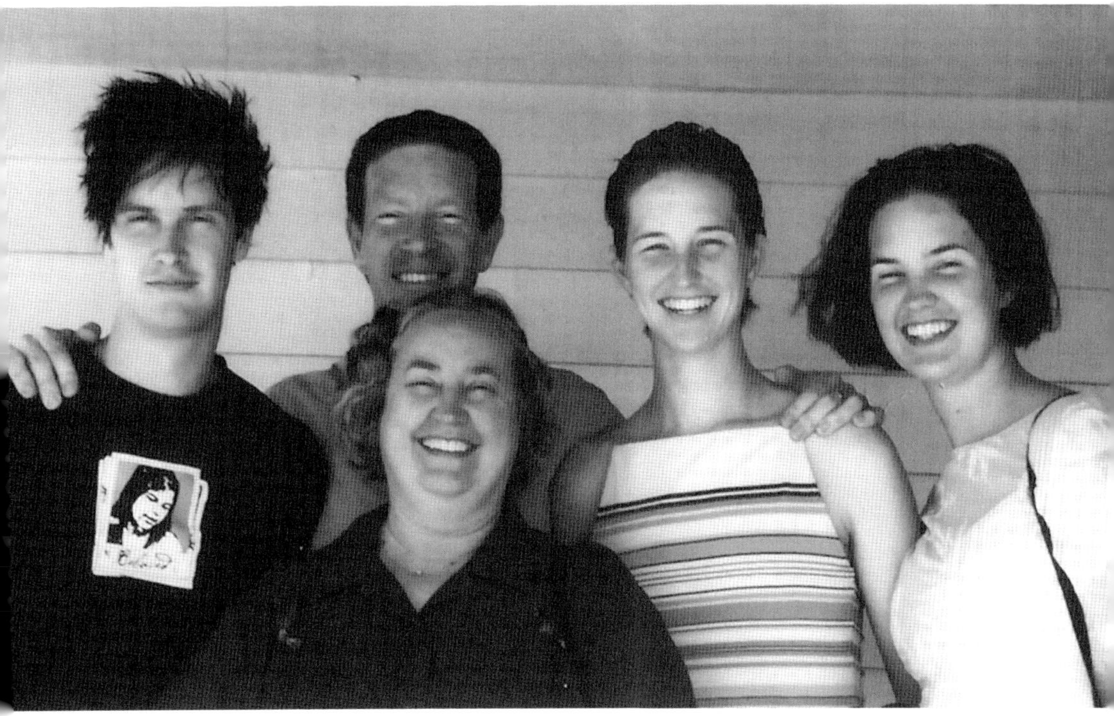

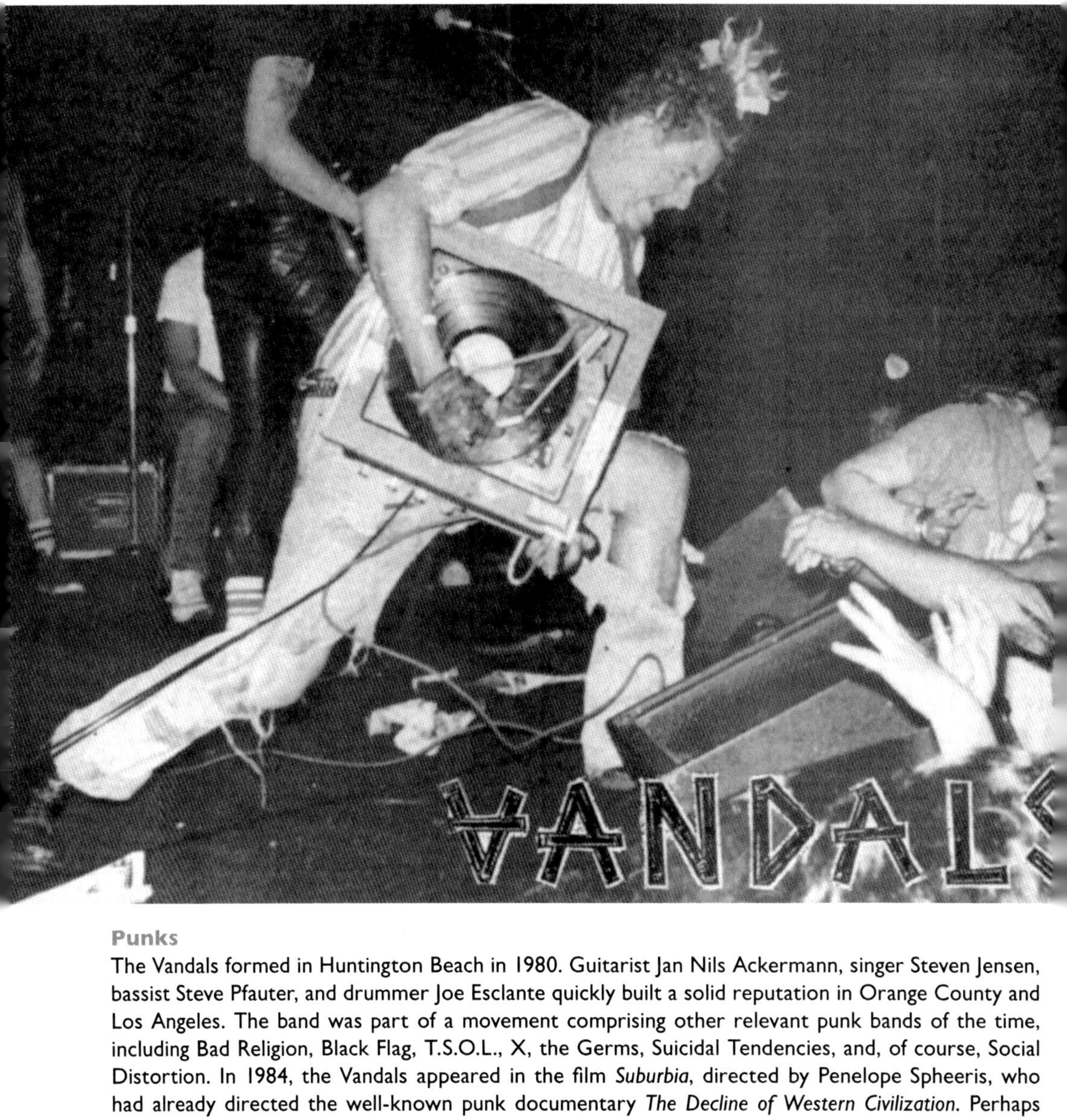

Punks

The Vandals formed in Huntington Beach in 1980. Guitarist Jan Nils Ackermann, singer Steven Jensen, bassist Steve Pfauter, and drummer Joe Esclante quickly built a solid reputation in Orange County and Los Angeles. The band was part of a movement comprising other relevant punk bands of the time, including Bad Religion, Black Flag, T.S.O.L., X, the Germs, Suicidal Tendencies, and, of course, Social Distortion. In 1984, the Vandals appeared in the film *Suburbia*, directed by Penelope Spheeris, who had already directed the well-known punk documentary *The Decline of Western Civilization*. Perhaps infamously, the Vandals played a benefit concert that year in Orange County for the Cypress College Young Republicans, being joined with other punk stalwarts the Circle Jerks and the Dickies, among others. The performance drew heavy criticism from the anarchy-driven punk community.

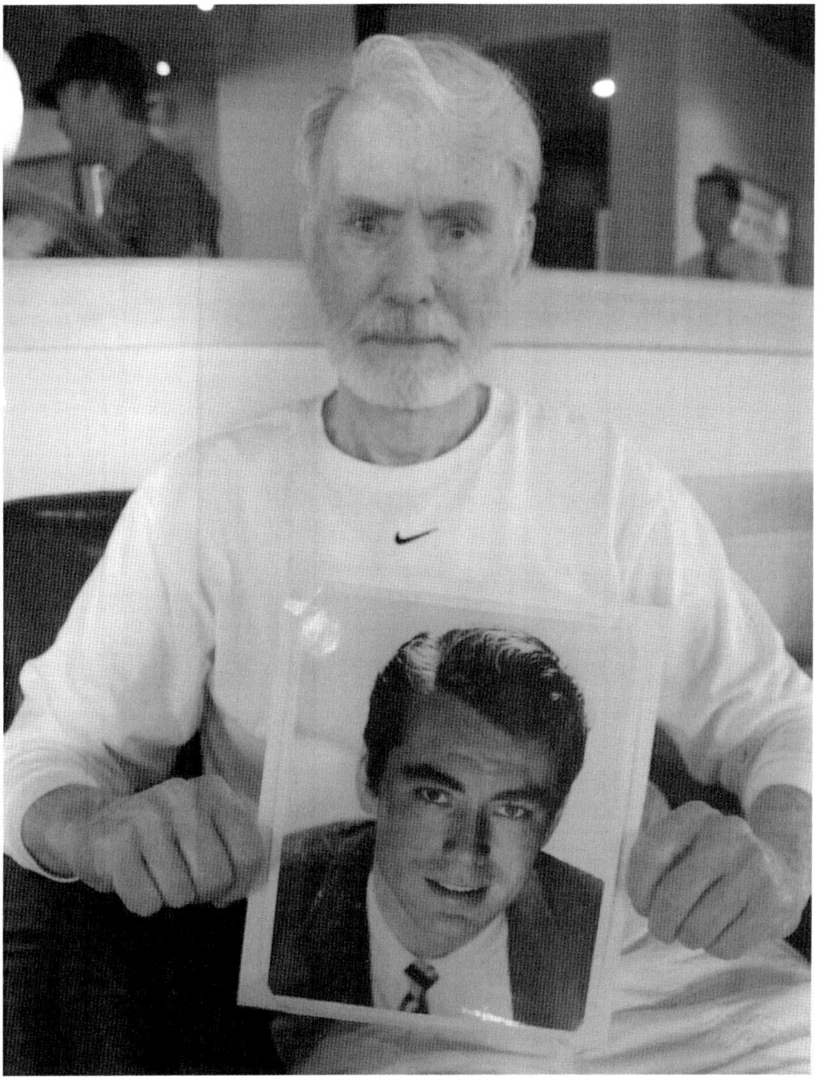

Actor and Writer

"I was working at Googies the Sunday Dean was killed and as you now know, I knew him fairly well, and I swear it was as if a meteor had crashed into Hollywood killing thousands. People on the street who had no connection to the industry were weeping." Steve Hayes is referring to James Dean. He also recounts the death of another Hollywood icon: "Same with [Marilyn] Monroe. I knew women who wore black for weeks in mourning. My then-wife Janet summed it up perfectly when she said: 'Hell, had she'd known it would cause this much of a stir, she would have killed herself years ago!' And remember, Janet and I knew her pretty well." Hayes, an author, actor, painter, and raconteur, is so blessed with the art of storytelling (and of living life!) that he has already filled two books of memoirs, *Googies, Coffeeshop to the Stars*, parts one and two. Hayes's life is almost comically rich with provocative, romantic escapades and adventures. But, as interesting as his past is, it is his current life and, no doubt, his future that make him most compelling. Hayes, 83, works out at the gym from about 4:00 to 6:00 a.m., six days a week. In the 1950s, Hayes's dashing, matinee-idol looks landed him plenty of small parts. But the writer in him won out, and, to date, he has penned countless screenplays for television and film, almost two dozen fiction books, and his two-part, all-but-impossible-to-put-down memoir.

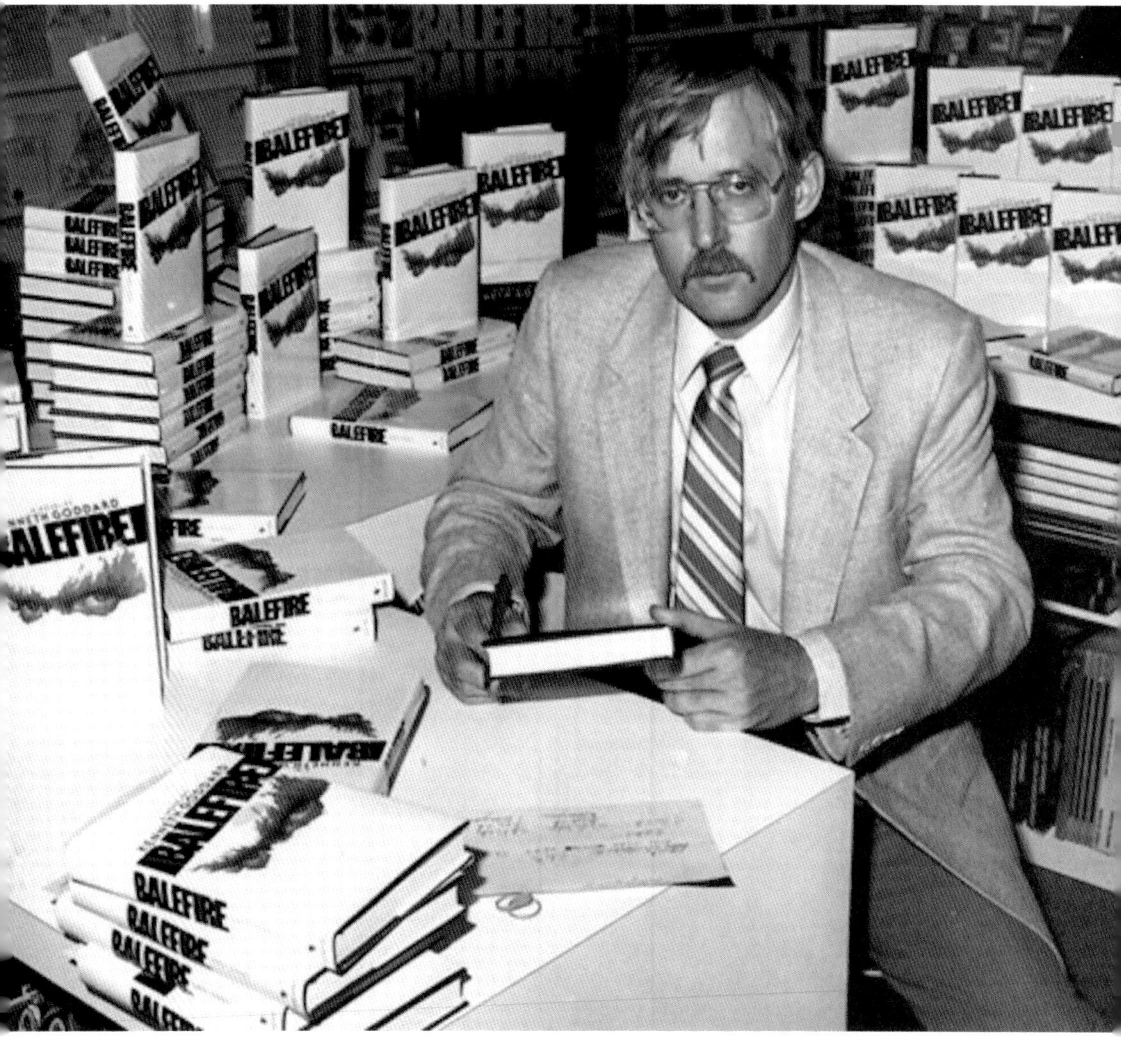

Bestselling Author

That a terrorist group would choose Huntington Beach not just as its base of operations, but also as ground zero for one of the most cataclysmic attacks in US history, is hard to fathom. Yet, reading the story, it all seems frighteningly simple and realistic. How could this happen right here? Ken Goddard, who wrote the classic 1984 *New York Times* bestseller *Balefire*, is the man who knows. Seeds for the story were planted in 1978 while Goddard was the primary crime-scene investigator in Huntington Beach. The story in the book actually takes place on the eve of the 1984 Los Angeles Olympics. Goddard got the inspiration from a lecture by his boss, Chief Earl Robitaille. "Chief Robitaille, who has retired but I think still lives in Huntington Beach, didn't think the HBPD was taking his warning about terrorism in regards to the Olympics seriously, and he was a real expert," Goddard said. "So this concerned him. I was in charge of the force's Scientific Investigation Bureau—I was the chief criminalist then—and what he said caught my ear. And it really scared me. And that's what made me start thinking about writing a story. His presentations to us inspired me, because of how scary they were." Goddard is still writing novels, and *Balefire* will soon be coming to the big screen.

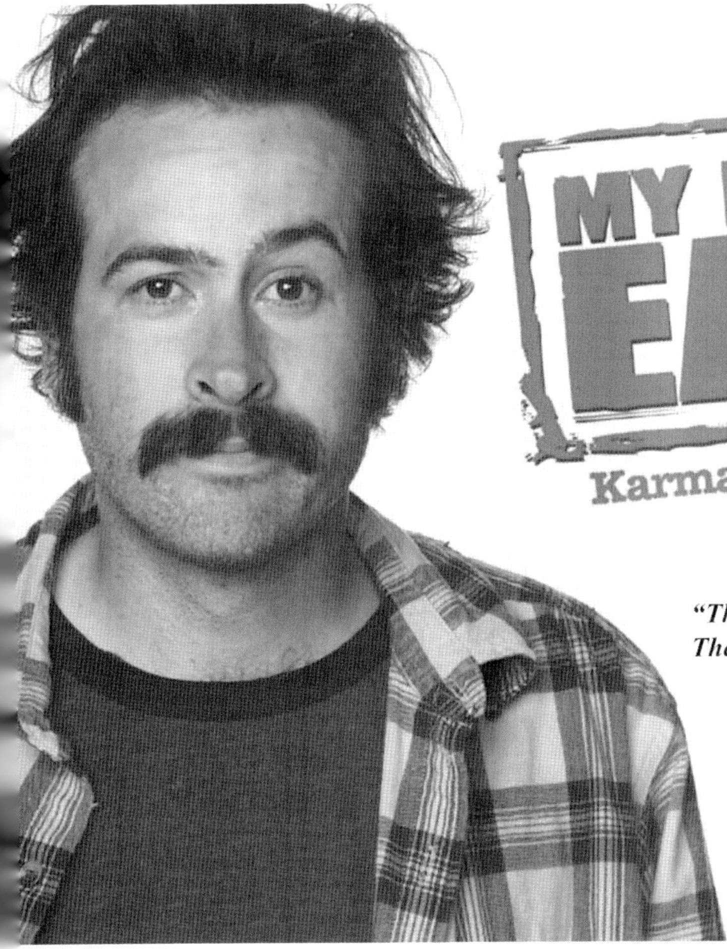

MY NAME IS EARL

Karma is a funny thing.

"The Secret To Life Is Fixing All The Bad Things That You've Done"

His Name Was Earl

Actor Jason Lee, probably best known for his role as the title character on the NBC hit series *My Name Is Earl*, is a Huntington Beach local who attended Oceanview High School. Before becoming an actor, Lee developed a stellar reputation as a professional skateboarder. In the late 1980s, he cofounded Stereo Skateboards and, along with Tony Hawk, was one of the first two skateboarders to receive his own signature shoe with the Air Walk company. He started his acting career in the early 1990s, eventually landing roles in the films *Vanilla Sky* and *Almost Famous*. But, no doubt, the world knows Lee best as Earl Hickey, a petty thief who, after discovering karma, goes on a mission to right all of his past wrongs. He also played Dave in the Alvin and the Chipmunks films.

Stone Temple Pilots

Rock 'n' roll front man Scott Weiland, best known as the lead singer for Stone Temple Pilots and the supergroup Velvet Revolver, attended Edison High School in Huntington Beach. His family had moved to the city when he was a teenager. Soon after graduating, Weiland enrolled at nearby Orange Coast College. In the mid-1980s, Weiland met Robert DeLeo, a bass player, at a Black Flag show in Long Beach. The seeds were planted that night for the band that would make them both famous, Stone Temple Pilots. The band also featured Robert's brother, Dean, on guitar. STP, as they were known, achieved international success, but Weiland's drug problems were a constant challenge for the band. After a series of breakups and reunions, Weiland was finally fired from the band in February 2013. Stone Temple Pilots continues today with Chester Bennington from Linkin Park on lead vocals.

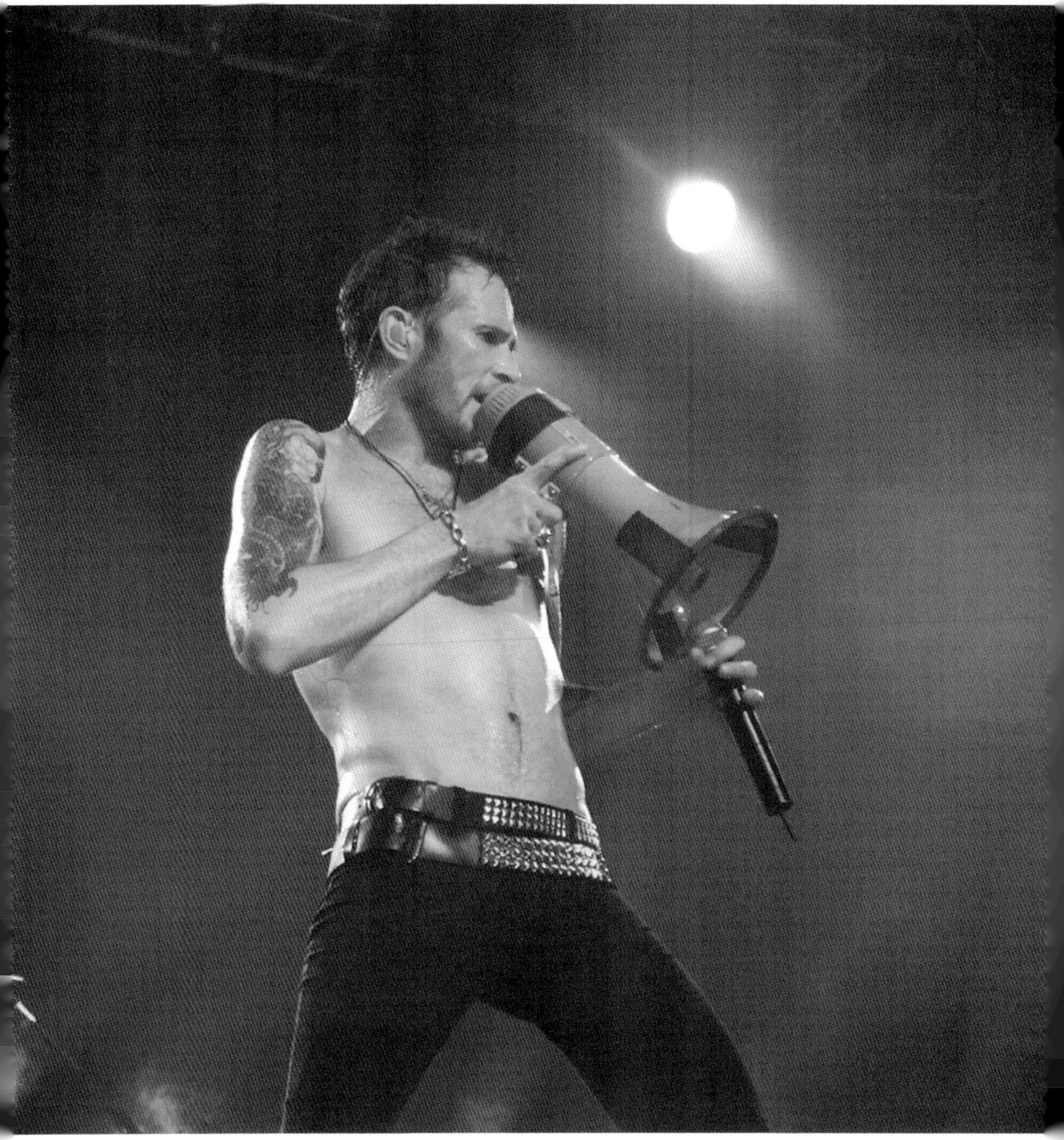

CHAPTER FOUR

Surfing

It all started in 1914, when George Freeth, widely regarded as the first surfer in the United States, demonstrated surfing at the dedication of Huntington Beach's new 1,350-foot-long concrete pier. In 1927, Delbert "Bud" Higgins and Gene Belshe hand-carved the first surfboards from solid redwood, thus creating more interest in the sport. Soon after that, the legendary Hawaiian surfer Duke Kahanamoku came to surf in Huntington Beach with both Higgins and Belshe. Within 10 years or so, Huntington Beach had begun to embrace surfing as a special part of the city. In a chamber of commerce brochure, the following quote appeared: "A real thrill experienced by surfboard riders. Long rolling breakers make Huntington beach an ideal spot for this thrilling sport."

In the 1930s and 1940s, surfing became even more popular in Huntington Beach. This was due in part to lighter wood surfboards and the return of soldiers who had learned how to surf in the Pacific Islands. In 1945, the first rubber wet suit was manufactured in Huntington Beach, making surfing a year-round sport.

As time wore on, there were more firsts. Gordie Duane opened Huntington Beach's first surfboard-shaping shop under the pier in 1956. And when Jack Hokanson opened Jack's Surfboards in 1957, a true industry was under way. In 1959, the first West Coast Surfboard Championship was held in Huntington Beach. In 1964, it became known as the United States Surfing Championships, and then, in 1982, the OP Pro, named for its sponsor, Ocean Pacific. In 1994, the event was rechristened the US Open of Surfing, a name it retains today. In the 1960s and 1970s, the competition was held over Labor Day weekend. However, after riots broke out in 1986, the event was pushed back to July.

In the 1960s, the popular event was covered extensively by ABC-TV's *Wide World of Sports*. Today, surfing is memorialized in downtown Huntington Beach in several ways. The Surfing Walk of Fame is the world's first and only such tribute. It was dedicated in 1994, and today, dozens of renowned surfing legends have been honored in the sidewalks near Main Street and Pacific Coast Highway. Also at Main Street and PCH is a bronze bust of Duke Kahanamoku, created by the surf artist Edmond Shumpert, who also created the famous Ultimate Challenge surfer art along the coast highway, just across the street at the Hilton. And, there is the International Surfing Museum, which attracts visitors from all over the world, all year long.

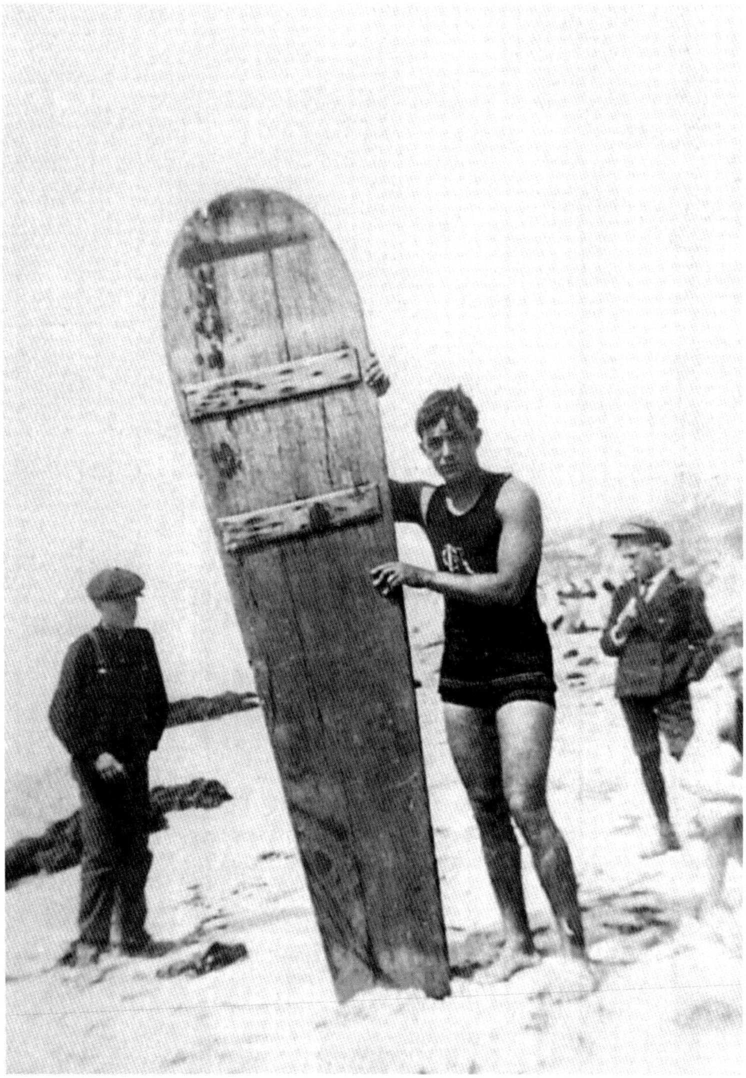

The Father of Modern Surfing
George Freeth is considered the father of modern surfing and is even credited by some with developing the rescue paddleboard, the device still most commonly used by lifeguards to rescue people. He was born in 1883 and lived only to the age of 35, succumbing to the global flu pandemic in 1919. He grew up in Hawaii. After seeing an old Polynesian painting the depicted his parents' ancestors riding surfboards, Freeth decided on his own to revive the art of surfing. However, the huge, 16-foot hardwood boards in style at the time were too hard to manage. So he cut them in half and inadvertently created the original version of the longboard. In 1907, Henry Huntington, on vacation in Hawaii, saw Freeth and commissioned him to come surf in Redondo Beach, where Huntington was investing heavily, to demonstrate the art and thus make the area more attractive and interesting. On the same day the new concrete pier opened in 1914, legendary surfer George Freeth paid a visit and gave the first surfing demonstration in town. Carrying a heavy, eight-foot surfboard made of redwood into the ocean, Freeth performed dazzling feats of balance and dexterity that people had never seen before. His wave-riding earned him a brief mention in the local paper. But that first demonstration made a lasting impression on Huntington Beach.

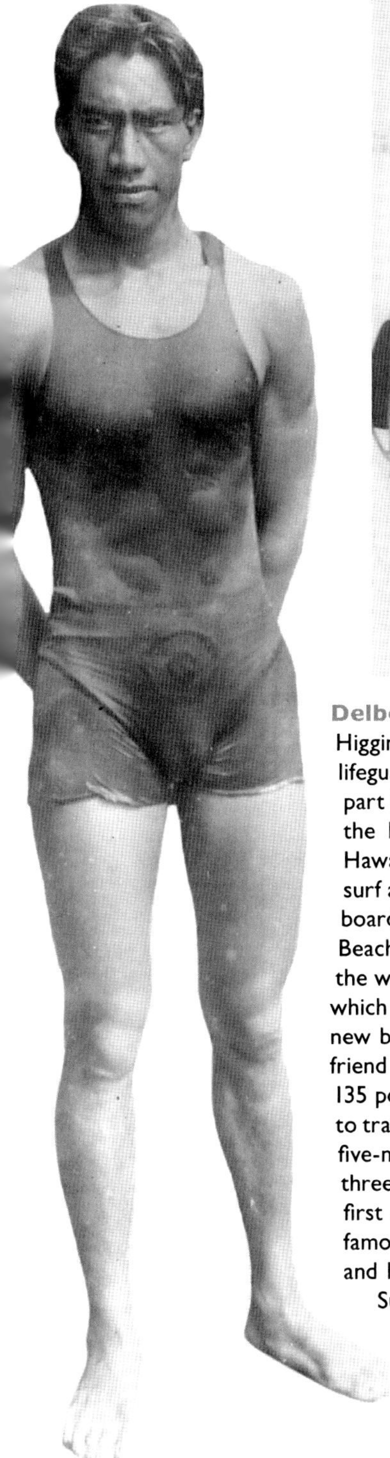

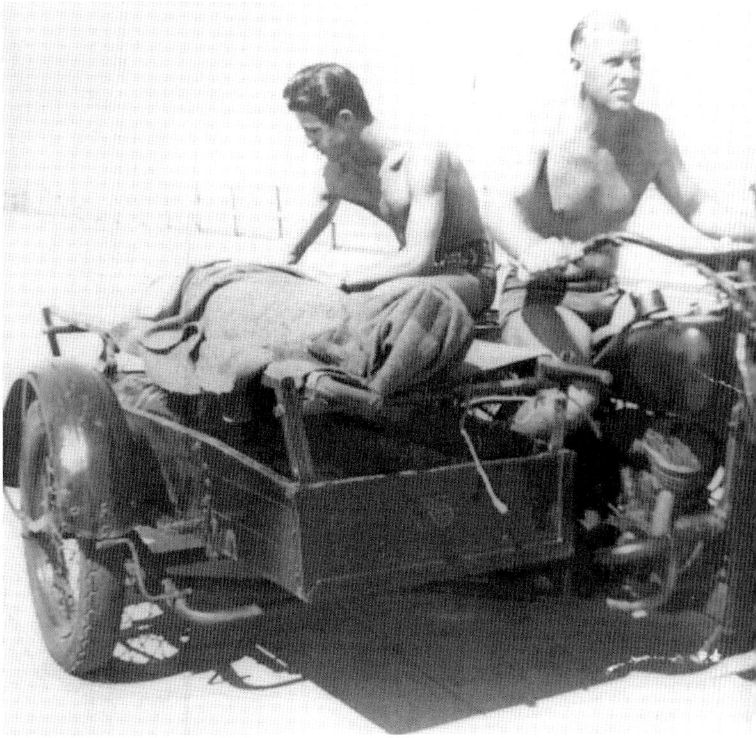

Delbert "Bud" Higgins
Higgins (above right), born in 1908, became a Huntington Beach lifeguard when he came of age. But he was also a trailblazing surfer, in part because of what he witnessed in the 1920s. As Higgins wrote in the 1960s, "Duke Kahanamoku [left] from Kahaliana and two other Hawaiians came over from Hawaii to make a movie and spotted the surf at Corona Del Mar, surfed there. . . . It was there I first saw their boards, talked to the Hawaiians and invited them to surf the Huntington Beach Pier." Higgins says, "They visited here on several occasions surfing the west side of the pier. After surfing here they stashed their boards, which were 11 feet long and 18 inches wide; they said if we should make new boards, they should not be longer then 10 feet." So Bud and his friend Gene Belshe made their first redwood boards, which weighed 135 pounds each. As lifeguards, Belshe and Higgins created a program to train other individuals. One student, Herb Barthels, won the world's five-mile swim record in 1932. Another, Wally O'Connor, became a three-time Olympic champion. Higgins was eventually credited as the first surfer to shoot the pier. He also became chief of lifeguards, a famous fire chief, and even the city historian. Eventually, Bud Higgins and his brother Gordie, a surfboard shaper, were inducted into the Surfing Walk of Fame in 1997. Both are since deceased.

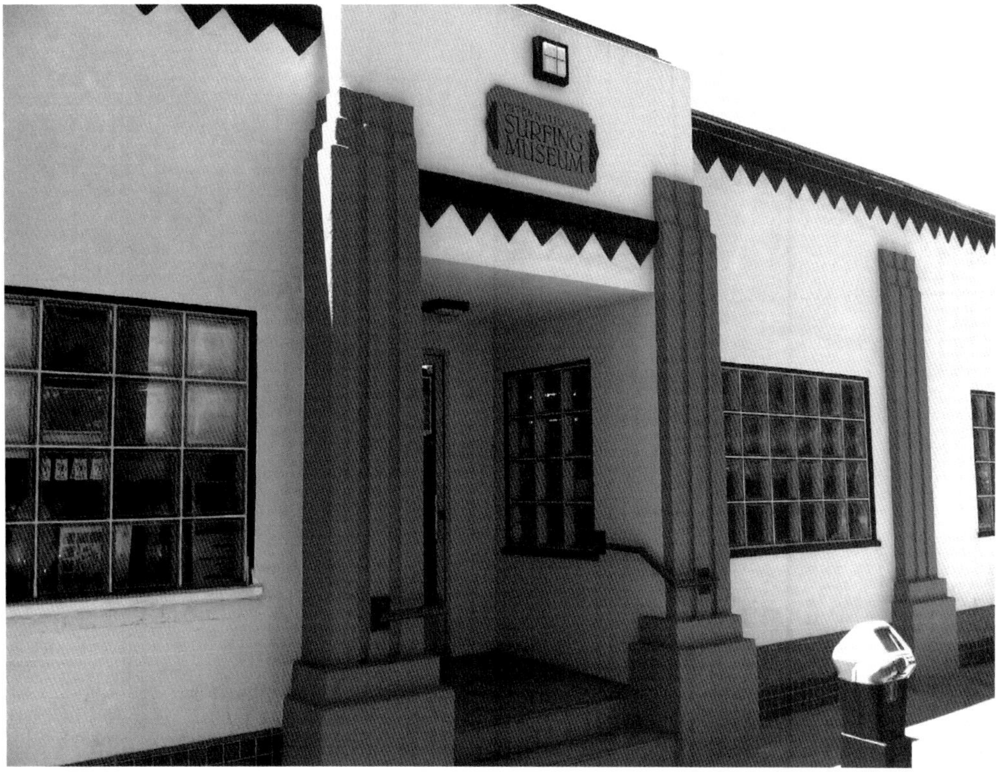

Surfer Girl

When Natalie Kotsch arrived in Huntington Beach in 1976, she found not just a place to live, she found a new life. Raised on a farm in Canada, Kotsch had been a teacher, exercising her creativity in the local community theater. An advocate of foster parenting, she produced the first Foster Parent Convention at McMaster University. In Huntington Beach, with her two daughters in high school, she decided to embark on a new career, real estate, that would offer her the flexibility to commit time and energy to her new hometown. She jumped in with both feet! Kotsch chaired the committee to develop the first ordinance for mobile home park conversion, chaired the Downtown Merchants Guild, and organized the Tenant Relocation Committee. And, in the early 1980s, the vision that would become her life's work and passion began to take shape: a museum celebrating the surfing culture that had put Huntington Beach on the map. She enlisted the assistance of Don Strout, an art director of a surfing magazine, and plans were developed for a museum that would tell the story of surfing and its historic link to "Surf City." In 1987, the city administrator, Paul Cook, offered a small, city-owned building on Walnut Avenue as a location, and in 1987, the Huntington Beach International Surfing Museum was officially opened. It moved to its current home, at the corner of Olive Avenue and Fifth Street, in 1992. Kotsch earned the distinctions of Citizen of the Year in 1991, Realtor of the Year in 1992, and was inducted into the Surfing Walk of Fame in 1998. But her most cherished titles are those of "mom" to daughters Simone, Julie, and foster daughter Kate and "nana" to grandchildren Sarah, Taylor, and Ashley and great-grandchildren Cameo and Cole. Natalie Kotsch passed away in 2014, and the outpouring of love and admiration from the surfing world came from around the globe. The farm girl from Canada, who never surfed, had a bigger impact than she would have ever imagined, and she left a legacy beyond her wildest dreams.

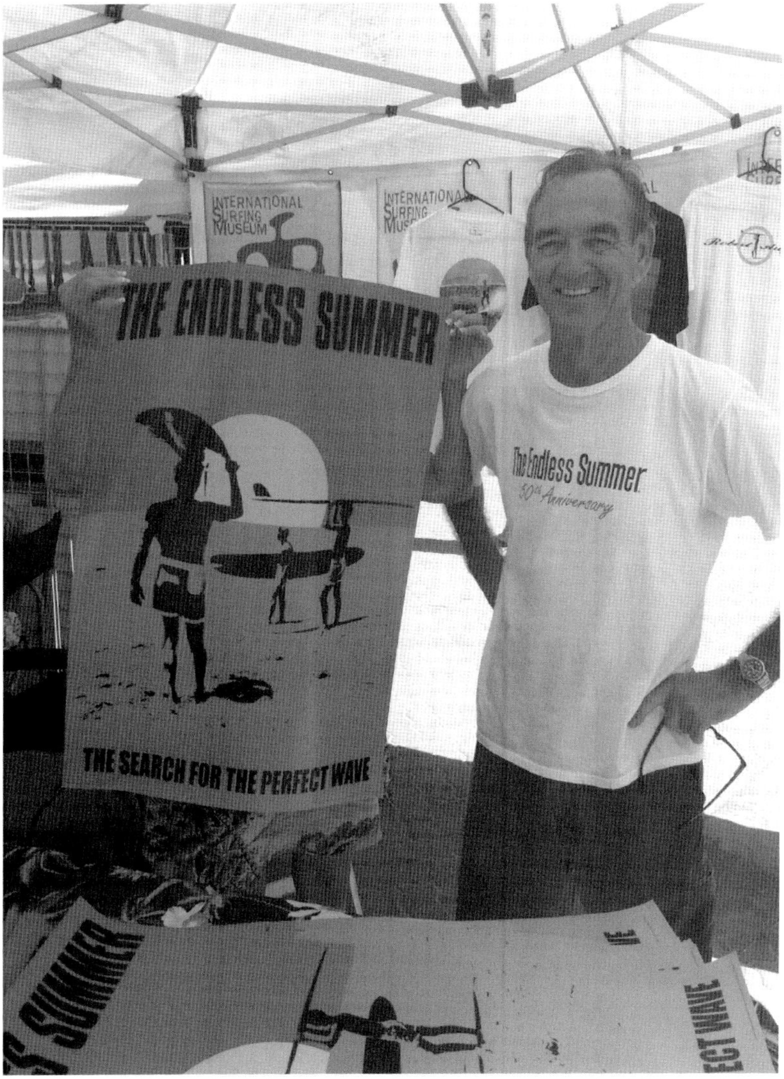

Robert August

It was 1963, and Robert August was set to graduate from Huntington Beach High School, where he served as Associated Student Body president. He planned to attend college and become a dentist. A call from friend and filmmaker Bruce Brown changed his plans and his life. The call was an invitation to undertake the surfing journey of a lifetime, resulting in the most iconic surf film of all time, *The Endless Summer.*

Encouraged to go by his parents, Patricia and surfing legend Blackie August, Robert logged over 35,000 miles on a single surfboard and returned to California a star. He warmed up to the industry side of surfing, ultimately starting his own line. In the ensuing decades, Robert August Surfboards became synonymous with the Huntington Beach surf scene.

The goofy-foot icon moved to Costa Rica several years ago, but frequent visits to Surf City have kept his legend and popularity alive among the locals. August plans to move back to his hometown this year.

He recently accompanied the Huntington Beach High School surf team to South Africa, sharing the "Endless Summer" dream with a new generation.

Robert August has two sons, Sam (who runs Robert August Surfboards) and Byron, and one daughter, Christine.

Corky Carroll

Corky Carroll, the original pioneer of professional surfing, was the first person to be paid to surf and the first to receive endorsements. He won all the events that gave away prize money in the early years. Carroll started surfing in the mid-1950s in Surfside, California, while in the first grade. He competed professionally from 1959 until 1972, when he retired at the age of 24. In that time, he won five overall US Championships, three International Professional Championships, one International Big Wave Championship, and one World Small Wave Championship. He won over 100 titles in all. He was named "Best Surfer in the World" in a *Surfer* magazine readers' poll in 1968. Following his surfing career, Carroll began writing a column about surfing and the surfing lifestyle for the *Orange County Register.* He also dabbled in music, recording a couple of CDs and becoming a popular draw at places like Duke's Barefoot Bar at the Huntington Beach Pier. Carroll, along with David Nuuhiwa, holds the distinction of being inducted into the Surfing Walk of Fame as both Surf Champion and Local Hero. He now resides in Costa Rica.

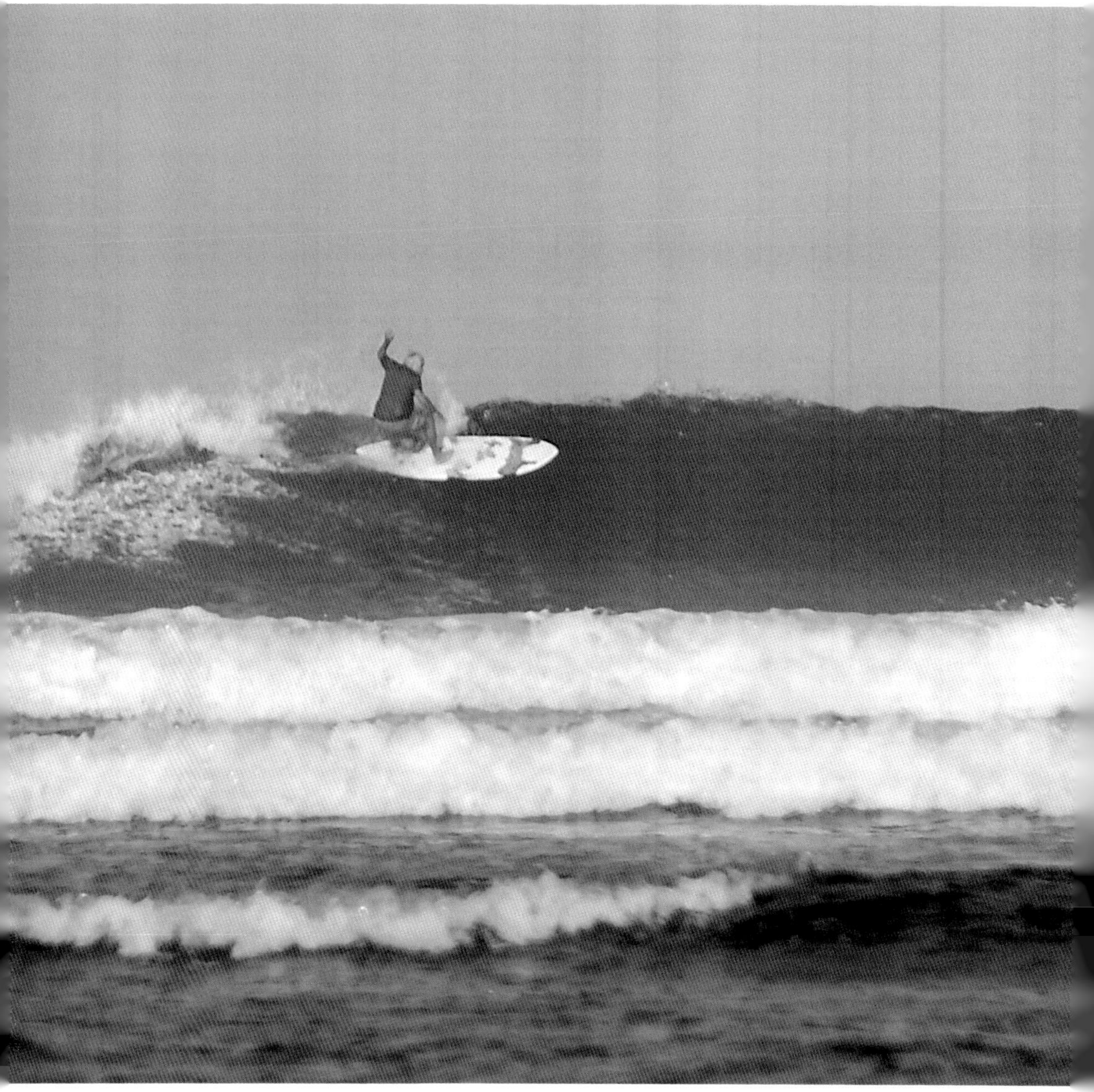

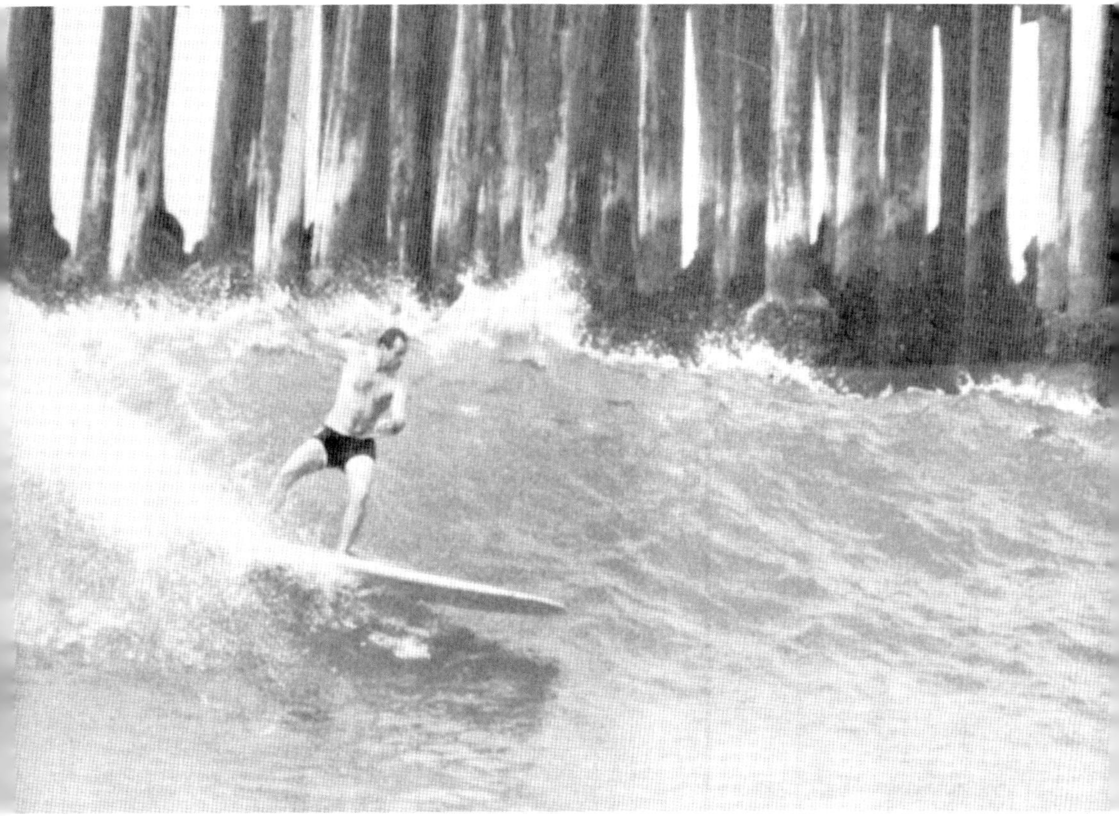

Gordon Duane

"Gordie" Duane achieved a lot of firsts related to Huntington Beach and surfing, including receiving the city's first ticket for surfing illegally. He opened the first surfboard shop, at the foot of the Huntington Beach Pier, in 1956. It was so popular with the burgeoning surf community that kids would skip school to hang out there. This caused the city to ban surfing until after 10:00 a.m. and to issue a statement citing Gordie as the first official scofflaw. He was recognized as the biggest name in surfboards when Surf City was the board-making center of the universe. Gordon Patrick Duane was born on February 2, 1931, in Los Angeles and learned to surf in his early 20s while serving in the Navy at Pearl Harbor. He made his first surfboard out of surplus balsa wood from Navy rafts. As wood gave way to foam surfboards, Duane was among the first to strengthen them by incorporating a thin strip of wood down the center, from nose to tail. This "stringer" is still used today by almost every shaper and manufacturer. After a 1958 fire destroyed Duane's shop, he reopened nearby on Pacific Coast Highway, remaining in business until 1988.

In the 1970s, Duane surfed with the "Hole in the Wall Gang," a group of Huntington Beach's best. The amateur team, ranging in age from 23 to 54, dominated the scene, winning over 20 consecutive Western Surfing Association contests. Decades later, teammates still spoke with equal parts reverence and joy at having surfed with Gordie Duane. He died in 2011 at the age of 80.

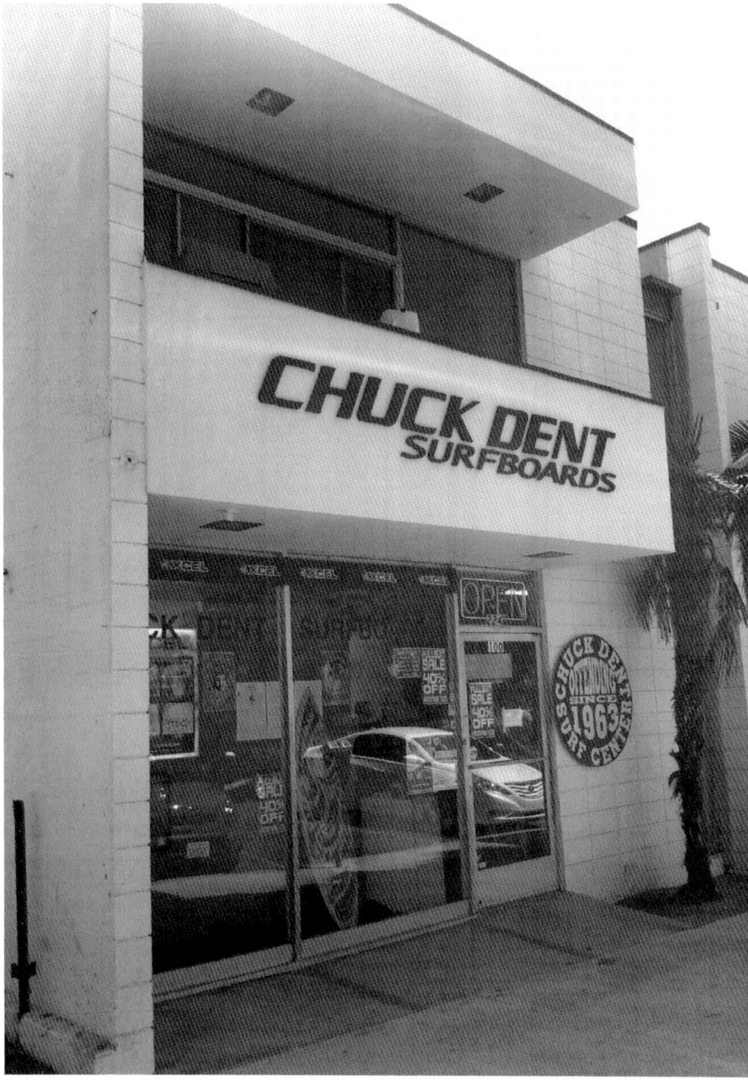

Chuck Dent

Chuck Dent was not the best surfer in town, but he knew how to attract attention. Soon, the tiny storefront he opened in 1964 became the hangout for surfers young and old. The establishment remains at the same spot on Fifth Street. Dent once described himself as "the original angry young man of surfing," and his acid-tongued wit was both stinging and hilarious. His invectives against the surf industry in the 1972 classic film *Five Summer Stories* are vintage Dent. He drove around town in his chocolate-brown Caddy, hung out at his shop telling stories to whomever and however many could squeeze in the door, and watched his cult following swell. It was Dent who gave employee Rick Fignetti his famous "Rockin' Fig" moniker. One slow winter day at Dent's shop, the boys cranked up the stereo, and Fignetti jumped up on the counter, dancing crazily. "You're really rockin' Fig!" Dent exclaimed. And the rest is history. Chuck Dent, wild man, cult leader, and storyteller extraordinaire, was also a visionary who modernized the surf industry, turning the standard concept of the surf shop—selling boards, leashes, and wax—into full-service retailers. Soon, all shops adopted this model. In the end, the character fell victim to the demons of a very real man. Chuck Dent died of drug and alcohol-related heart failure in 1980. He was 36 years old.

Bud Llamas

Ask people in the surfing community to name the mayor of Huntington Beach, and chances are good that they will answer without hesitation: Bud Llamas. The popular owner of the Seventeenth Street Board Shop is a fixture in the waters off the pier and an enthusiastic ambassador for the sport that put Surf City on the map. Burton "Bud" Llamas won the first NSSA (National Scholastic Surfing Association) championships before graduating from Huntington Beach High School in 1979, and he landed on the US National Team the same year. He turned pro at 18 and immediately went on the Association of Surfing Professionals (ASP) Tour for the next seven years. Bud's aggressive mastery of the famous break at the Huntington Beach Pier was studied and honed into the modern-day aerial attack practiced by today's best. Inducted into both the Surfers Hall of Fame and the Surfing Walk of Fame, this hometown favorite has graced the covers of both *Surfing* and *Surfer* magazines.

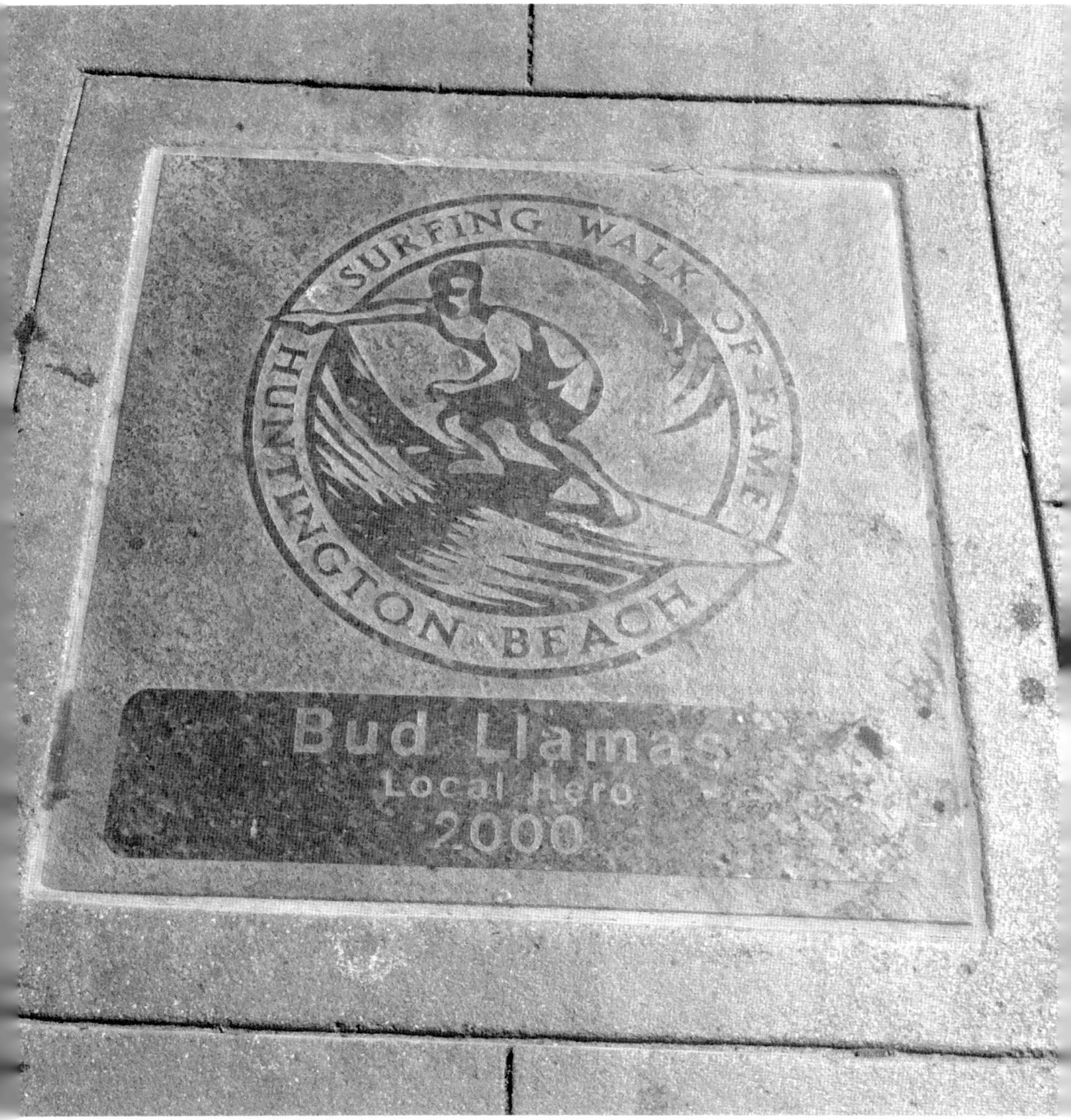

Carl Hayward

At six feet, four inches, there was no mistaking the formidable figure of Carl Hayward as he dominated the lineup on the south side of the Huntington Beach Pier in the 1970s. But his imposing frame and wingspan were a small part of what made Hayward so well liked among his peers and so respected in the industry. He was an authentic gentleman and a devout man of faith devoted to his family. In a sport riddled with overwrought egos and braggadocio, he was sincere and humble. Hayward moved to Huntington Beach in 1969 and quickly became one of the best young surfers in the city. After graduating from Edison High School in 1974, Hayward shaped first for Infinity and then Wayne Brown Surfboards before opening Carl Hayward Surfboards on Main Street in 1979. He spent the next 10 years running the shop and refining the "rocket fish" design that would become his claim to fame as both a surfer and shaper. He coached the Marina High School surf team and embraced the role of mentor and role model. Hayward closed his shop in 1991 and worked for longtime friend Bob Hurley, eventually rising to director of printables at Hurley International. Some say his life really began when he first took his place in the lineup at the pier. In January 2005, Carl Hayward passed away from a brain aneurism doing what he loved, where he loved it: surfing the south side of the pier.

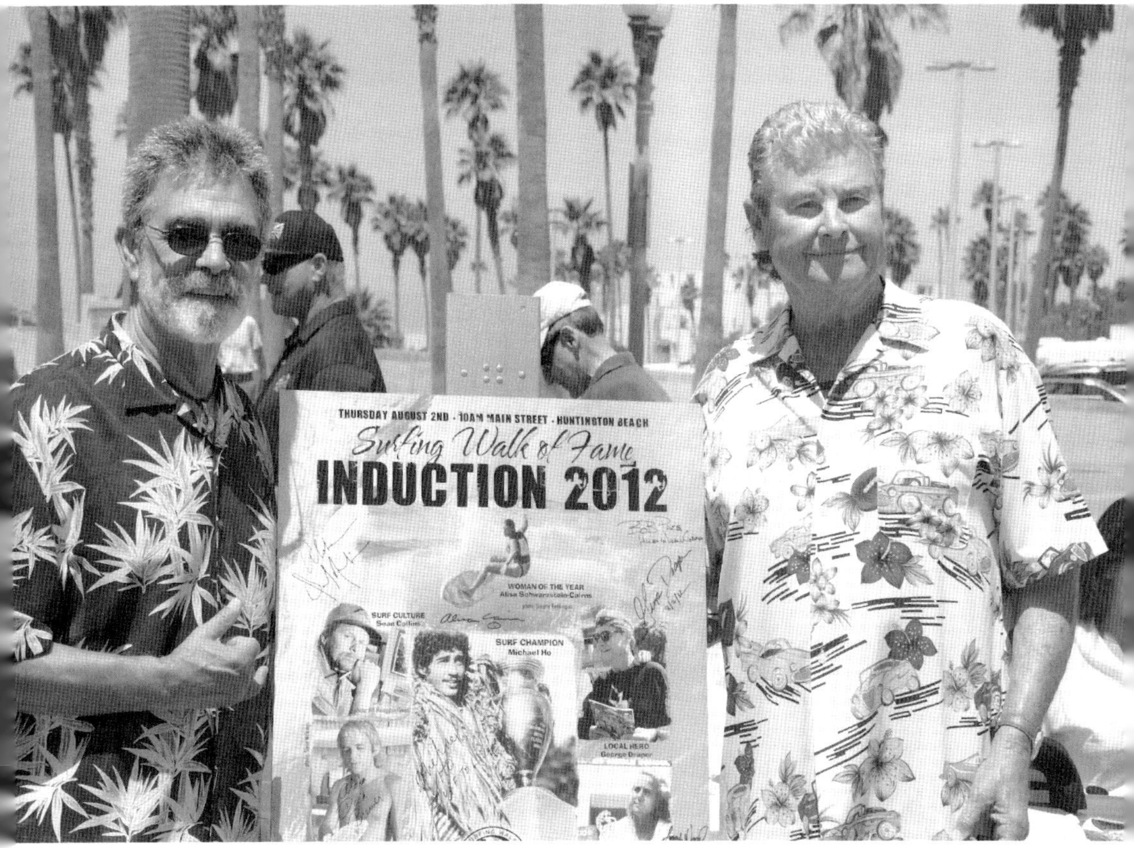

Bob Bolen

Bob "the Greek" Bolen (left) started surfing in 1958 and made his first surfboard in 1959 while still a student at Bolsa Grande High School in Garden Grove, California. A local bike shop owner asked him to make boards to sell in his shop and paid for the materials needed, and Bolen built the boards in his father's garage. Bolen opened his own surf shop in Huntington Beach in 1960, calling it Surfboards by the Greek. He acquired his nickname in high school as a nod to his heritage. The shop became a Surf City icon, and Bolen became one of the top builders in the business, with popular models like the Eliminator and Liquidator. After closing the shop in 1980, Bolen went on to become a successful real estate broker and owner of Huntington Beach Realty on Main Street. But his love of surfing has never really taken a backseat. The real estate office is a mini-museum of artifacts, photographs, and boards. He invented the Turbo Tunnel fin system, which helps control the movement of the surfboard by channeling the water through a center "tunnel." He also created a modern longboard shape called the Stylemaster for Surf Tech's line of high-tech boards.

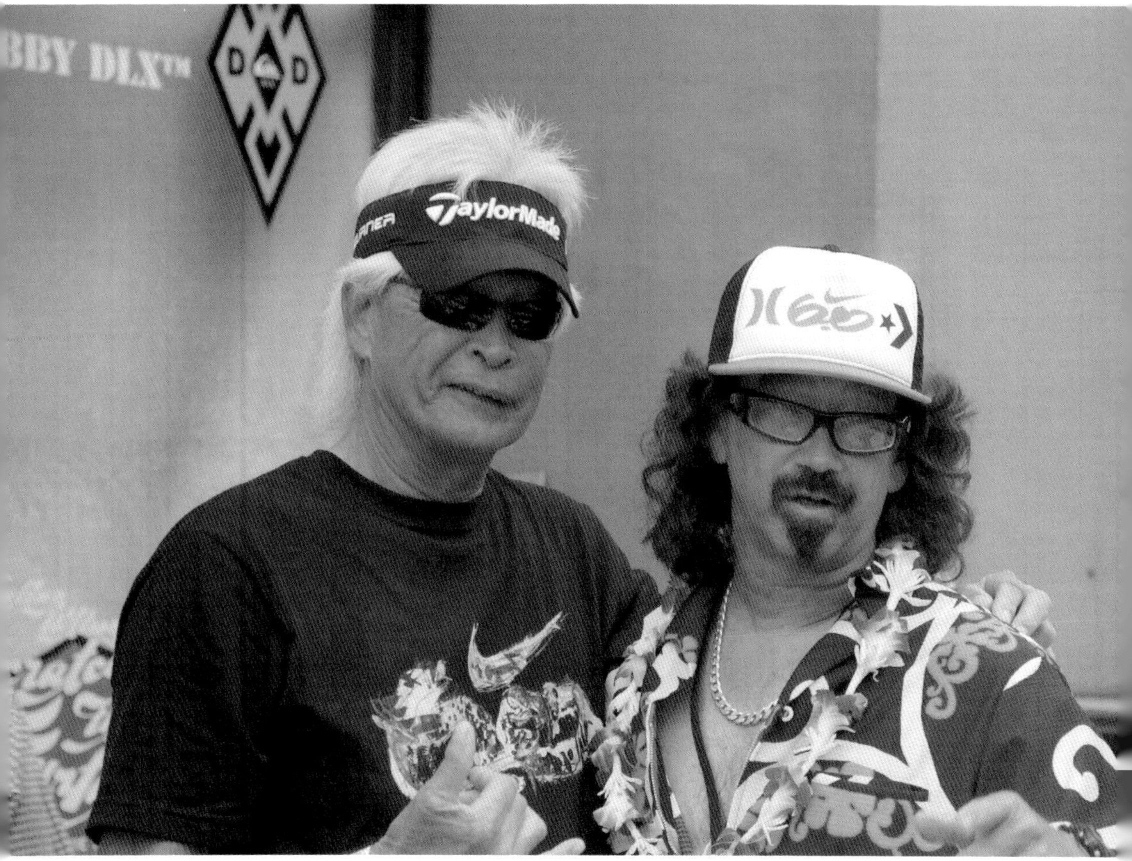

Rick Fignetti

With his trademark black-rimmed glasses, flowing black hair, and ever-present trucker cap, Rick Fignetti is instantly recognizable as he makes the almost daily trek from his surf shop to the famous Huntington Beach Pier and back again. It is clear that this is his town, and that the residents love him. Rick "Rockin' Fig" Fignetti is arguably the most visible, well-known surfer in Huntington Beach. A 15-time West Coast Surfing Champion and first member of the 1978 NSSA National Team, Fignetti has the rare distinction of being almost as well known by nonsurfers as by surfers. As the voice of the US Open of Surfing for 19 consecutive years, Fig peppered the worldwide audience with exciting commentary and provided the live crowd with entertaining trivia and cool trinkets. A generation grew up listening to his morning surf reports on KROQ-FM and reading his popular "Wet 'n' Wild" column in the *Huntington Beach Independent*. His "O.C. Live" in the *Los Angeles Times* expanded his audience even more. Fignetti received a lifetime membership in NSSA and was inducted into both the Surfing Walk of Fame and the Surfers Hall of Fame for his numerous contributions to the sport.

The Sunset Beach native got his first taste of surfing as a kid in the 1960s, when tenants at a home owned by his parents skipped out and left their belongings behind, an old longboard among them. Fignetti nabbed it and gave it a try. For nearly 25 years, he has run Rockin' Fig Surf Headquarters, a tiny establishment three blocks from the beach. The place is jam-packed with boards, artifacts, photographs, trophies, and people from every walk of life, buying boards, talking surfing, and enthralled by the enthusiastic Fignetti. And if he isn't in the shop, he can be found surfing his cherished north side of the pier almost every morning.

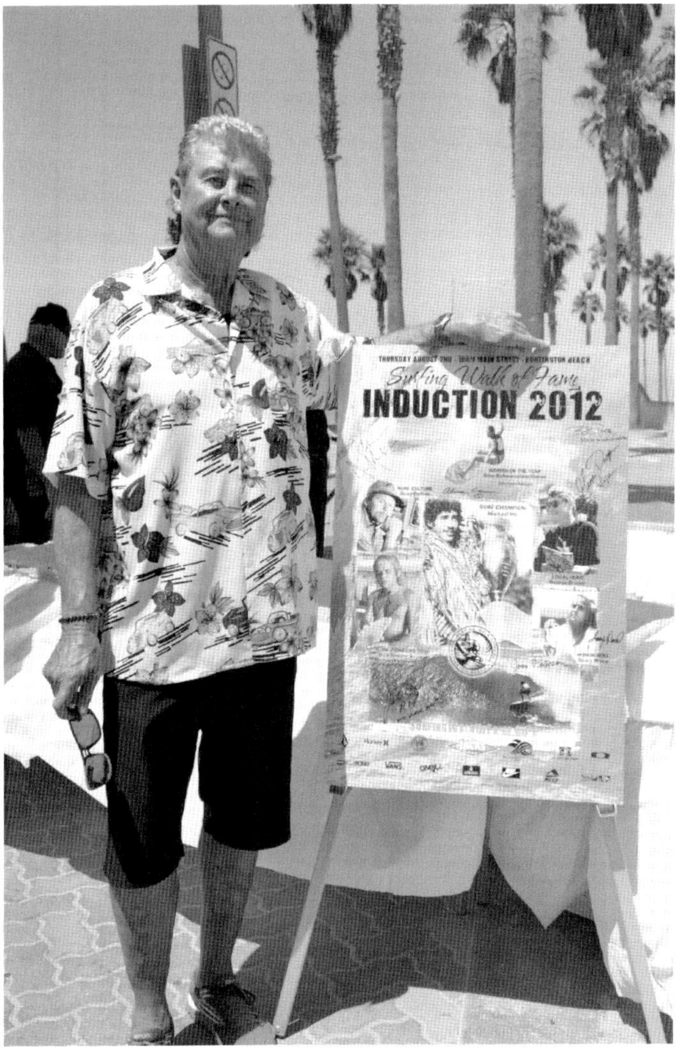

George Draper

The Kansas-born Draper began his love affair with surfing when his family moved to Carlsbad, California, in 1952 and the new kid in school hooked up with future surfing legends like Murph the Surf and Phil Edwards. Draper learned to surf on a board crafted for him by Edwards. Draper eventually became the first lifeguard at Tamarack in Carlsbad. He taught Don Hansen (Hansen Surfboards) how to surf and did a stint as a delivery driver for Clark Foam. Then, in 1967, Draper opened his own surf shop on Huntington Beach's Main Street. The shop he acquired was called George's Surf Shop, named after the original owner, George Panton. Not only did Draper purchase it for a mere $1,000, he did not even have to change the signage. He did, however, expand the concept of a surf shop as a local gathering spot by adding Jan's Health Bar, offering up healthy sandwiches and juices. It was the height of surf-shop proliferation in Huntington Beach—there were over 20 shops within a few blocks of each other—but Draper had positioned his establishment as more than a shopping experience. George's Surf Shop was a mainstay for 27 years before closing in 1994. George Draper can be seen walking or riding his bike through the streets of downtown Surf City, where he was once declared the official Mayor of Main Street. In another odd twist, the title would eventually be handed down to another George: George Lambert III. Draper was inducted into the Surfing Walk of Fame in 2012.

Kim Hamrock

The only girl in a family of boys, Kim Hamrock grew up swimming, skateboarding, and rafting in the waves. But, it was not until she was 16 that she got her first surfboard. And it would be another 15 years before she would surf competitively—while raising a family, no less. Hamrock, small and wiry, earned the nickname "Danger Woman" somewhat facetiously from the guys she routinely had to battle with for a place in the lineup off Huntington, Newport, and other coastal locations. The name stuck, but the moniker came to describe a woman whose size belied her strength and whose aggressive assault on big waves made her a force to be reckoned with. During her career, Hamrock earned 12 US Championship titles, one World Longboard title, and was named Woman of the Year in the Surfing Walk of Fame in 2002. She was also the first woman to both paddle surf and tow-in surf at Dungeons, South Africa, some of the most dangerous and formidable waves in the world. At 45 years old, "Danger Woman" entered the first all-woman's competition at Banzai Pipeline, Hawaii, and placed first in the longboard division. She also earned a special Averal award for charging the hardest through the entire event. She was the oldest competitor there. These days, Kim Hamrock is a regular in the art and music scene in Huntington Beach and beyond and will be launching a series of e-books about surfing. She still competes from time to time and is a sought-after instructor, especially among young girls who are looking to be the next "Danger Woman" among the boys.

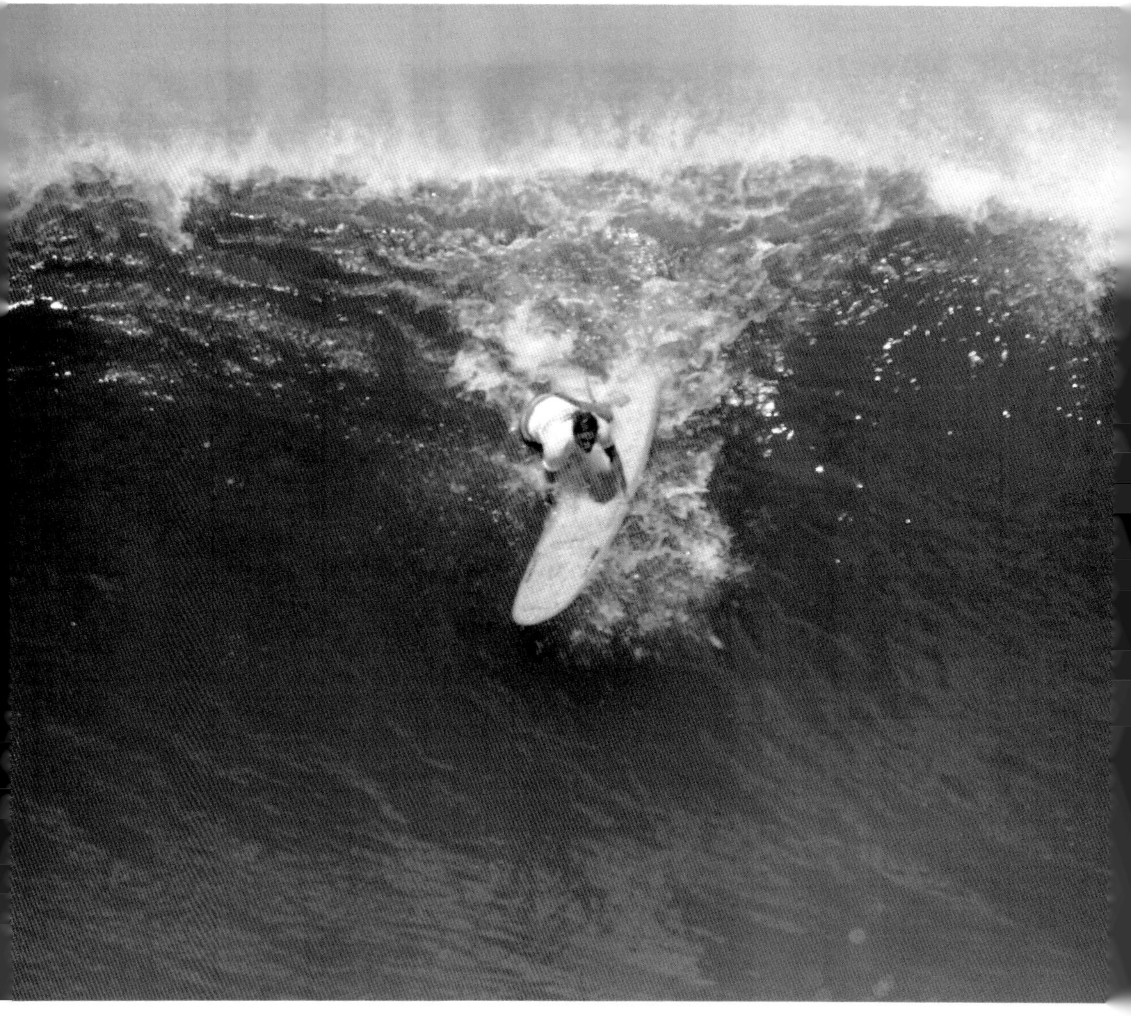

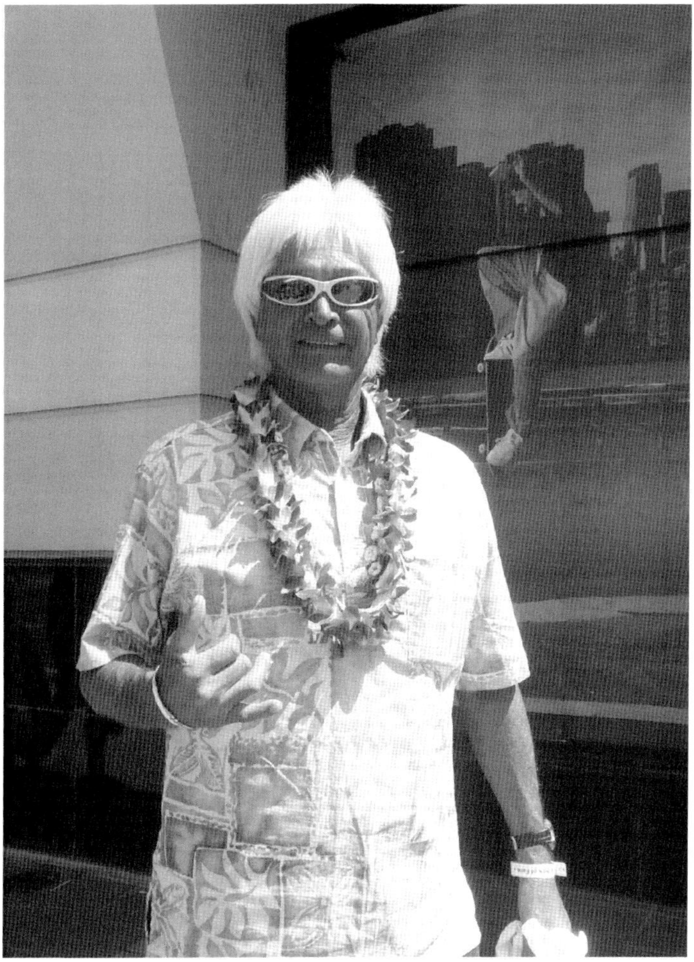

David Nuuhiwa

Born in 1948 in Honolulu, Hawaii, David Kealohalani Nuuhiwa III moved to Southern California and quickly rose to prominence as a teenager under the tutelage of legend Donald Takayama. His style was all smoothness and grace. Gliding to the nose of a longboard, Nuuhiwa would often stay on the tip for 20 seconds or more, looking relaxed, almost wistful. He made very difficult maneuvers look deceptively easy. He was considered one of the best surfers, if not the best, of his time. *Surfer* magazine once said of Nuuhiwa, "smoothness didn't come at a higher grade." His rides were jaw-dropping to watch. Couple that with movie-star good looks, a killer smile, and an engaging manner, and a true superstar emerged to take over the world of surfing. The crowds that came to see him surf often resembled those of rock concerts or football games, screaming his name, cheering his every move, sometimes even crying from the sheer "bigness" of it all. His battles against fellow longboarder Corky Carroll are legendary. Nuuhiwa could be a bit too aggressive in the lineup for some. But when he got on that board, the beauty and artistry overwhelmed the viewer, and all gladly worshipped at the altar of Nuuhiwa. In 1971, he appeared in the Jimi Hendrix film *Rainbow Bridge*. The following year, he placed second in the World Championships and appeared in *Five Summer Stories*. David Nuuhiwa still has a graceful gait and generous smile, although the dark crown of hair has been replaced with a sexy mop of white. He hangs out at favorite haunts on Main Street and visits the International Surfing Museum often. He gives surf lessons and judges contests on occasion. He may have been born in Hawaii, but David Nuuhiwa is one of Surf City's favorite sons.

Brett Simpson (OPPOSITE PAGE)

When Brett Simpson clinched a first-place finish at the 2009 US Open of Surfing, the crowd reaction rivaled the excitement (and volume) of a home team winning the seventh game of the World Series. "Simpo," the regular footer with the fast and fluid style and breathtaking aerial maneuvers, had beat reigning champ Mick Fanning in six-foot waves at his home break. Simpson returned in 2010 to claim back-to-back titles, this time upsetting South African prodigy Jordy Smith, ranked number one in the world at the time. Growing up in Huntington Beach, Simpson played football, basketball, and baseball before trying surfing at 12. His reputation as a small-wave master grew, but, like his idol, Michael Jordan, his strength and wizardry was in the air. He was named Orange County Surfer of the Year in 2008 and 2009. Brett Simpson excited the crowd once again with his strong showing in the 2014 Vans US Open of Surfing, but this time, the victory was not to be. But it did not stop social media from lighting up when Simpson hit the water, and it did not stop the crowd from showing up in droves to cheer on the hometown hero.

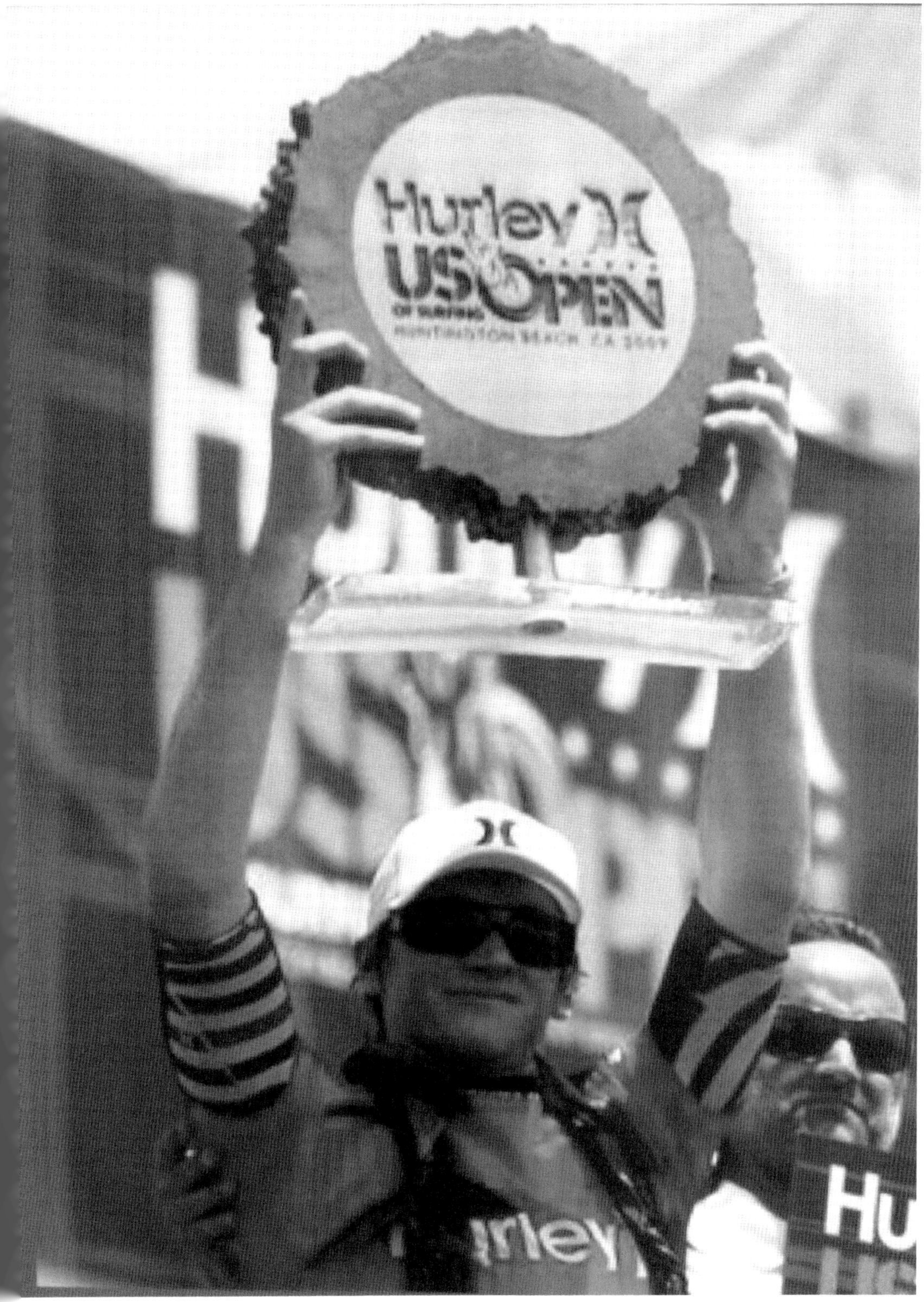
Hurley
US OPEN

PT (OPPOSITE PAGE)
Peter Townend has lived in Huntington Beach for the better part of 35 years, raised his three kids here, coached and competed here, and remains an integral part of the community—not just as a surfing icon but also as a board member for the Huntington Beach Marketing and Visitors Bureau. With his distinctive Australian accent, the always-affable, legendary surfer is a true treasure to the city. He has also been a journalist, stuntman, actor, and coach, among other things. Townend was born in Australia in 1953. Throughout the 1970s and 1980s, many considered him to be one of the best surfers in the world. In 1998, "PT," as he is known, was inducted into the Surfing Walk of Fame. In 2001, he was also inducted into the Australian Surfing Hall of Fame as well as the International Surfing Hall of Fame. And then, there is the color that he made so popular: pink. "My style on the board was influenced by Fred Astaire," he says. "And the color pink I adopted was influenced by David Bowie. I know that might sound a bit weird, but the whole thing about Bowie being a chameleon, ever changing, was always something that appealed to me. The color I chose just seems to embody that."

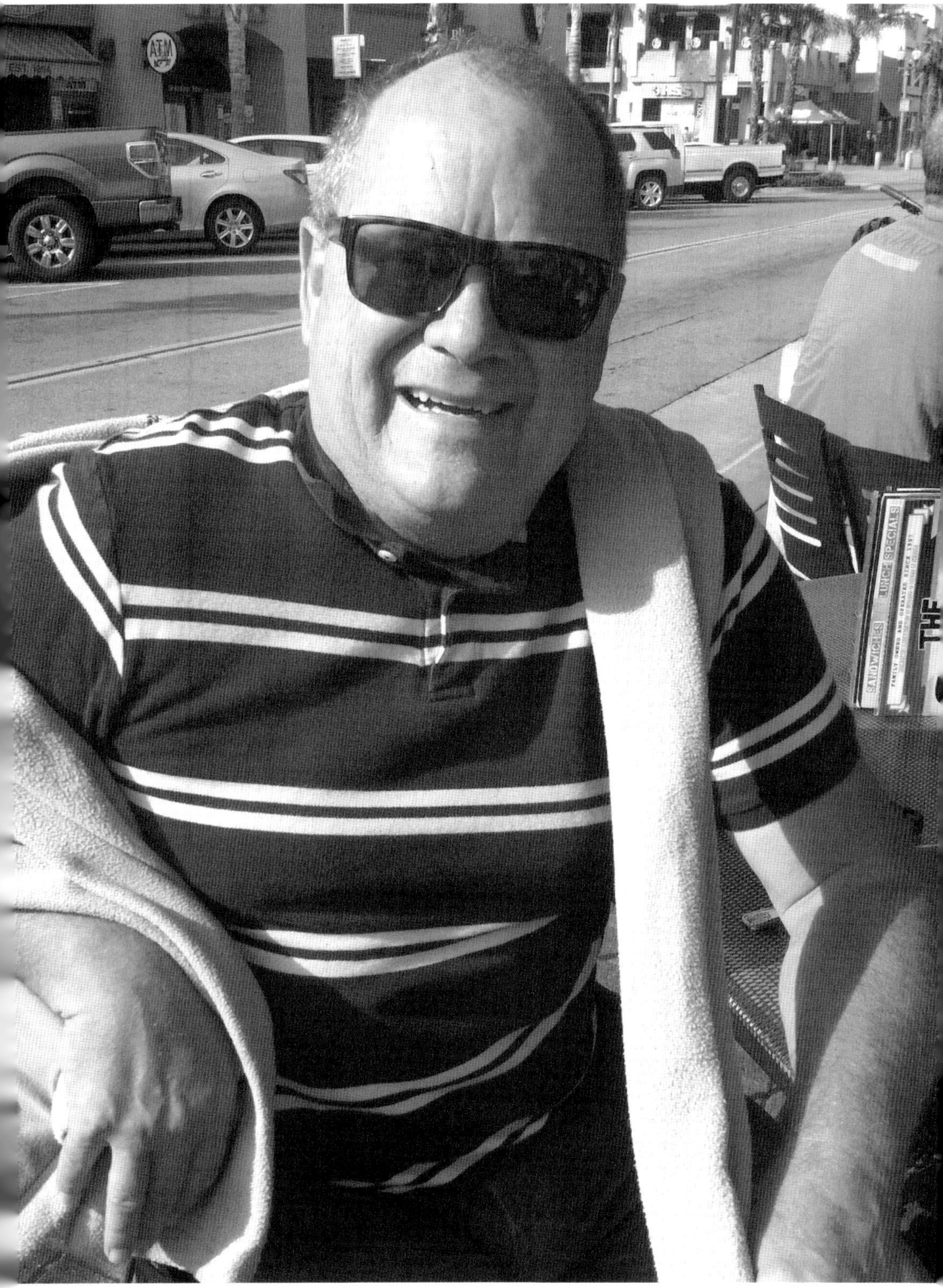
ATM
SANDWICHES
LUNCH SPECIALS
FAMILY OWNED AND OPERATED SINCE 1967
THE

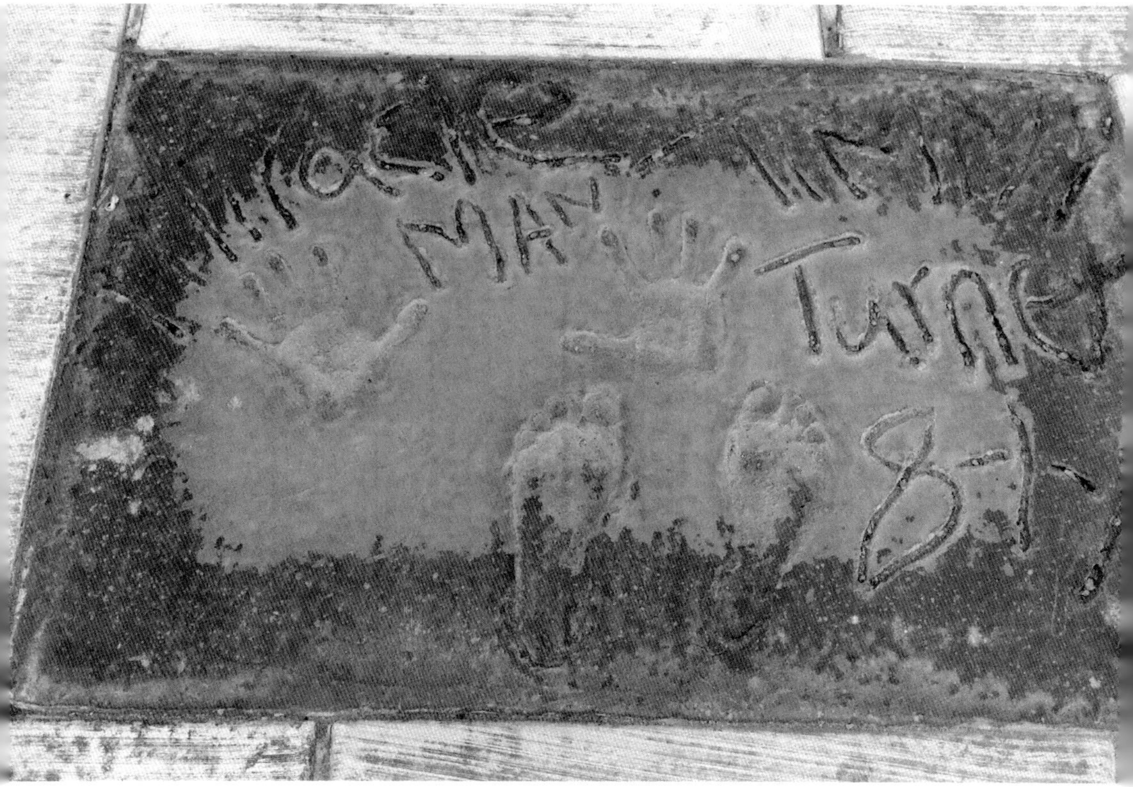

Timmy Turner

Turner attended Huntington Beach High School, where he served as the surf team captain during his senior year. Then, at age 17, he took off for Indonesia to make a film. *Second Thoughts*, which took three years and numerous trips to uncharted Indonesian islands to complete, captures the adventures of three guys surfing extreme waves and surviving on very little else. In 2004, it was named Best Video of the Year by *Surfer* magazine. The talented young filmmaker was off to a promising start and soon was back in Indonesia with photographer Dustin Humphries to chronicle relief efforts after the devastating 2004 tsunami. Surveying the damage, Turner and Humphries could not remain detached observers. They rented a boat to deliver medical supplies, food, and whatever else they could to the furthest areas affected. Shortly after returning, it was discovered that Turner had contracted an aggressive staph infection, which quickly went from his lungs, through the blood stream, and then into his brain. He endured six brain surgeries and months of rehabilitation before returning to a family and community that had seemingly been holding their collective breath until he came home. When *Tsunami Diaries* premiered in April 2006, the packed house of well-wishers exhaled in wild applause as a healthy, happy Timmy Turner entered the theater. Today, Turner continues to make films and can be found at the Sugar Shack, the legendary Main Street eatery owned by his family. In 2013, he returned to Indonesia and surfing. Timmy Turner was inducted into the Surfers Hall of Fame in 2014.

CHAPTER FIVE

Sports

Huntington Beach has long been a haven for many different sports and the home of well-known athletes. Local baseball teams formed here in the early 1900s, when oil companies organized competitive leagues up and down the coast. Various Little League teams from Huntington Beach have made it to the Little League World Series, and the major high schools, including Huntington Beach High School, Edison High School, and Marina High School, have produced standout athletes over the years.

But the town has not only produced conventional athletes, like well-known baseball, football, and basketball players. Huntington Beach has also been home to many professional skateboarders and surfers. This is not surprising, given that those sports came of age in the area and still remain popular here. In Huntington Beach, kids in many cases are practically born with boards in their hands. The city has also seen many coaches who have headed up winning high school teams over the years. Like many West Coast cities where sports are a year-round activity, competition and performance levels have always run very high.

This book covers many well-known athletes, including Ian Kennedy, Jeff Kent, Cherokee Parks, and Tony Gonzalez. But there are, of course, many other athletes who could have been featured in a book such as this. Were it not for the demands of space, the reader would also be learning about Collin Balester, a Huntington Beach High School product who plays professional baseball for the Washington Nationals. Then there is Bill Green, a former US record holder in the hammer throw who placed fifth in the 1984 Summer Olympics and who lived in Huntington Beach for a long time. There are the tennis players Scott Lipsky and David Martin, the mixed martial artists David Tank Abbott and James Irvin, and many others.

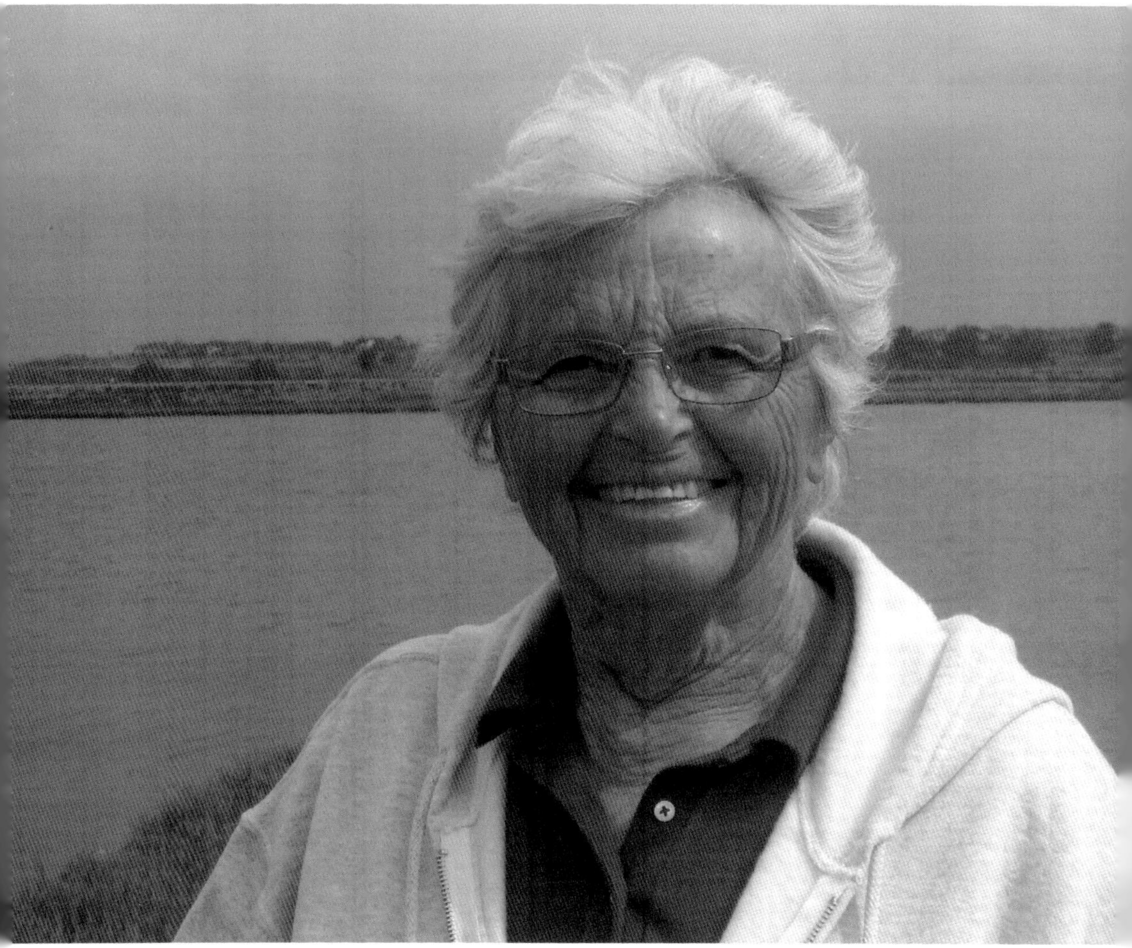

Olympian (ABOVE AND OPPOSITE PAGE)
Her eyes twinkle in the morning sun, and her smile beams. Looking out across the water while standing on the boardwalk at the Bolsa Chica Wetlands, Olga Connolly glances up as a large pelican swoops by, just several feet over her head. She laughs like a girl decades younger than 78, but then, age does not really mean too much to Connolly. Born Olga Fikotová in 1956, she won a gold medal in the discus competition at the 1956 Olympic Games in Melbourne, Australia. Also at those games, Connolly met and fell in love with well-known American athlete Harold Connolly. Throughout her career, Connolly captured five US national titles and raised the American record no less than four times, adding over 15 feet to the previous record. She has lived in Huntington Beach for many years. Several months ago, she joined the Miracles of the Marsh docent team from the Bolsa Chica Land Trust. She meets at the wetlands most weeks to teach visiting school kids about nature. As she wistfully described, nature, as much as athletics, has always played a big part in her life. "Since I was a young girl in Czechoslovakia, I've always respected nature. The peace and solitude, the sound of the streams on the rocks; it's always been vital to my life. I explain to my grandkids today what it was like to wander, plucking seeds from the ripening wheat and munching on them in the beautiful fields. It's so hard to find open places today. That's why I love it here."

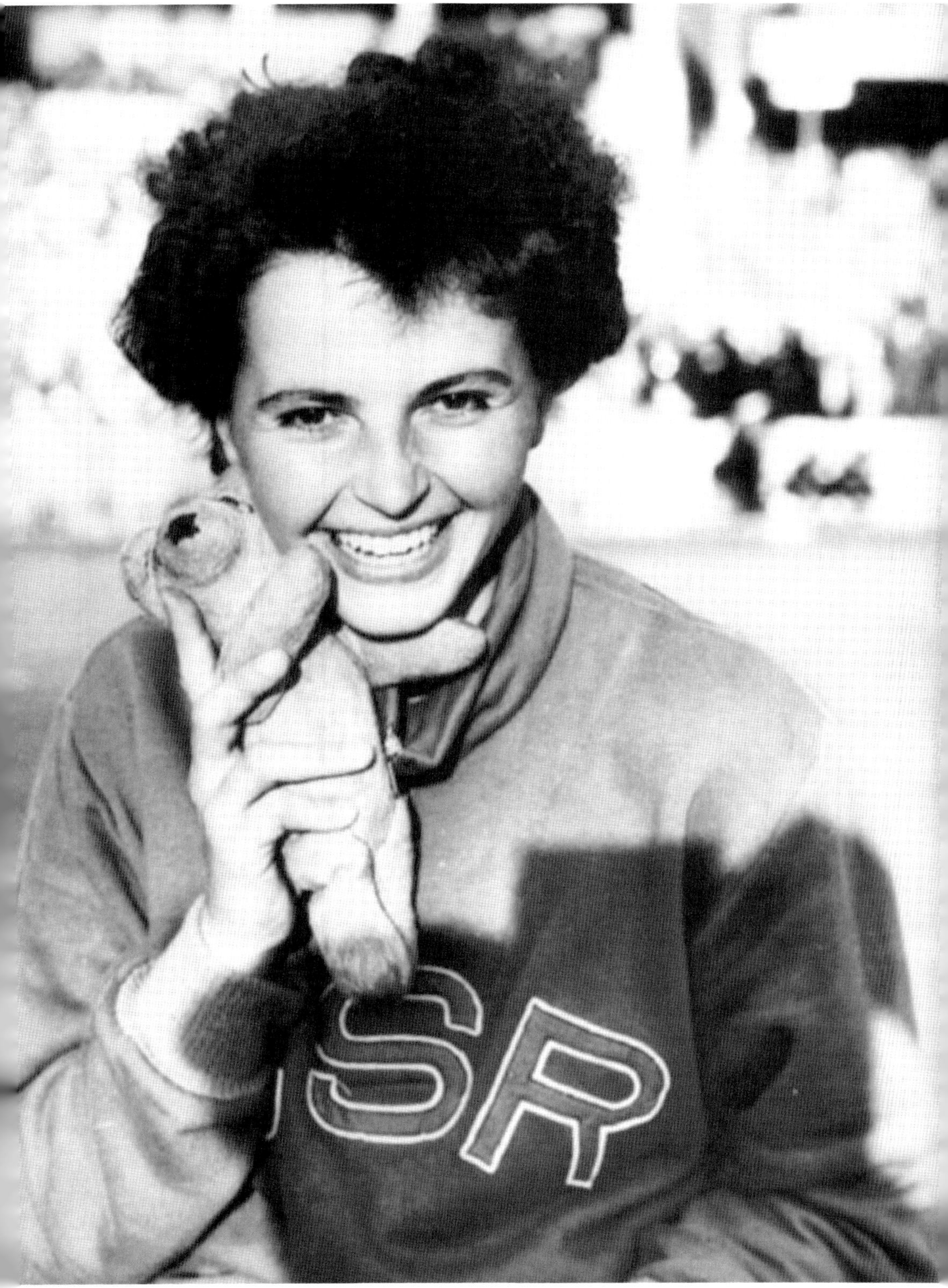
SR

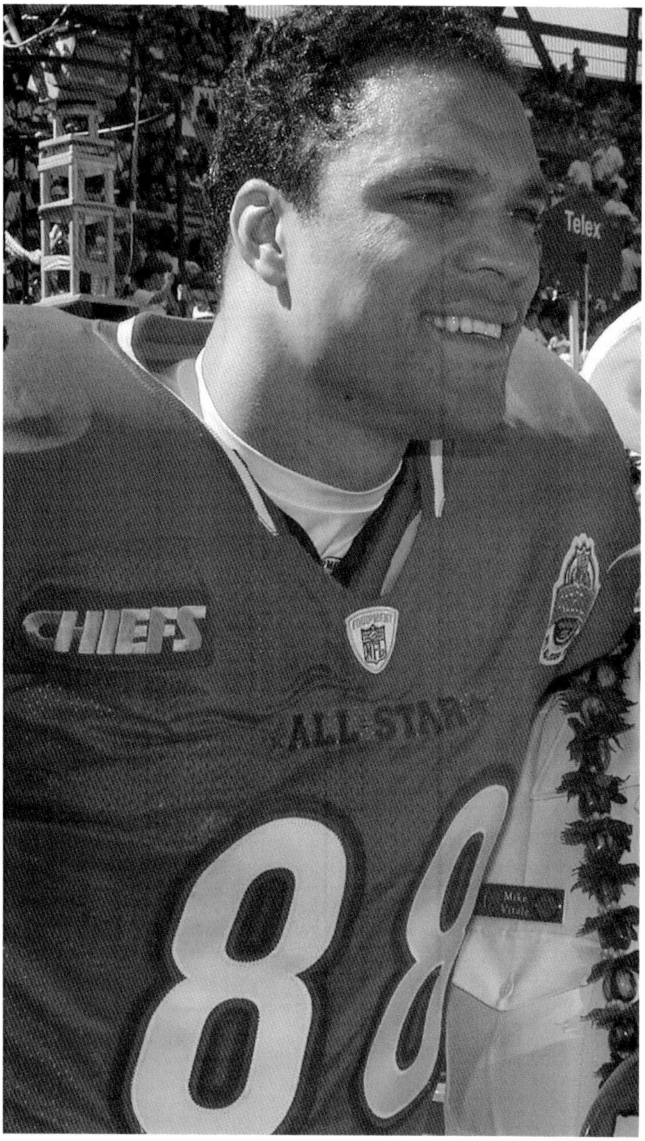

Future Hall of Famer

Many think that Tony Gonzalez will be enshrined in the Pro Football Hall of Fame in Canton, Ohio. He lettered in football, baseball, and basketball while attending Huntington Beach High School in the early 1990s, but it seems football was always going to be in the cards for Gonzalez. As a senior, he caught 62 passes for 945 yards and 13 touchdowns. At both tight end and linebacker, he was chosen as a first-team All-American. Also in his senior year, Gonzales shared the Orange County high school athlete of the year award with none other than golfer Tiger Woods. Ranked as one of the top tight ends in the 1997 NFL draft, Gonzalez wound up on the Kansas City Chiefs and began his professional career in 1997. In his rookie season, he had 33 receptions. As the years went on, his numbers continued to rise. In 2010, Gonzales was traded to the Atlanta Falcons. Among the many records he set, Gonzales was the first tight end to reach 15,000 receiving yards, he had the most career touchdown receptions for a tight end (111), and he had the most Pro Bowl selections of any player at any position (14). The list of records goes on and on. Gonzalez retired after the 2013 season. (Courtesy US Navy.)

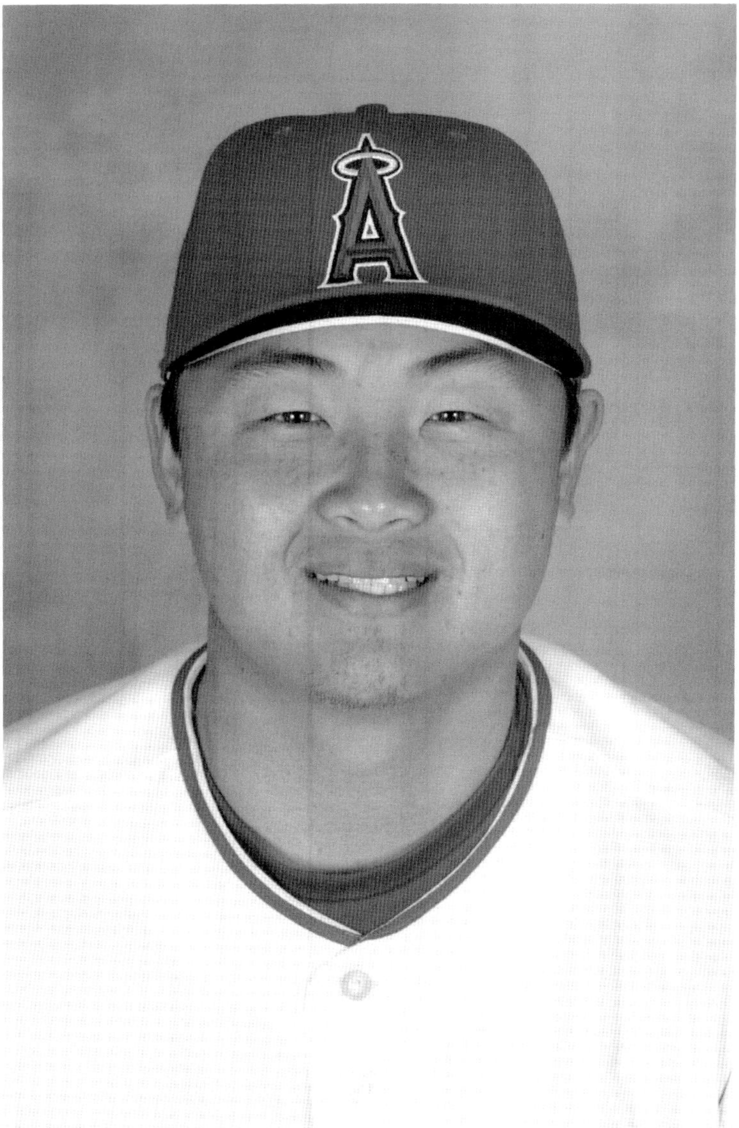

An Angel

"Jeff Mathis and Mike Napoli gave me lots of time and tips in terms of catching. And I also got to work with Mike Scioscia, which was amazing." Hank Conger grew up an Angels fan, so the experience of actually being part of the Angels organization still seems a bit surreal for him. "When I was a kid, I always followed Garret Anderson, [Darin] Erstad, Frankie Rodriguez and of course Tim Salmon. So having Tim come to camp this spring and talk to us about his love of the game, his passion for hitting—it was unbelievable," he said. The kid who made his mark at Ocean View Little League still loves to come home when he gets the chance, both to catch up with his buddies and to spend time with his family. Hank Conger's dad, Yun, is thrilled thus far with how the Angels organization has treated his son—and the entire family. "They are incredibly professional, just the best," Yun said. "Owner Arte Moreno has been wonderful, the scouts; everyone has gone out of their way to make this a great experience for my son and for us, too. The communication is very clear, and they really seem to care about their players. My wife, Eun, and I could not be happier."

The Boxer

In the late 1980s, at 5061 Warner Avenue, stood Latka's Golden Glove Tavern. George Latka, who ran the place, was a fairly well-known boxer, which is why the inside of the place looked not so much like a bar as it did a boxing museum. Nicknamed "The Professor," primarily because he was the first professional boxer to earn a college degree (UCLA, 1944), Latka competed in the 1930s and 1940s, winning 33 bouts, including 8 knockouts. In fact, in a total of 55 professional fights, he lost only six times. Originally from Colorado, Latka wound up settling in Huntington Beach and ran his tavern while in his late 70s. When he died in December 2007, this was a portion of the obituary that ran in the *Los Angeles Times*: "Latka was inducted into the World Boxing Hall of Fame. He also had bit parts in movies as a boxing referee, including in *Raging Bull*. Born in 1914, Latka grew up in Pueblo, Colo., and later moved with his family to Gary, Ind., where he learned to box and won Golden Gloves titles from 1934 to 1936. He earned a scholarship to box in the intercollegiate program at San Jose State but left school early to turn pro. He resumed his education and earned a bachelor's degree from UCLA. He worked as a teacher and at Douglas Aircraft. In recent years he owned a tavern in Huntington Beach, where his boxing memorabilia was displayed."

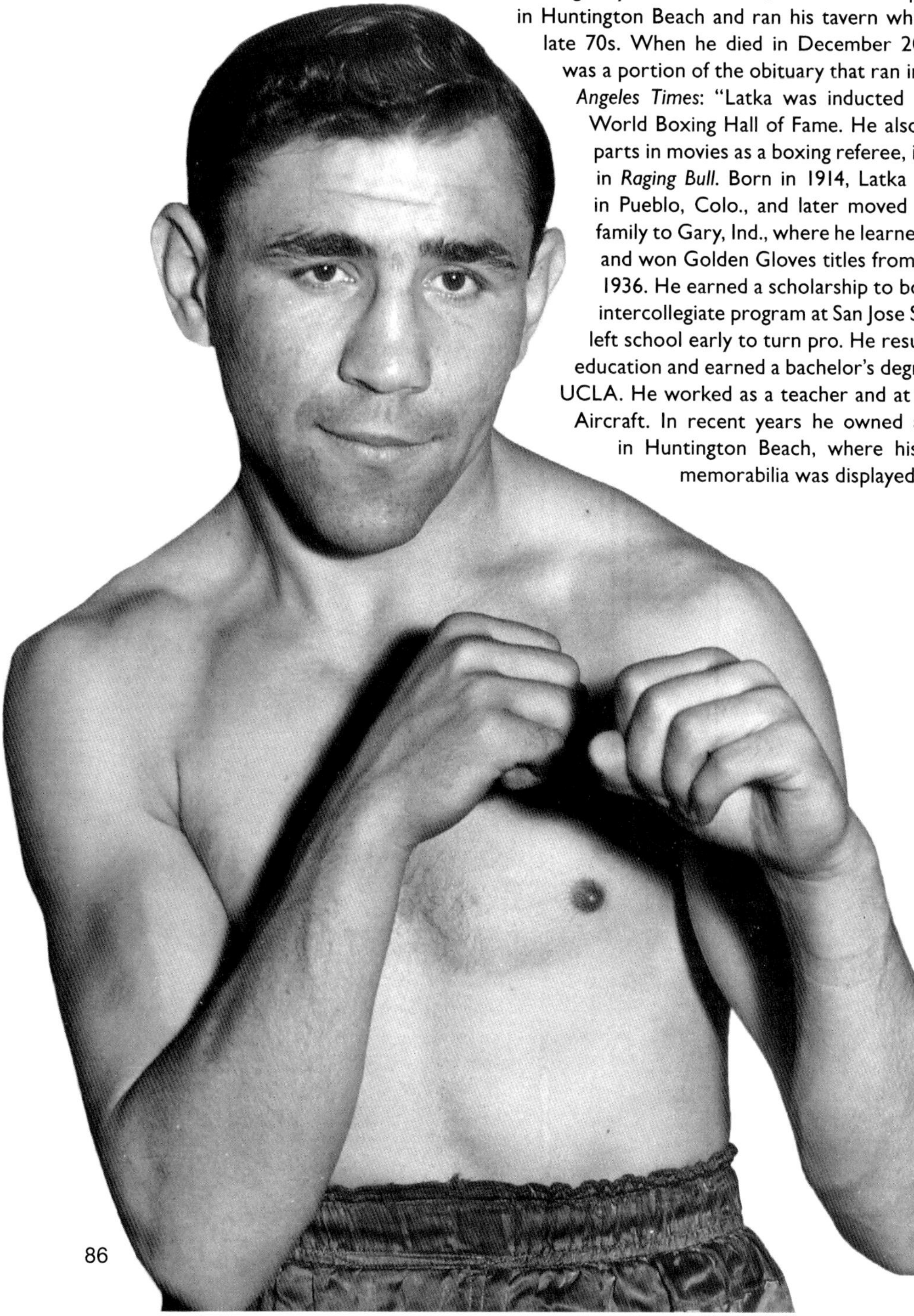

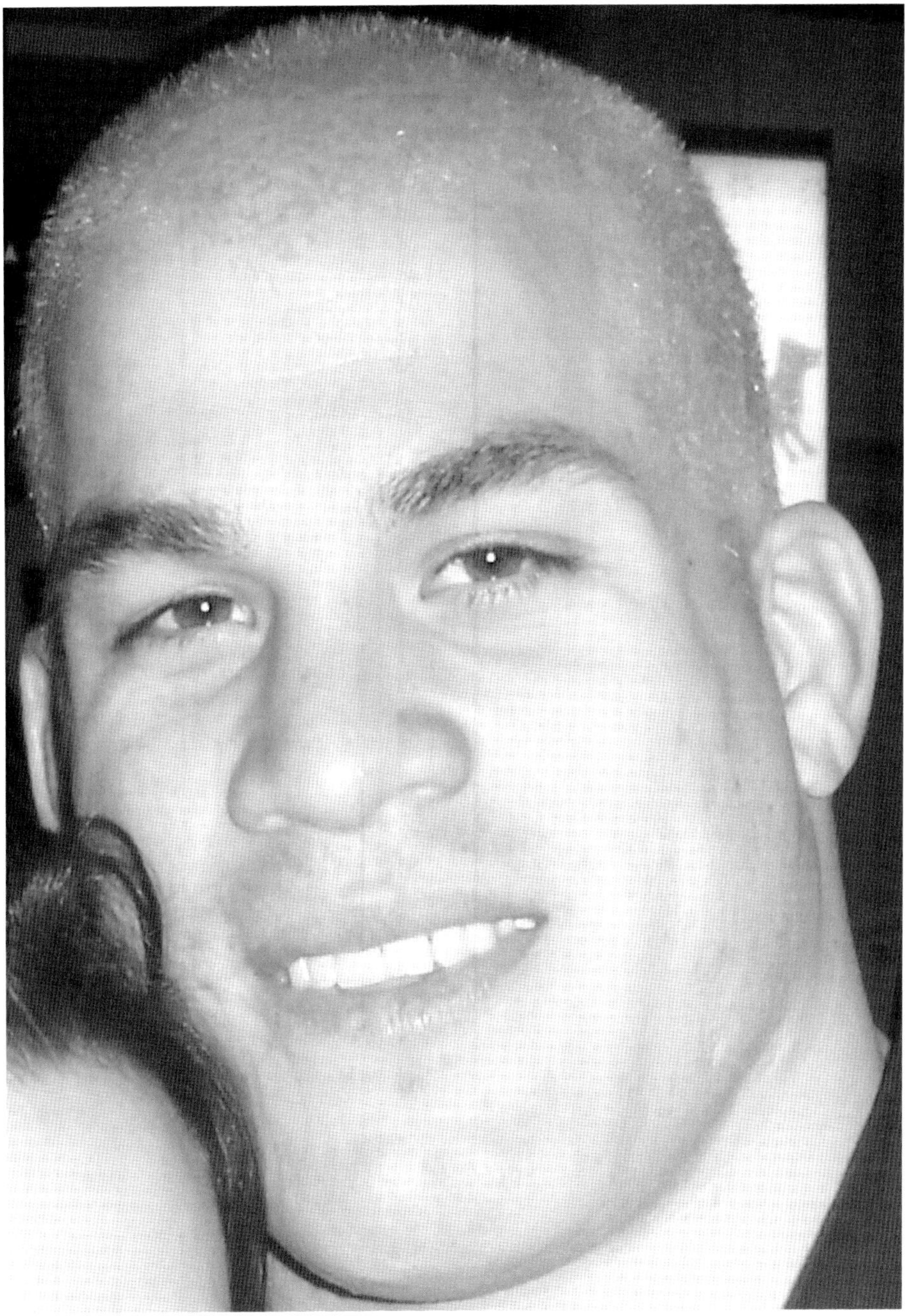

"The Huntington Beach Bad Boy"
Jacob Christopher "Tito" Ortiz was born in Huntington Beach on January 23, 1975. The product of a very tough upbringing, Ortiz would eventually attend Huntington Beach High School, where he began wrestling. He excelled at the sport and, after attending Golden West College, he became NJCAA state champion before transferring to California State University at Bakersfield. His mixed martial arts debut was at UFC in 1997, and within two years, he became the world champion. Ortiz went on to do some acting, run a clothing line, and perform charity work with inner-city children after retiring.

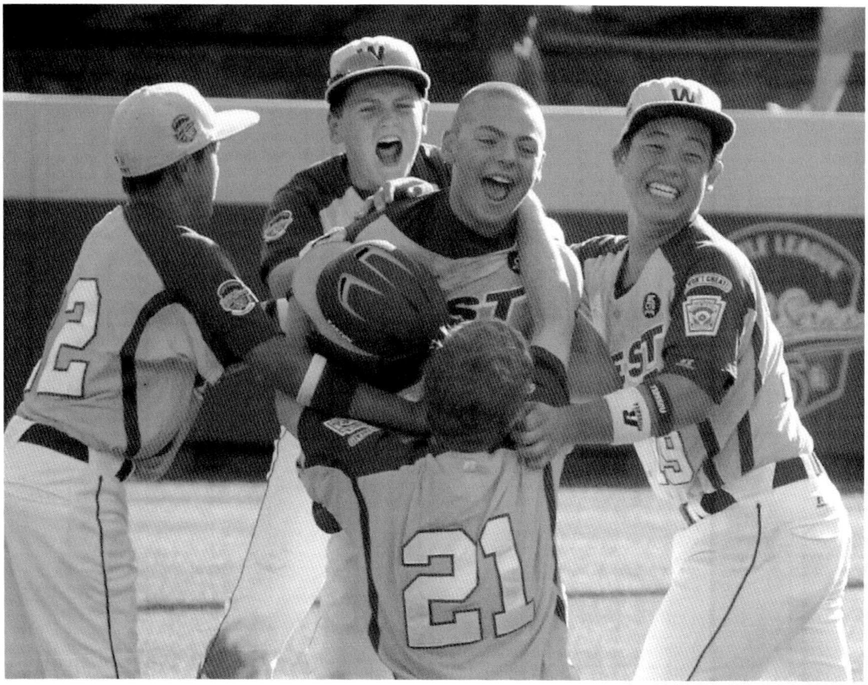

The Boys of Summer

In 2011, Ocean View Little League manager Jeff Pratto found himself in a raucous environment as he and his team arrived in Williamsport, Pennsylvania, hallowed home of the Little League World Series. The team was about to take part in a parade featuring all of the squads from around the world that had earned their place in the sun (or, as it turned out, some rain, too). Such was the dreamlike path for the Surf City boys of summer, a poised, disciplined group of young players who, under Pratto and his equally poised and disciplined coaching staff, found themselves sitting on the cusp of that rarest of baseball achievements—a World Series championship.

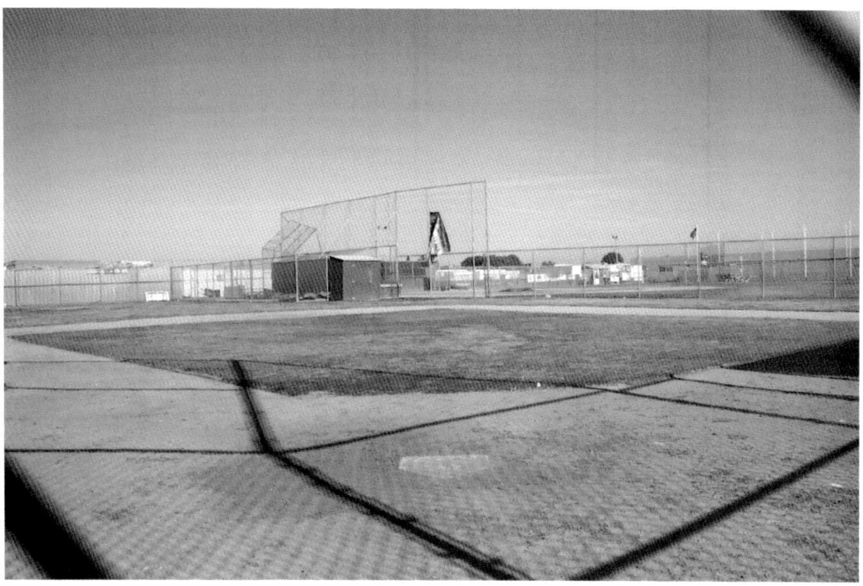

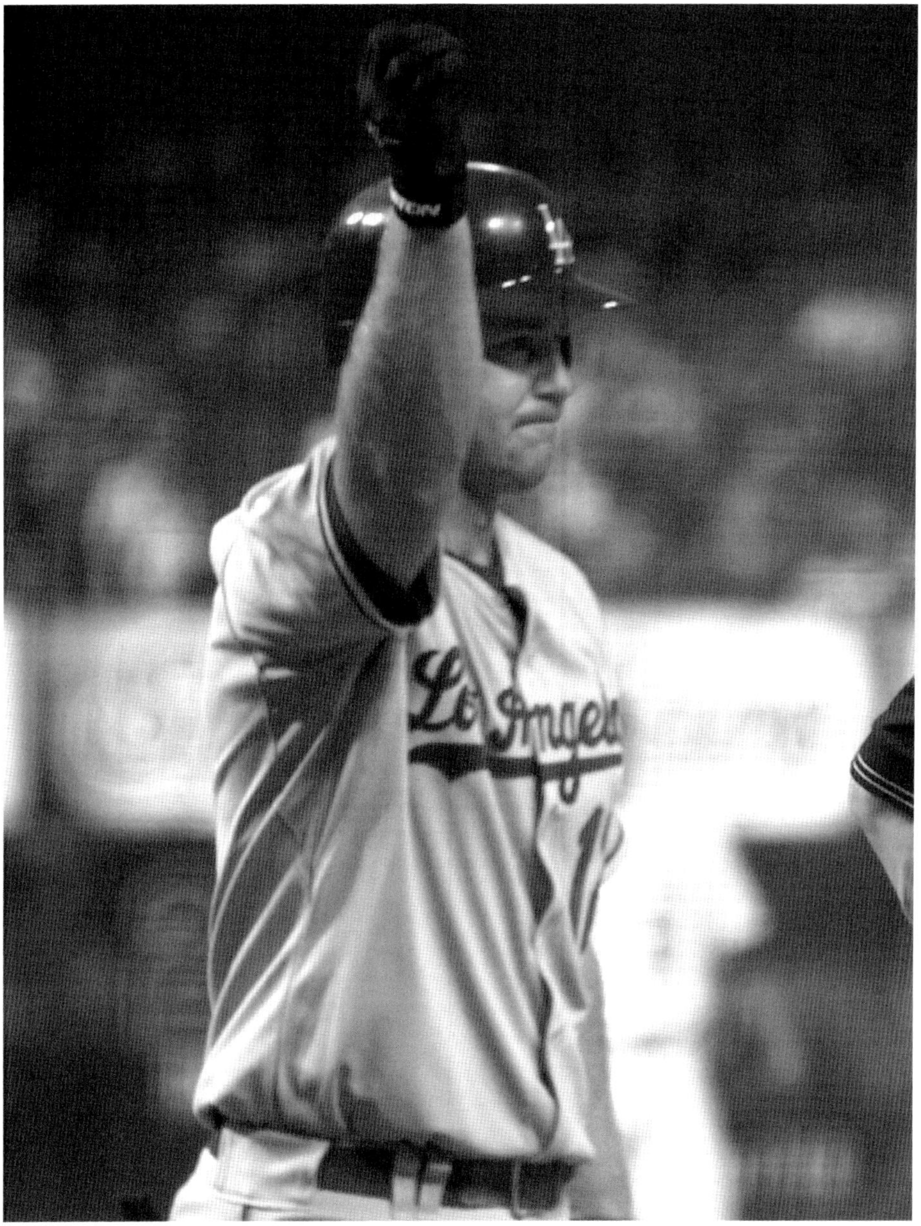

All-Star

Baseball star Jeff Kent has a long list of accomplishments within the sport. The second baseman won the National League MVP award in 2000 while playing for the San Francisco Giants, and he is the all-time leader in home runs for second basemen. A five-time All-Star, Kent drove in 90 or more runs from 1997 to 2005, a streak that has never been done by another second baseman. Kent entered Edison High School in Huntington Beach in the fall of 1982, but he did not make the varsity team until his junior year. That did not matter, though. A run-in with the coaching staff during his senior season cost Kent a spot on the team. Thankfully, after entering Berkeley, he got another shot. Though his defense has probably kept him out of the National Baseball Hall of Fame, he was one of the most dependable run producers of his generation.

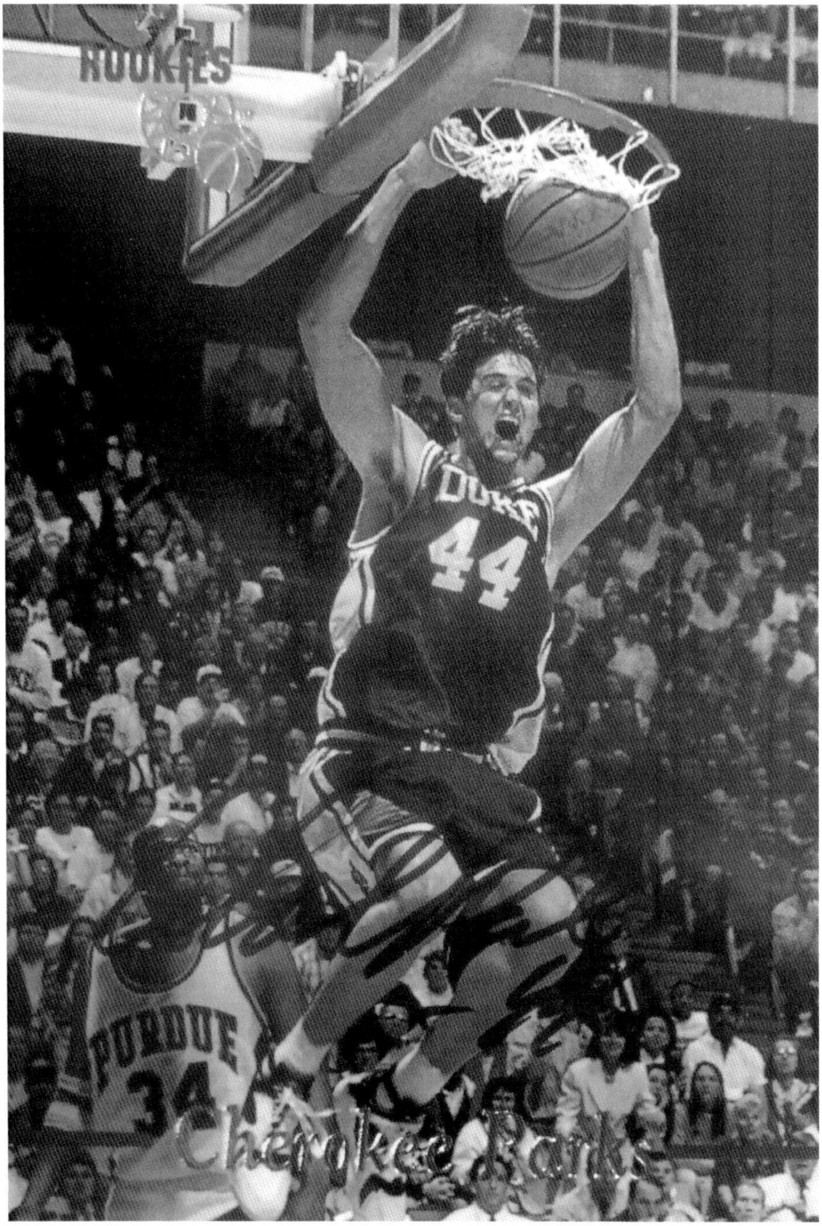

NBA Star

Cherokee Parks was a standout center at Marina High School in Huntington Beach before graduating in 1991 and then heading off to Duke University, where he helped win the 1992 national title in his freshman year. Following his college career, Parks was selected by the Dallas Mavericks in the first round, and he went on to have a 10-season NBA career, playing for the Mavericks, Minnesota Timberwolves, Vancouver Grizzlies, Los Angeles Clippers, San Antonio Spurs, Washington Wizards, and Golden State Warriors. Parks had career-high averages of 7.1 points per game and 5.5 rebounds per game during the 1997–1998 season with the Timberwolves. Named in honor of his great-grandmother, a member of the Cherokee tribe, Parks returned to Huntington Beach after his NBA career ended and became a businessman.

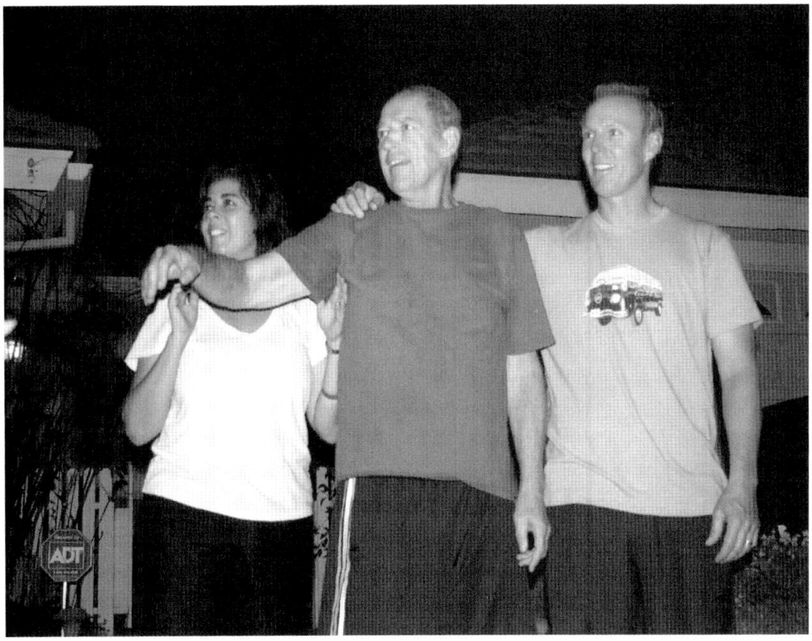

The Coach

Jim Harris (above, center, with his wife and son) coached at Ocean View High School for 33 years, beginning when the school opened. His teams have won 19 boys' basketball league championships, and, several years ago, he had a five-season stint coaching Ocean View's girls' basketball team, winning four league titles in that time. But, for alumni, it is not the numbers that made Harris's legend, it is the man. His leadership skills, combined with his compassion and concern for students, resulted in a remarkable small-town love affair among players, students, parents, and coach. Sadly, he died in the fall of 2011 from cancer. Harris was so beloved and respected in his community that a candlelight vigil was held on his block (below), and a prayer service took place in the school gym. School officials met with players and students Monday morning to inform them of Harris's passing.

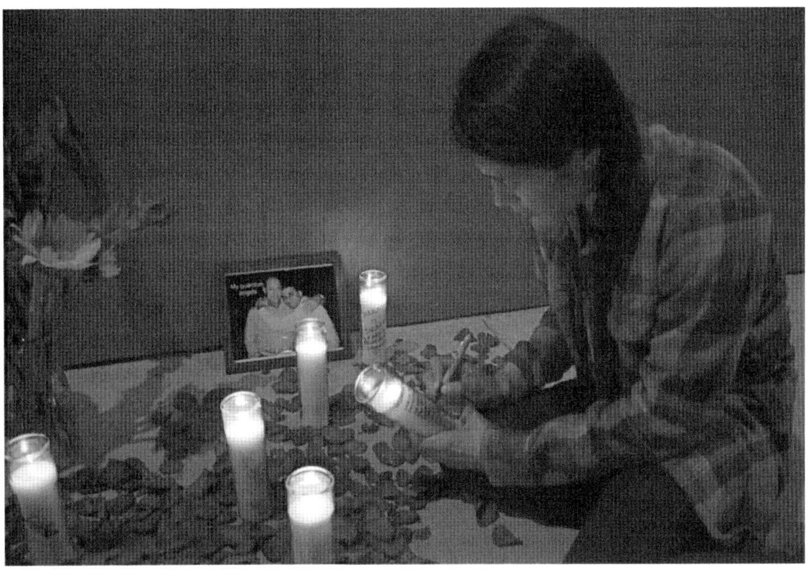

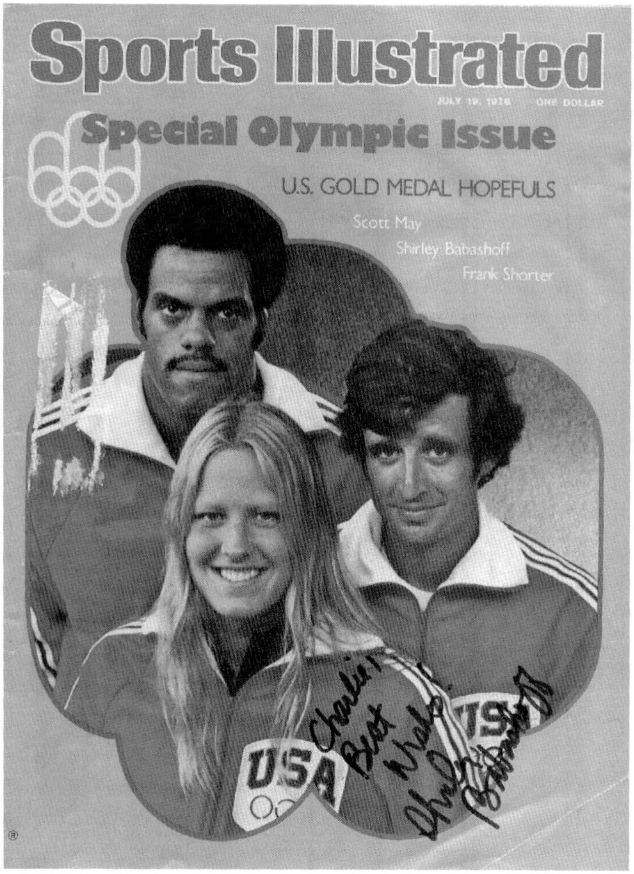

Golden Girl (ABOVE AND OPPOSITE PAGE)

With a total of eight Olympic medals to her name, Huntington Beach's Shirley Babashoff was the most successful US female Olympian prior to the 1990s. Although she never won an individual Olympic title, she is recognized as one of the greatest freestyle swimmers. Babashoff set six world records in individual events and shared in an additional five in relays. She also set 37 US records (17 individual and 20 relay) and, at one time, held the US freestyle record at every distance from 100 meters to 800 meters. Apart from her record-breaking feats, Babashoff had a fine competitive record in major championships, winning 27 Amateur Athletic Union (AAU) titles, including relays, in addition to taking the 200-meter and 400-meter individual gold medals at the 1975 World Championships. Her greatest performance came at the 1976 Olympic trials, when she won every freestyle event and the 400-meter individual medley. She set three US records in the heats, three more in the finals, and broke the world record in the 800-meter freestyle. This performance ranks among the great swimming feats of all time.

Babashoff was vilified by many in the media in 1976 after she accused the East German swimmers who defeated her, notably Kornelia Ender, of using performance-enhancing drugs (PEDs). After the fall of the Berlin Wall in 1990, documents from the East German secret police, the Stasi, were found that confirmed Babashoff's suspicions. On April 30, 2005, Shirley Babashoff received the Olympic Order, the highest award of the Olympic Movement, during the inaugural Olympic Assembly luncheon. International Olympic Committee members Bob Ctvrtlik, Anita DeFrantz, and Jim Easton presented the award. The IOC established the Olympic Order in 1974 to honor individuals who have illustrated the Olympic ideals through their actions, have achieved remarkable merit in the sporting world, or have rendered outstanding services to the Olympic cause, either through personal achievements or contributions to the development of sport.

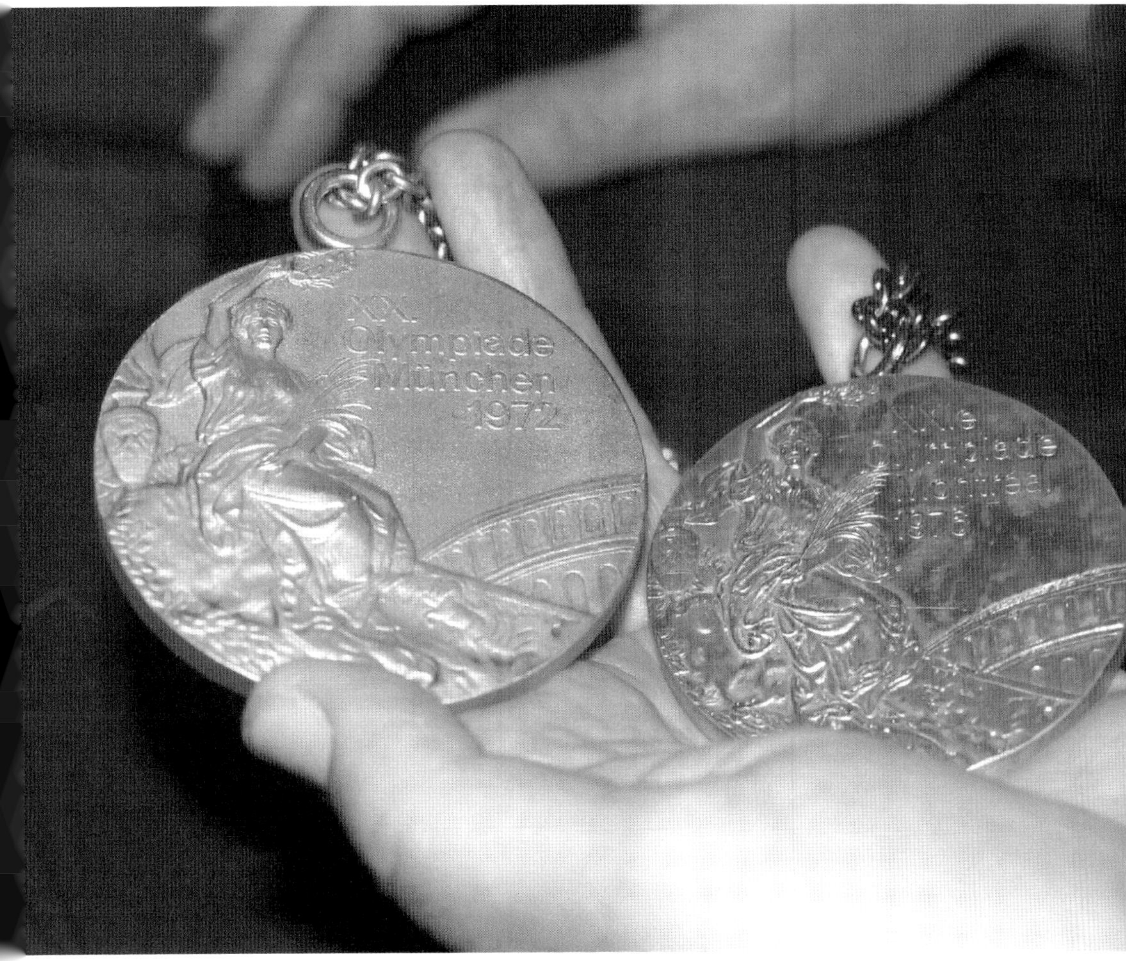
XX.
Olympiade
München
1972

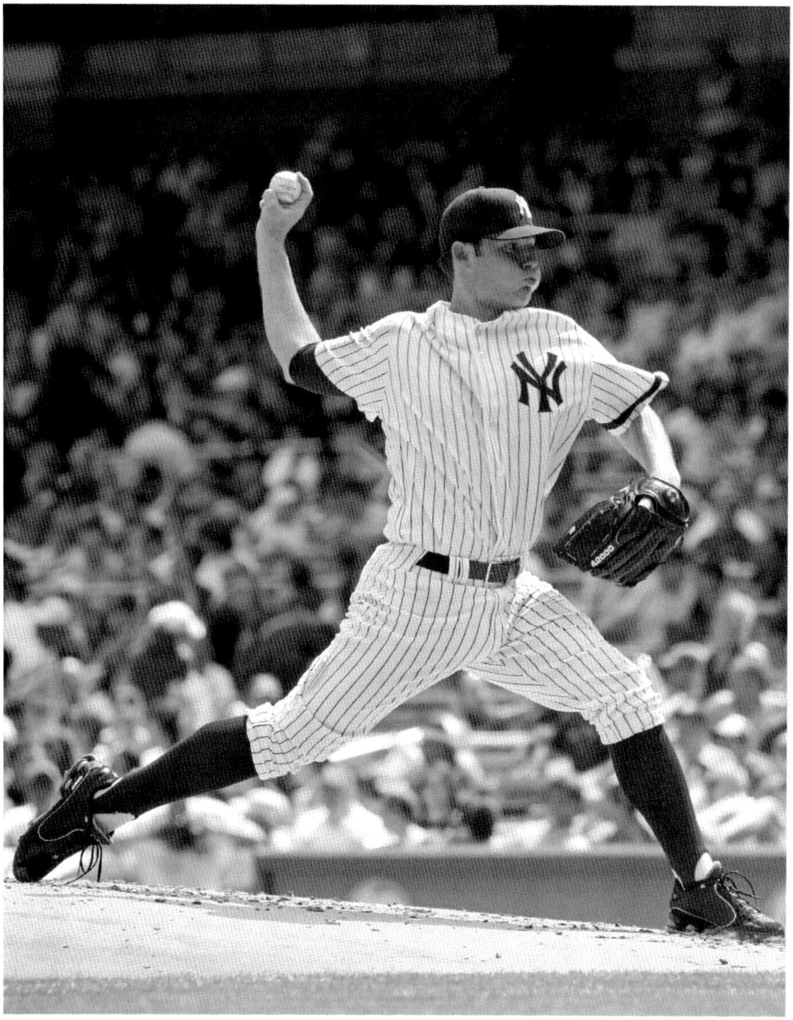

The Pitcher

Ian Kennedy grew up in Huntington Beach and attended La Quinta High School in Westminster. He went on to star at USC and then was drafted by the New York Yankees in the 2006 draft (first round, 21st pick overall). Kennedy pitched for the Staten Island Yankees of the New York–Penn League, the Class A Tampa Yankees of the Florida State League, and the AA Trenton Thunder of the Eastern League. On July 24, 2007, Kennedy was promoted to the AAA Scranton/Wilkes-Barre Yankees. Several weeks later, on September 1, he made his sparkling debut at Yankee Stadium in place of Mike Mussina. He got the win by allowing just one earned run and striking out six in seven innings. Asked what it was like to make his debut in perhaps the most hallowed of stadiums, Kennedy, standing in the locker room in the House that Ruth Built, replied, "It was amazing." He went on, "I don't know a whole lot about baseball history, but I know about that place and it was unforgettable." Was he nervous? "Not really," Kennedy said. "I had Roger Clemens talking to me about how to be tough and handle the better hitters. Plus, Moose [Mussina] was real supportive, so I was in good hands." To say the least. Kennedy said his entire family was on hand and said what a thrill it was to see them after the game. He does not get back to Huntington Beach too much, so seeing friendly faces on the road is a good way to help settle him down. His alma mater produced other major-league players, including Bobby Crosby, Gerald Laird, and Ian Stewart.

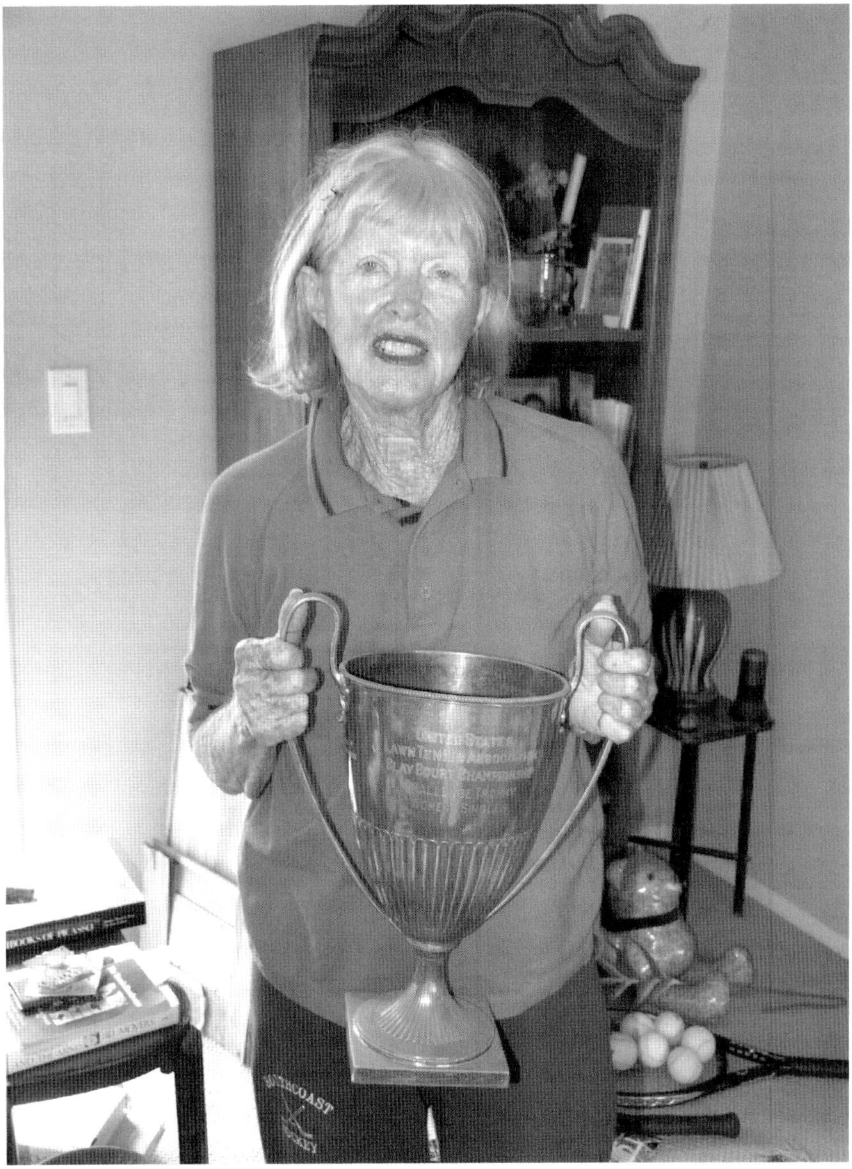

The Tennis Player

The three-time French Open finalist moves fluidly across the tennis court, setting her opponent up with a well-disguised drop shot and then finishing the point with a crosscourt overhead. This is taking place not on the Tennis Channel, nor at Roland Garros near Paris, France, where the French Open is played. Rather, the action is happening at a local tennis center, where a legend is doing what she has done for nearly 70 years: play tennis with grace, energy, and smarts. Dorothy Knode, 81, lives in Huntington Beach. On her wall are old photographs that reveal how much tennis styles have changed since the 1950s, before the game's elegance and formality gave way to neon-colored costumes and space-age rackets. But Knode does not bemoan the current state of tennis. "I really enjoy following Roger Federer, James Blake, and Maria Sharapova, among some others," she says in her musical, lilting voice. "Of course I wish we could have made their money, but it was a different time and we did incredibly interesting things and met wonderful people."

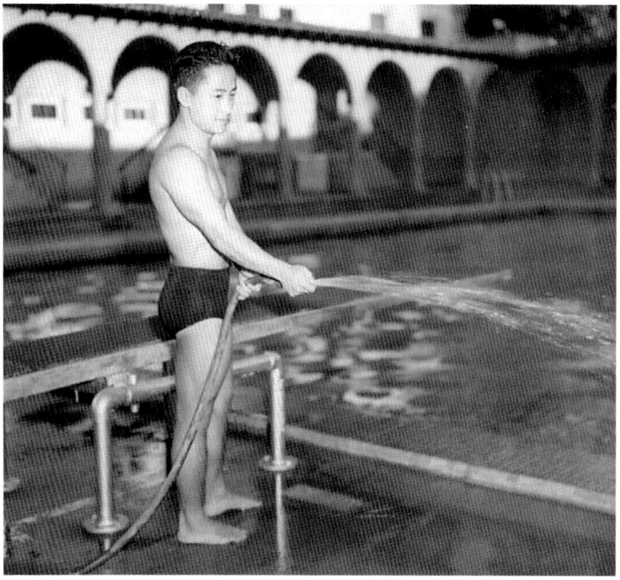

The Diver
Longtime Huntington Beach resident Sammy Lee was the first Asian American to win an Olympic gold medal. It happened at the 1948 games in London, when he won for one of his performances on the 10-meter platform. He then won the gold in the 10-meter springboard and the bronze in the 3-meter springboard at the Helsinki Olympics. As a doctor, he served in the US Army Medical Corps in Korea from 1953 to 1955. In 1968, Dr. Lee was elected to the International Swimming Hall of Fame. Now in his early 90s, he still makes speaking appearances in the area.

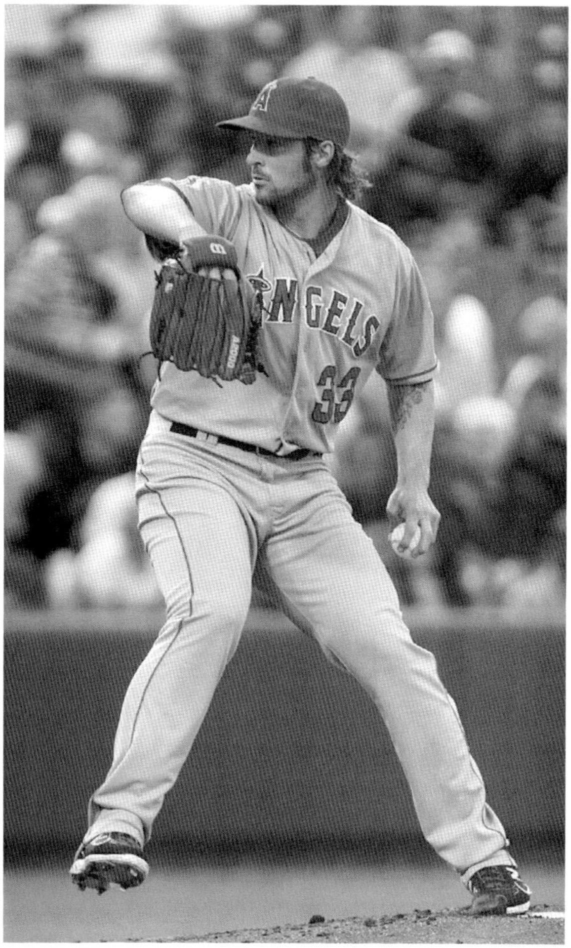

The Little Leaguer
C.J. Wilson grew up in Huntington Beach, starring in the Seaview Little League. After going to high school in Fountain Valley, he started playing baseball at Santa Ana Junior College. There, the left-handed hurler developed into one of the 20 best players in the area. From Santa Ana, he gained a scholarship at Loyola Marymount University and, in 2005, found himself in the major leagues, pitching for the Texas Rangers. Today, he pitches closer to his original home as a starter for the Los Angeles Angels of Anaheim.

CHAPTER SIX

Special Citizens

Every community, no matter how large or small, has them. They are the citizens that somehow always manage to go a little bit above and beyond. They might be the hardest working, or the most inspired, or the most talented. They might be the most dedicated public servants, the most loyal, the most knowledgeable, or the most passionate about a particular topic. Some have gone too soon, but they have left something profound behind.

Huntington Beach residents know who they are and are usually better for having known them. These special citizens all share that knack of being able to both create awareness and generate enlightenment in their particular area of expertise.

In that sense, this was the most difficult chapter in the book to put together, because many books could be filled with the stories of these people that have made such dramatic differences in Huntington Beach. They are the shopkeepers and the historians, the teachers, the volunteers, the advocates, and the activists.

They are the people that take chances, knowing no other way to make a difference. Since becoming a city more than 100 years ago, Huntington Beach has never been at a lack for personalities like this. As much as any other group in the city, they have helped shape, mold, and inspire many people. And they have all left a positive mark.

It was extremely hard to cull the list down to what appears in this book, and there will be some oversights. Originally, several political figures were to be included. However, due to limited space, politics has for the most part been left out. Rather, the chapter focuses on individuals that have made a difference on their own.

Huntington Beach is a wildly open and diverse community that allows for free expression and self-driven involvement. Some of these people are more connected than others, but they all share those rare and unique qualities of individualism, energy, and tenacity. They are the people that hopefully, in 100 years, readers will look back on and say, "I wish I had known all of them."

For those that are not included in this collection, the author hope at some point to create another volume in which they can take their deserved place among the special citizens that have made Huntington Beach such a special city for both residents and tourists alike.

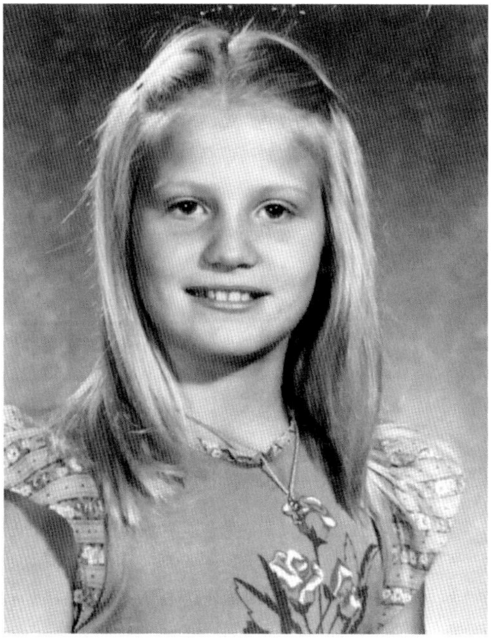

Robin Samsoe

In the summer of 1979, thirteen-year-old Robin Samsoe was abducted in Huntington Beach and, several days later, was found dead in a nearby mountain range. This tragedy galvanized the public, resulting in the capture of one of the nation's most demonic serial killers. As of this writing, there are plans for a Robin Samsoe memorial by the pier. This eloquent entry was written by Robin's niece, 18-year-old Jaydenn Grace Samsoe.

> Although the opportunity to meet my aunt, Robin Samsoe, was stolen away by a monster who's now serving his time, I've never heard anything but positive things about her. Robin was a beautiful, smart, and happy young girl who lived in Huntington Beach with her family—my family. My father, uncle, grandmother, and anyone who knew her will tell you what a sweet and incredible person she was. And although I'd have loved the chance to get to know her, and am terribly saddened that she was taken away; I'm glad that her death had a huge and positive impact on many people's lives. Robin's death led police to a serial killer who was wanted for many other murders and prevented this monster from taking more lives, and also served as a warning to other parents who, during this time, would let their kids go out and play all day with their friends at the beach because crimes like this weren't as prevalent as they are today. It was not uncommon for Robin to be out at Huntington Beach, with friends at the pier, playing in the water, or riding around on her bike because there was not much reason to worry about letting your children go out alone or with friends. After Robin's death, parents were wary about letting their kids out of their sights, and even police became more aware of these kinds of situations. I think that Robin would be glad to know that she did not die in vain, that her death actually meant something. To me, Robin has always been the reason my friends and I needed parental supervision to do things, and the reason my mom would pick us up from school every day even though we lived down the street. My grandmother speaks of Robin as an Angel sent to her from Heaven and she loved Robin with all of her heart. My father has a million stories of him and Robin growing up together. My uncle still gets tears in his eyes when he thinks about her. And my siblings and cousins will all tell you that they really wish they'd gotten the chance to meet such an amazing person. Robin and her story will forever live on in our hearts.

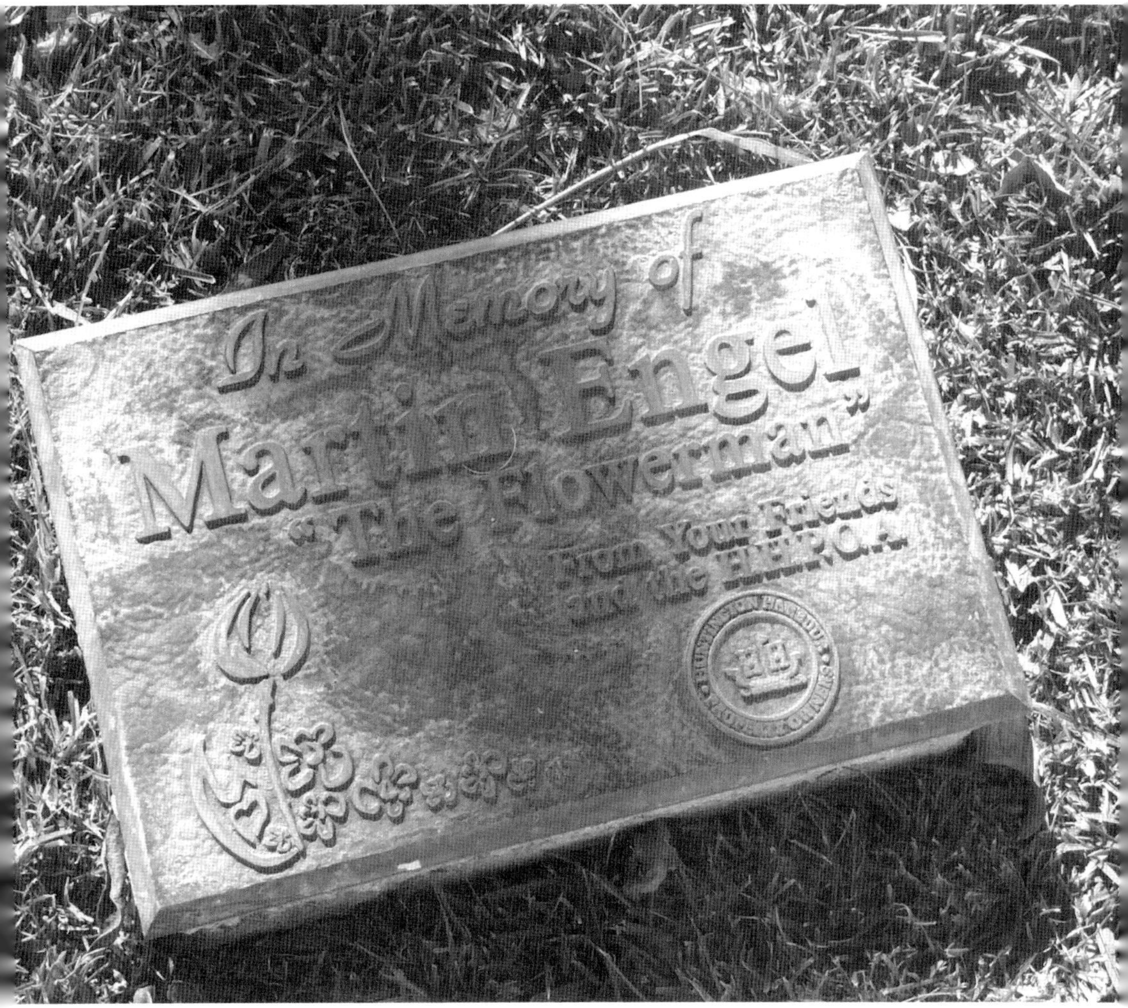

The Flower Man

On Humboldt Island, in the community of Huntington Harbour, there is a small plaque in the grass near the foot of the bridge that leads onto the island. It was placed there in honor of a man named Martin Engel. Well known throughout the city, he was certainly a legend in his small neighborhood. Starting when he was in his early 70s, Engel planted flowers and trees to help beautify the community where he lived for 30 years. And then, tragically, in 1995, Engel was killed when his car collided with a van as it was pulling out of a local home supply store parking lot in Huntington Beach. Ironically, Engel's car was filled that day with flowers he had just purchased to bring home and plant around his island neighborhood. The marker dedicated to this man is small and easy to miss, and those walking by may not know who he was or what he did. Martin Engel spent a lot of his own time and money to make things look prettier. Today, many of the fruits of his labors still bloom throughout the year, colorful reminders of one generous man's time.

The Discoverer

On this day, lifelong Huntington Beach resident Bill Kettler walks to the end of Bolsa Chica Street, where the Trails at Brightwater starts. "There were no houses out there," Kettler, 90, says. "It was all rural. Far as you could see. I graduated from Springdale Elementary as class valedictorian—though there were only two of us in the class." With a chuckle, Kettler motions down at the soft dirt studded with seashell fragments. "These shells are all part of the Indian middens; their garbage heaps. This is where they discarded all their shells. I'd come up here as a young boy after the rains and look for arrowheads." He kept moving ahead as he looked for a special spot. "Things have grown over a lot, changed over the years," he said to himself. Then he stopped near the thick, towering wild mustard. "It was here, right in here," he said softly. Kettler has come to the spot where, as a teenager in the early 1930s, he made a discovery. "I saw something shiny," he said. "Got closer and saw it was a skull. Then I saw another." The rain had uncovered two complete Indian skeletons, most likely at least several thousand years old. He knew, after witnessing several scientific exhumations in the area, that he had come upon part of a burial site. Soon, hundreds of skeletons were found. Today, within view of where Kettler discovered his skeletons, is located one of the most significant archaeological sites in Southern California. Known as ORA-83, it contains evidence of an 8,000-year-old village and burial ground. Does Kettler realize his discoveries probably helped thwart the building of 4,800 homes on the mesa? "Well, I guess it didn't hurt," he chuckles. "And I mean, I hope it helped. We have to respect this history—how we can learn from it and also protect the legacy of the Indians and their families."

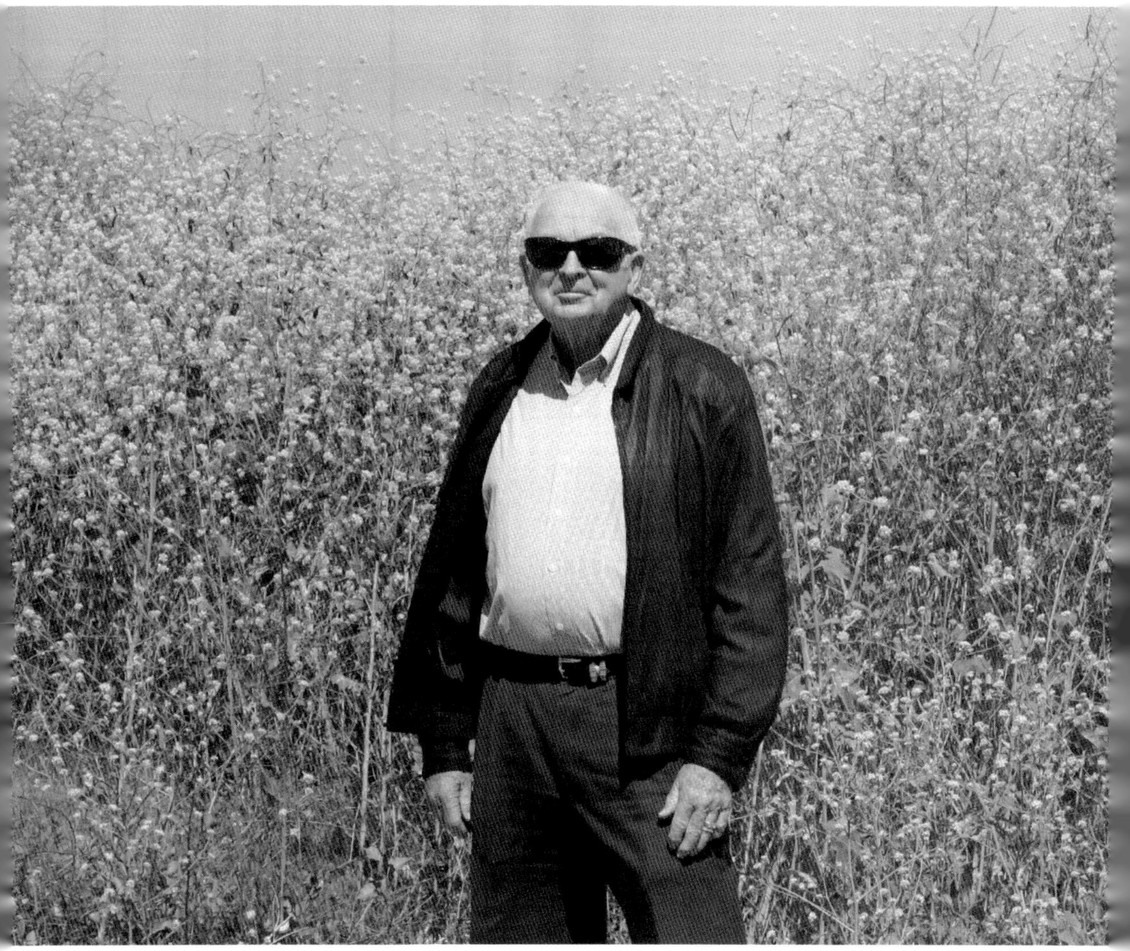

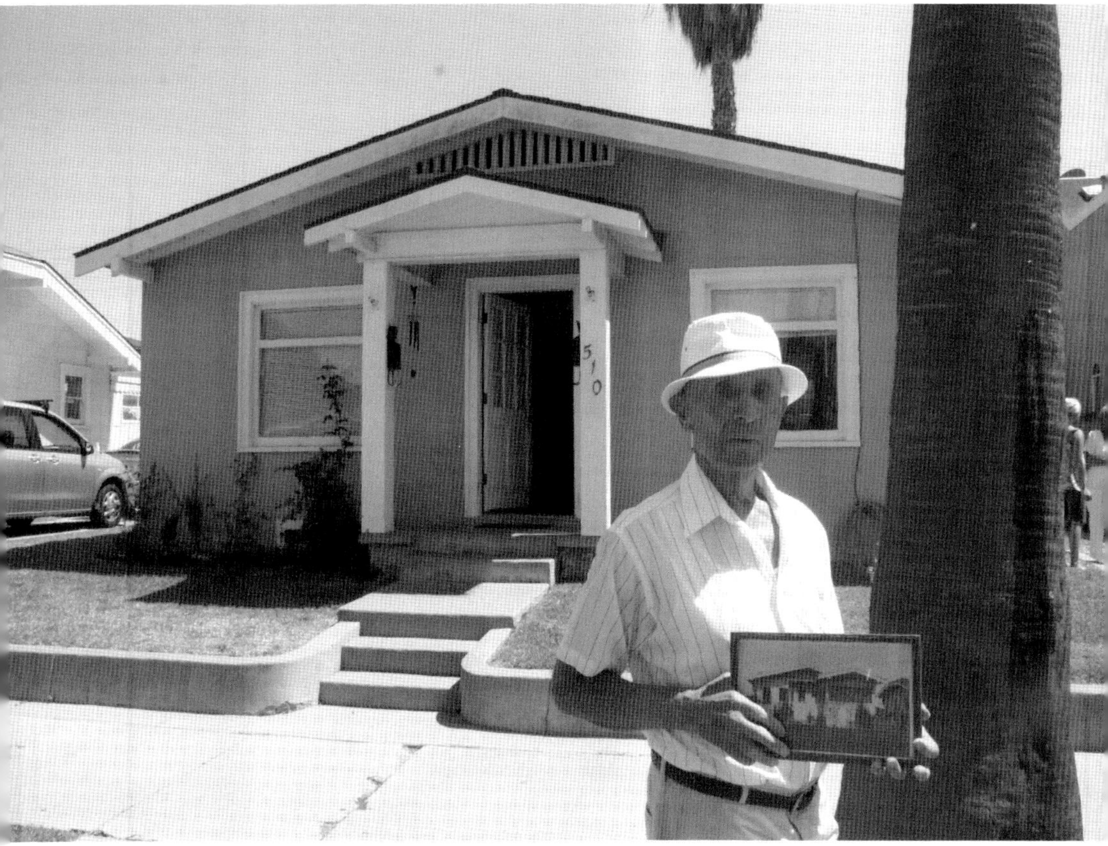

Special Palm Trees

There are many palm trees in Huntington Beach, but few as meaningful as the pair of graceful and slender Mexican fan palms that scrape the sky just several blocks from the ocean on Eighth Street. Like the house they sway in front of, the trees date to the early 1920s.

What makes them so special? They were planted by a father to honor the day his son, Leroy Jauman, was born. It was an effort to create two lasting monuments to mark his baby boy's entry to this world. Today, almost 89, Jauman lives in town with his wife of 61 years, Yvonne. His memories of old-time Huntington Beach are as sharp and vivid as the bright green fronds that grow in his honor atop the thin trunks. Looking down the block at the structure that was once the Evangeline Hotel, Jauman fondly recalled visits to the large building. "The roughnecks from the oil fields stayed there," he said. "And I'd bring bouquets of sweet pea flowers from my backyard to the lady that ran the place so she could decorate the dinner tables for them." Visitors to Eighth Street near Pecan Avenue who happen to notice those two palms should stare up high and consider what they represent. They are not just any trees. They are a lasting gesture of love, a proud new father's way of saying, "Welcome, my son. To this world. To this family. To this town."

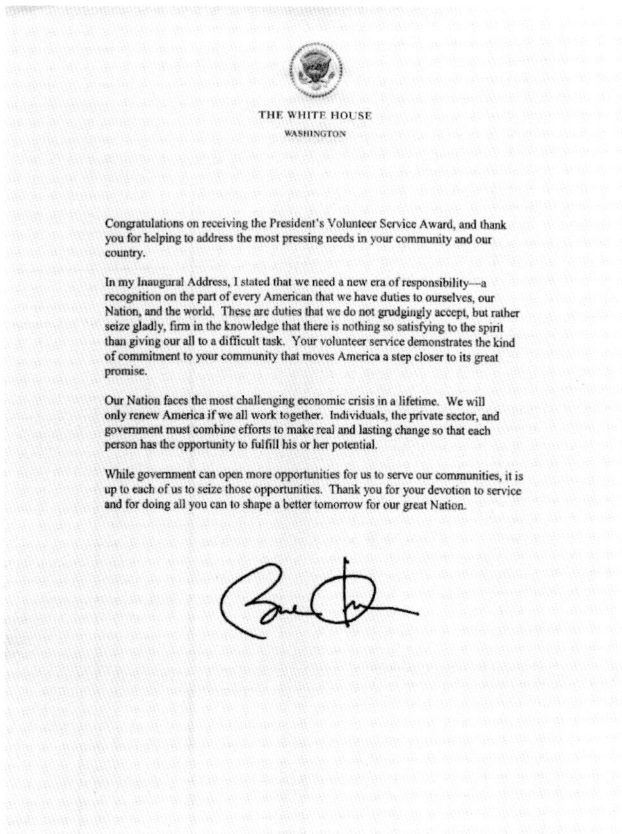

THE WHITE HOUSE
WASHINGTON

Congratulations on receiving the President's Volunteer Service Award, and thank you for helping to address the most pressing needs in your community and our country.

In my Inaugural Address, I stated that we need a new era of responsibility—a recognition on the part of every American that we have duties to ourselves, our Nation, and the world. These are duties that we do not grudgingly accept, but rather seize gladly, firm in the knowledge that there is nothing so satisfying to the spirit than giving our all to a difficult task. Your volunteer service demonstrates the kind of commitment to your community that moves America a step closer to its great promise.

Our Nation faces the most challenging economic crisis in a lifetime. We will only renew America if we all work together. Individuals, the private sector, and government must combine efforts to make real and lasting change so that each person has the opportunity to fulfill his or her potential.

While government can open more opportunities for us to serve our communities, it is up to each of us to seize those opportunities. Thank you for your devotion to service and for doing all you can to shape a better tomorrow for our great Nation.

Friend of the Library

Gail Page came to Huntington Beach after a long career as an Army wife. The stops along the way had included Asia and Europe and several postings in the United States. A few years later, when her sons went off to college, she turned her attention to the community and her passion: children's literacy. Joining the Friends of the Children's Library, a group that supports the children's department of the Huntington Beach Public Library, Page quickly became a leader in several of its projects to enhance the library experience for children. As one of her first contributions, she became the chair of the annual festival of children's authors. In this role, she refined an existing event to improve its benefit for children. This event sends children's authors to local schools to conduct reading-enrichment programs. In conjunction with the festival, Page began a children's writing contest that has become very popular. Awards are presented to the children by a city official. She also authored a grant request to the Boeing Company's Employee Community Fund, and the festival has received an annual grant from the fund. As a result of Page's work, the annual Authors Festival has become a highlight of the children's program of the Huntington Beach Public Library. Perhaps her most lasting contribution to the children's department of the library has been her work with the Taste of Huntington Beach. This is the major fundraiser for the children's library. Page has helped turn it into one of the city's premier events.

As a result of her efforts, Gail Page has been recognized several times, including receiving the Volunteer Service Award from the president of the United States in 2009. The presidential citation (pictured) reads, in part, "Your volunteer service demonstrates the kind of commitment to your community that moves America a step closer to its great promise." Most remarkable about all these achievements is the fact that Page has been confined to a wheelchair for over 20 years. Her battle with multiple sclerosis has not sidetracked her drive to support the children of Huntington Beach with her work at the children's department of the Huntington Beach Public Library.

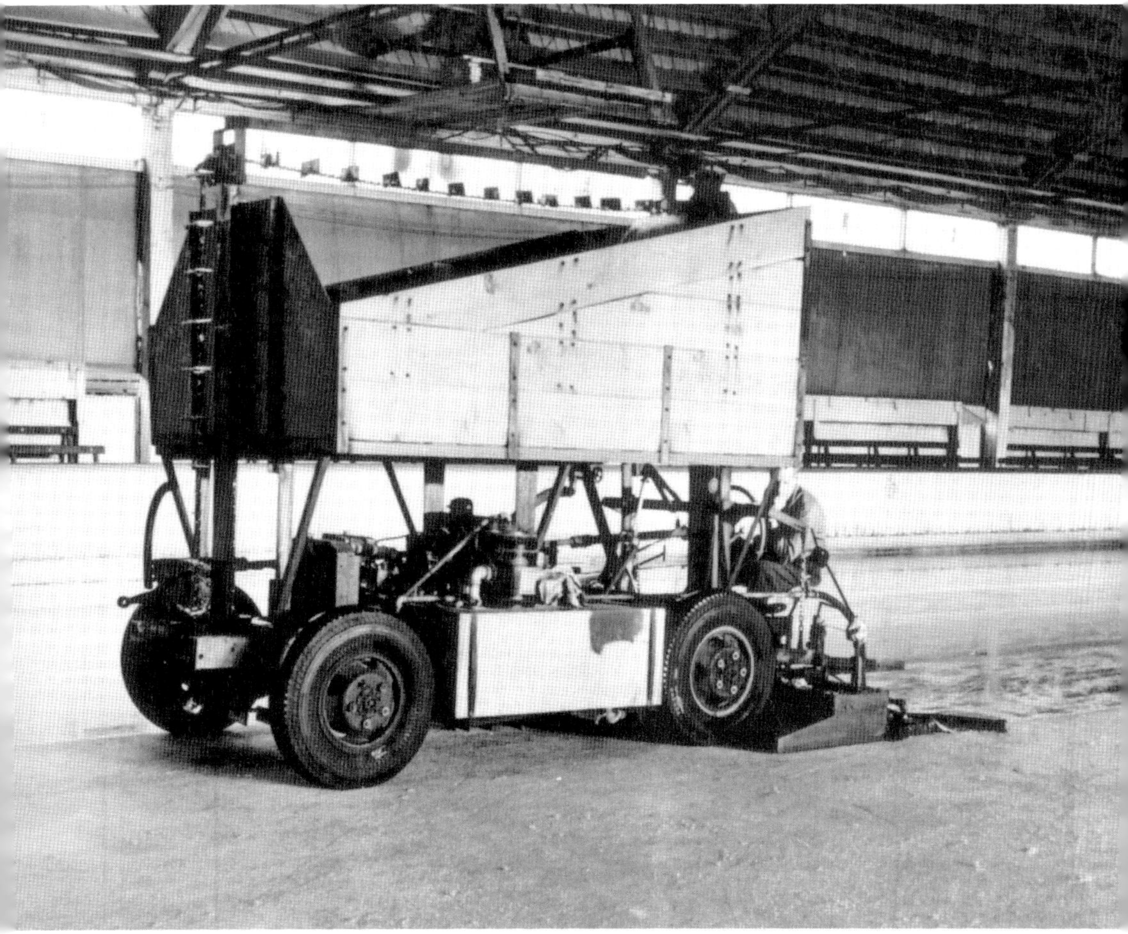

The Iceman

Richard Zamboni's, dad, Frank, invented the Zamboni, the machine that resurfaces ice-skating rinks. The family has a fascinating history. Frank Zamboni and his brother were in the refrigeration and ice business. They built an ice rink, which opened in Paramount in 1940. Frank found that the process of resurfacing the ice was labor intensive, so he began to experiment with various prototypes until the Zamboni Model A ice resurfacer produced a good sheet of ice in the summer of 1949. Richard, a longtime Huntington Beach resident, helps run the family company today, and the business has never been stronger. The ice-skating rink that Richard's dad opened is still in business. Visitors can even see the very first Zamboni machine (pictured).

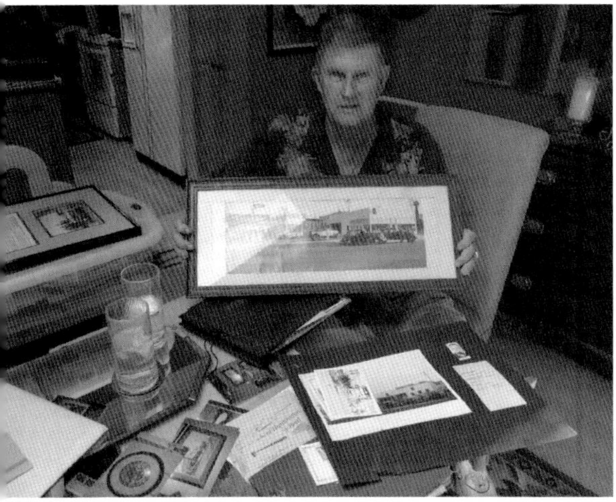

The Car Guy
Bob Terry was born in 1937, the year his dad, Collins "Pop" Terry, opened his new showroom. Pop had started as a Pontiac dealer in 1926. The family started in Huntington Beach in 1909, when an aunt arrived, and the Terrys clearly made a lasting impact. Relatives eventually owned many buildings and businesses in town, so much so that the area near the car dealership and family gas station was dubbed "Terryville" in the 1960s. For years, Bob's family ran one of the best-known businesses in city history, the venerable Terry Buick, just off Pacific Coast Highway on Fifth Street, across from another local institution, the Surf Theater.

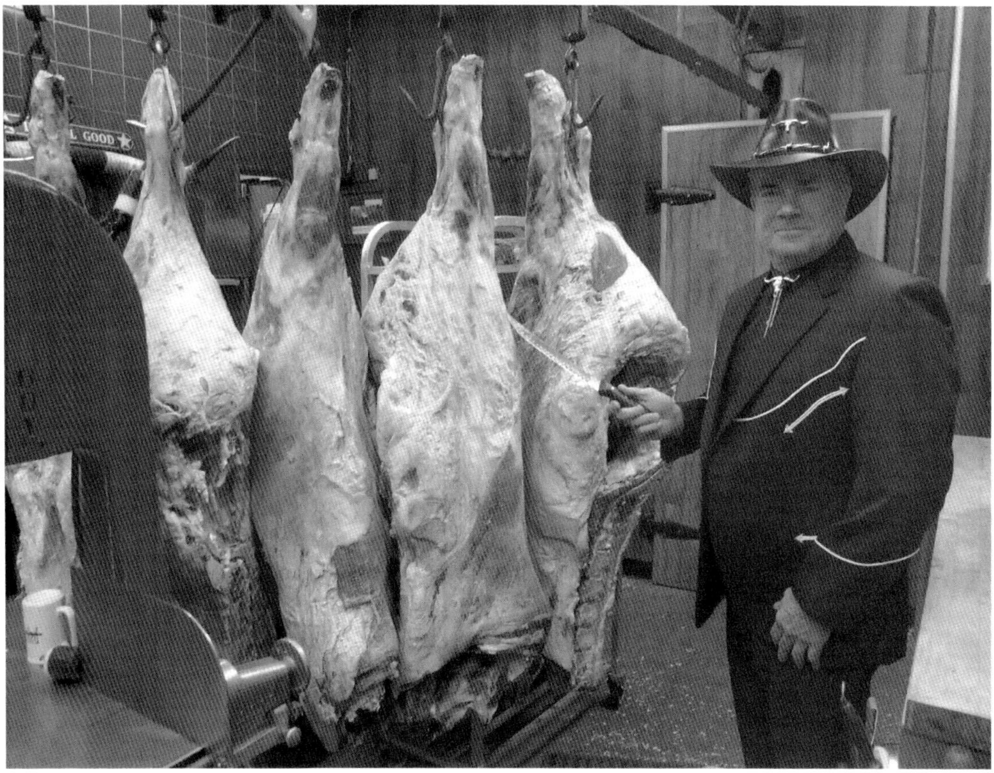

The Butcher
"I don't know how many tons," Calvin Free says pensively. This big, solid man dressed all in black, with jet-black hair and silver, longhorn-shaped bolo tie, continues. "Near six tons—and that's just prime rib." Free is seen here at the Beef Palace, a meat-worshiper's mecca that has been in Huntington Beach for 40 years. It was opened by Calvin Free's dad, the legendary butcher Melvin Free. Several years ago, the city asked if Calvin would donate hamburgers for a Fourth of July barbecue for Marines at the Newland House. "Hamburger?" Free laughs. "'Not for the Marines,' I said. 'They eat rib eyes, and I'm cooking them.' " Since then, the city has adopted the 3rd Battalion, 1st Marine Regiment, 1st Marine Division at Camp Pendleton. Free often keeps them fed—with steaks.

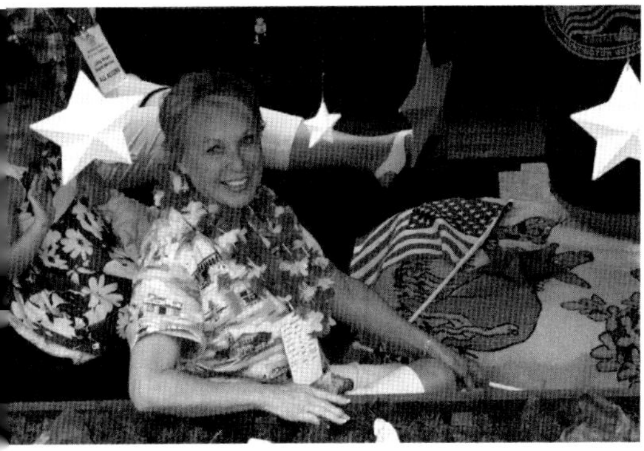

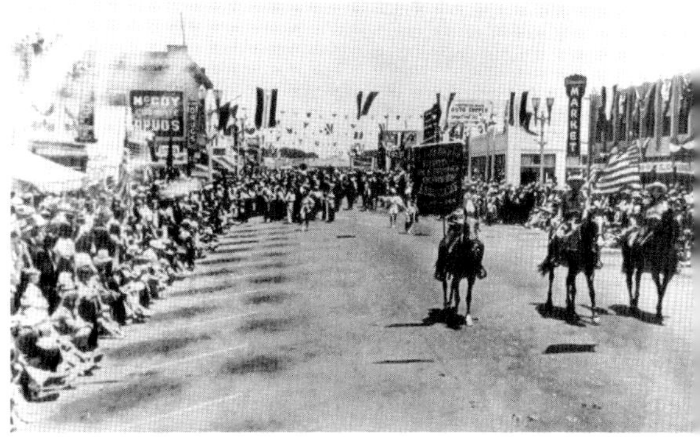

The Parade Lady

Patricia "Pat" Stier is the director for the Fourth of July Executive Board, in charge of the city's most famed annual event. In her own words, "I have been involved with the parade since 1993. I moved here from Duluth, Minnesota, in 1973 and never looked back. I fell in love with Huntington Beach immediately. I have lived in Huntington Beach for the past 41 years with my dog Molly. Along with Stacey Newton, we oversee the parade, 5K run, fireworks, festival, coordinates logistics, entertainment, Lake Park, and anything else associated with the words 'parade' and 'Fourth of July.' We team up to give the city of Huntington Beach the best parade in California every year."

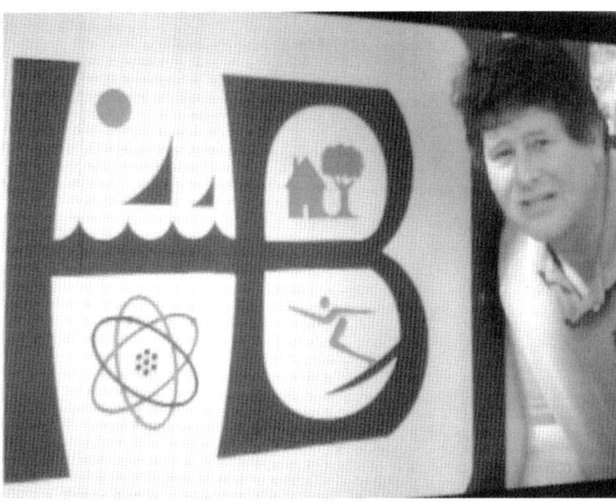

The Hyper-Local Host

To witness a community in action is one thing. To see it through the lens of a video camera takes on an entirely different "angle." This is the case with Matt Liffreing, Huntington's man on the streets (and galleries, sports venues, playhouses, and coastlines). Huntington Beach's cable television industry has been around for 31 years, and Liffreing began when most residents did not know what cable television was all about. He has captured the highs and lows of most everything involving Huntington Beach for HBTV-3 and for the city's website, with such programs as *Made in Huntington Beach* and *Surf City Highlights*, now in its eighth year. Additionally, *Journey to Pasadena* and *Centennial Yearbook* featured the city's centennial 2009 celebration. Whether he is in front of the camera or acting as his own producer/editor, Liffreing has brought the community together, showcasing its people, causes, and prospects.

"This city is like no other, and I feel blessed to compliment our friends in print or canvas, who share similar responsibilities for documenting individual, corporate and community experiences," said the award-winning producer. In addition, thousands know Matt Liffreing as the voice of the famed Fourth of July parade.

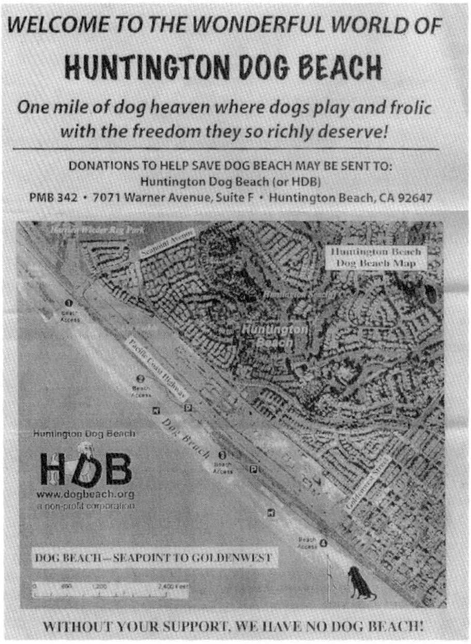

DownTown, USA

To watch Martin Senat walk Dog Beach was to watch a great conductor direct his favorite orchestra. He engaged nearly everyone who walked by, checked the bag dispensers, then dispensed treats for passing pups. Senat gave away T-shirts and offered quips, bits of gossip, and wry observations. He was as at home at Dog Beach as the dogs themselves. And that is why it was never the same after he died in 2010. The Englishman founded the nonprofit society in 1997 to preserve Dog Beach, a strip of shoreline in Huntington Beach where dogs can run and play without a leash. Today, Senat's group still maintains, cleans, and raises funds for the dog beach.

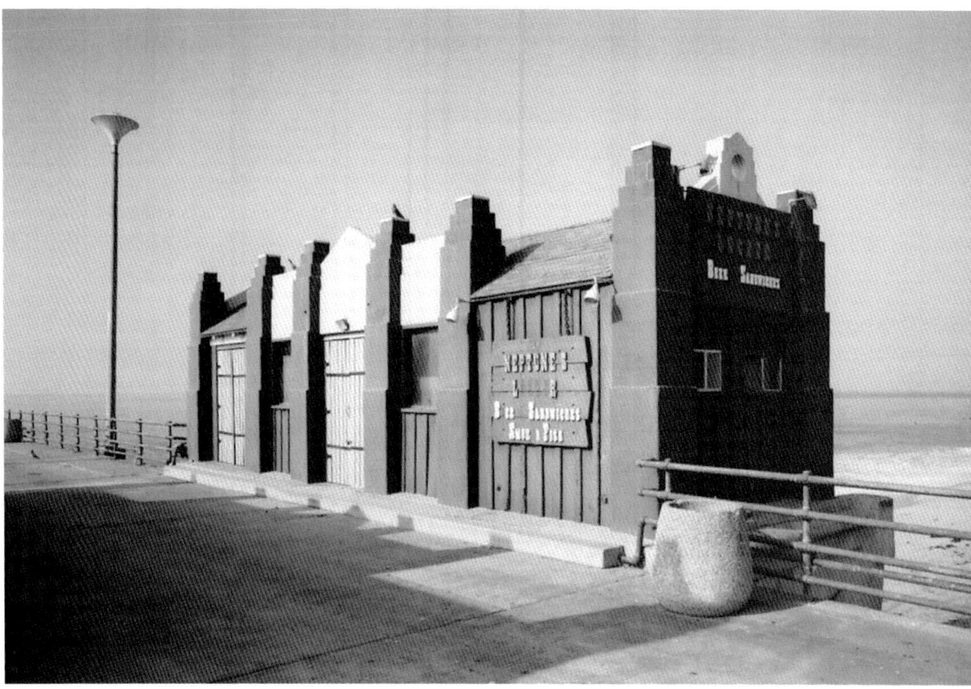

Queen of the Pier

Ella Christensen and her husband, Carl, purchased the Tackle Box bait shop in 1951. They successfully ran the shop, located near the end of the pier. Then, in 1969, the Christensens' daughter Joy purchased Neptune's Locker (pictured), a tiny pub on the pier. Ella took that over in the early 1970s and ran it until it closed in the late 1980s. There was also the Captain's Galley, a former lifeguard station and card room that Ella purchased in 1975 and turned into a fast-food restaurant. She was not happy when, in 1988, officials decided to close the 74-year-old pier. Ella passed away in 2003 at the age of 89.

The Singing Goodtimers

Each Wednesday morning at the Michael E. Rodgers Senior Center, the dulcet sounds of people singing from their hearts can be heard loud and clear, full of passion and exuberance. That is how the Singing Goodtimers do it. Formed by vaudeville entertainer Esther Rivelli Brown in 1971, the group today boasts about 60 seniors, ranging in age from the early 60s all the way up to 90. A plaque outside the room acknowledges Rivelli, who died in 1998. It reads, "Esther's charm and vitality will be missed. Her dedication to the seniors in Huntington Beach made a difference." Dianne Shirley, one of the coordinators of the group (and a lovely singer herself), describes the Singing Goodtimers: "Our singing group was formed in 1971 as a voluntary service organization, hopefully to bring pleasure to our community, especially our seniors. We entertain in senior community centers, retirement homes, convalescent hospitals, care homes, and adult day-care centers. We are a voluntary service organization, and we are all seniors. We hope that we will inspire and encourage some of the seniors who listen to us to join in the fun, have a few chuckles, and make life a little merrier. If we can encourage them to join us in singing, then we feel rewarded for our effort."

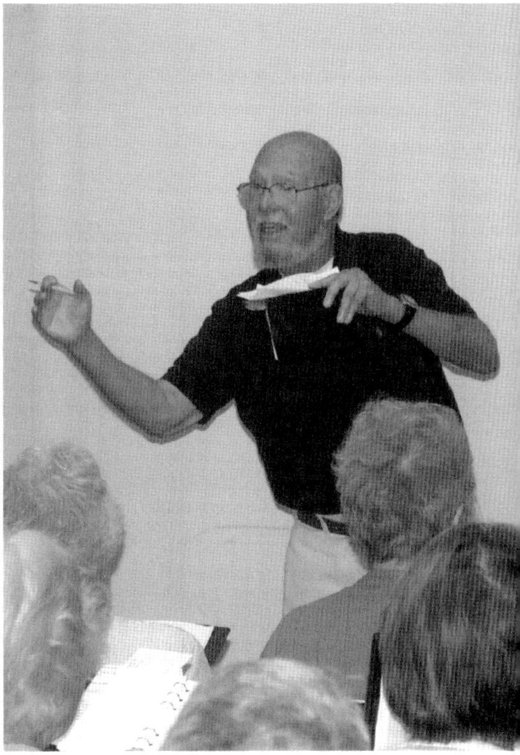

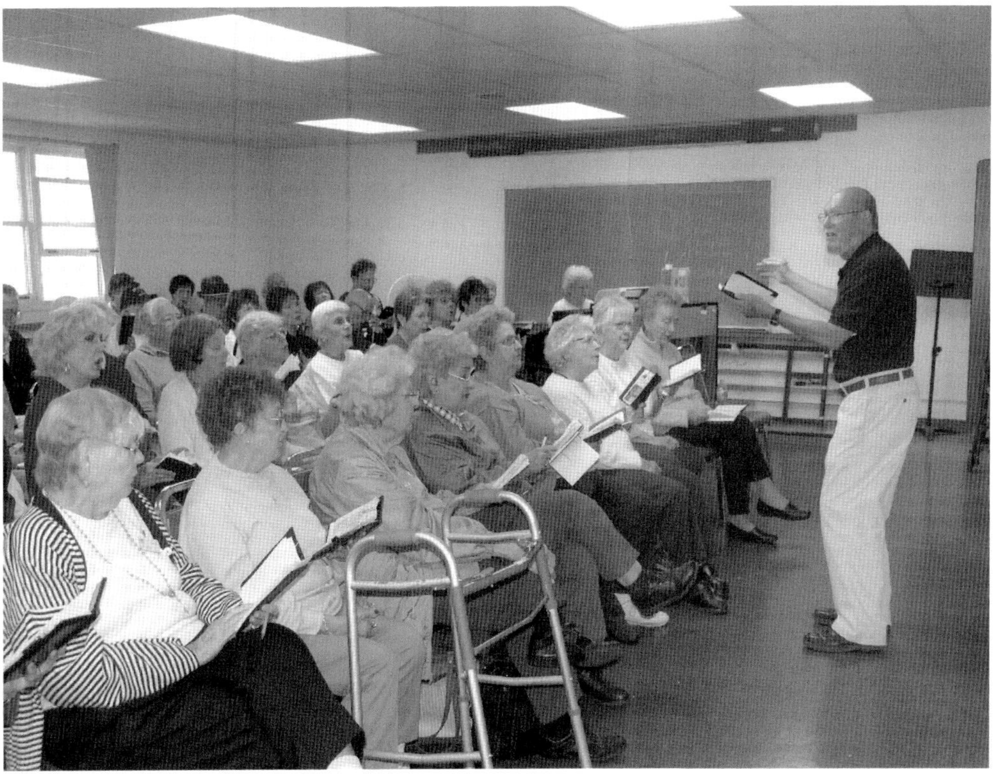

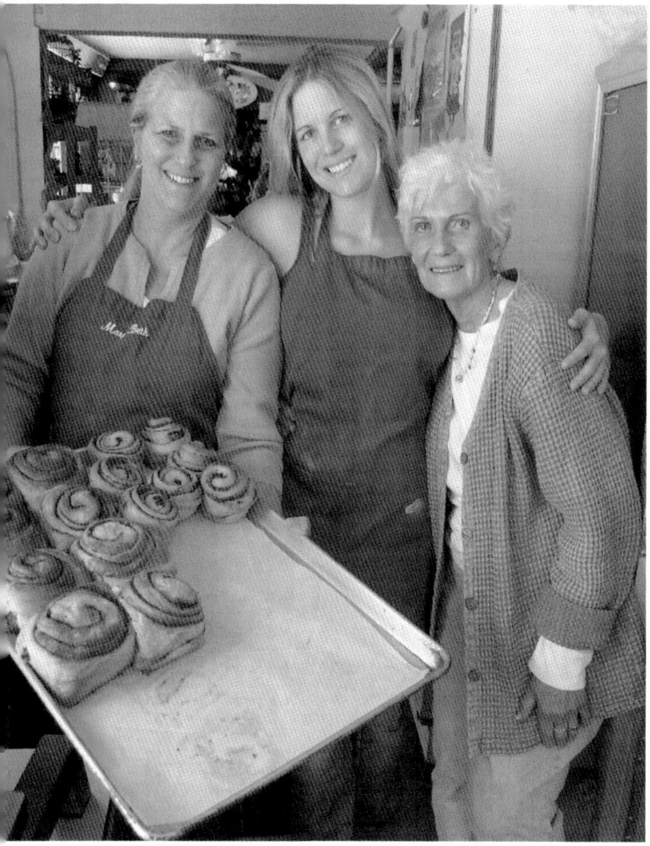

The Gustafsons

"Mary Beth Gustafson, 'Baker Extraordinaire,' " as her card says, is shown at left in the photograph on the left. She is posing in the kitchen with her 21-year-old daughter, Kerstin, and her mother, Alice, baking more of her legendary, mouth-watering cinnamon rolls from scratch, the way they have always been made. It seems pretty much everything at Alice's Breakfast in the Park restaurant (below) is made in a way that would cause any old-fashioned grandma to rejoice: from scratch and with love. Inside the small dining room, famously cluttered with charming bits of Americana, Alice, 77, talks about her husband, John, who co-owned their successful End Café at the edge of the pier. She misses him since he passed away, and she also misses her restaurant, one of Huntington Beach's favorite establishments, since it closed. As of today, Mary Beth is still baking her famous cinnamon rolls and selling them wherever she can. She is always up for having a cup of coffee and reminiscing about her restaurant and her family, two classic pieces of Huntington Beach history.

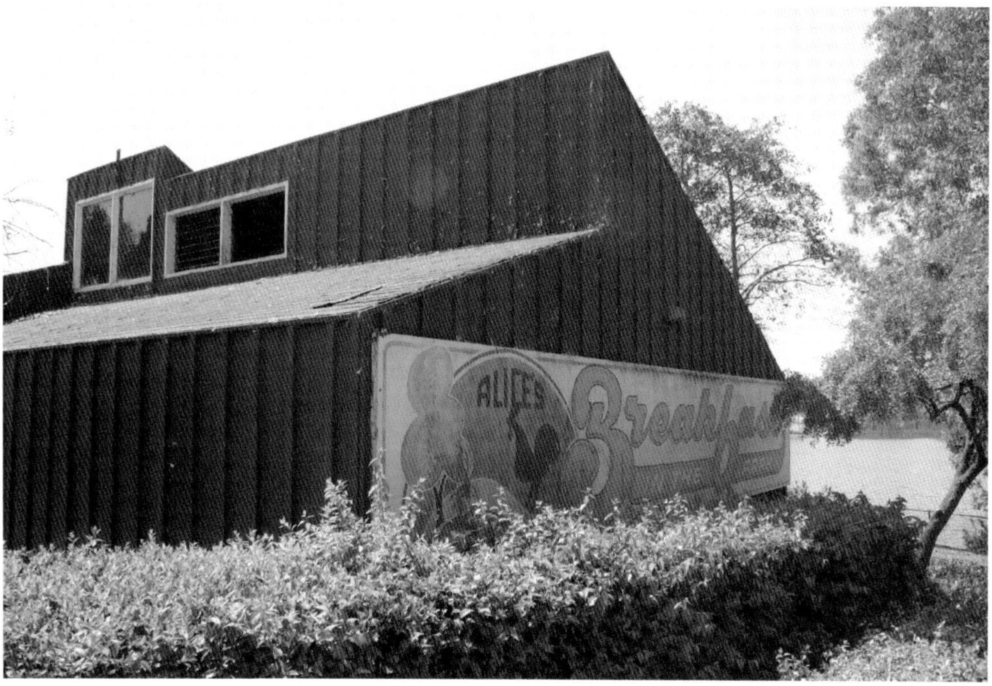

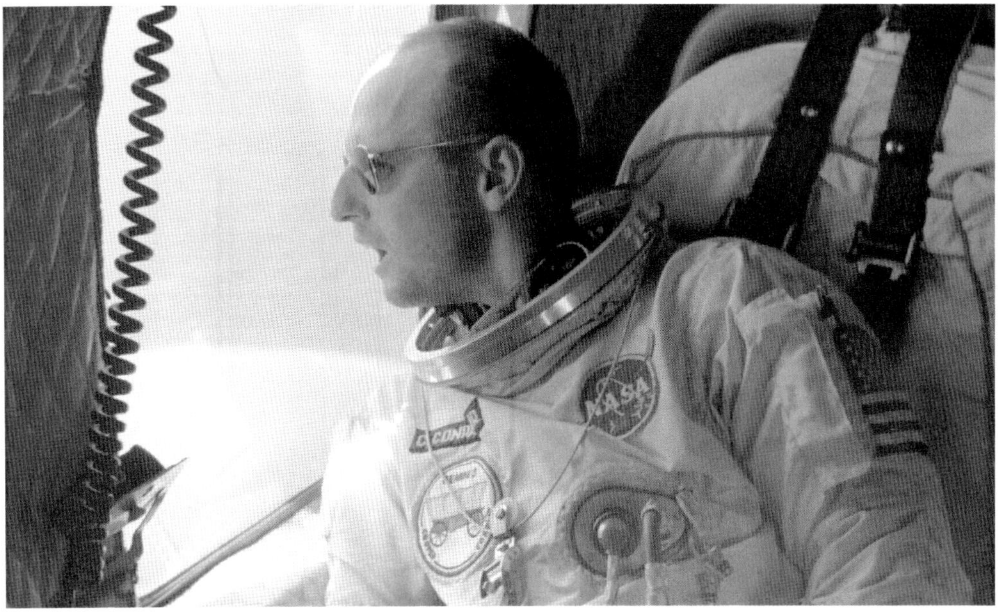

The Astronaut

Longtime Huntington Beach resident Pete Conrad is one of the most famous astronauts of all time. He was the commander on the first manned mission of Skylab, the first US orbital space station. Conrad was the third man to walk on the moon, as commander of Apollo XII. On the Gemini V mission, Conrad and his commander, pilot Gordon Cooper, set an eight-day space endurance record. Conrad also commanded Gemini XI. In 1978, he was given the Congressional Space Medal of Honor by Pres. Jimmy Carter. Tragically, Conrad was killed in July 1999, less than three weeks before the celebrations of the 30th anniversary of the first moon landing. He had been in Ojai, California, on a motorcycle tour with his wife and some friends when he suffered what was thought to be a minor crash. However, undetected internal bleeding killed him approximately six hours after the accident. Conrad was buried with full honors in Washington, DC, at Arlington National Cemetery, with many of his fellow Apollo astronauts in attendance.

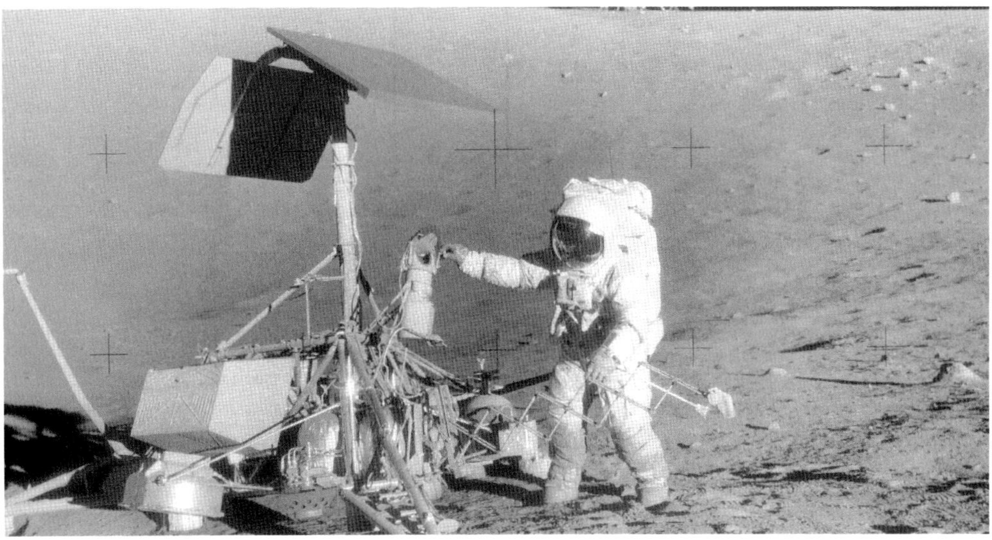

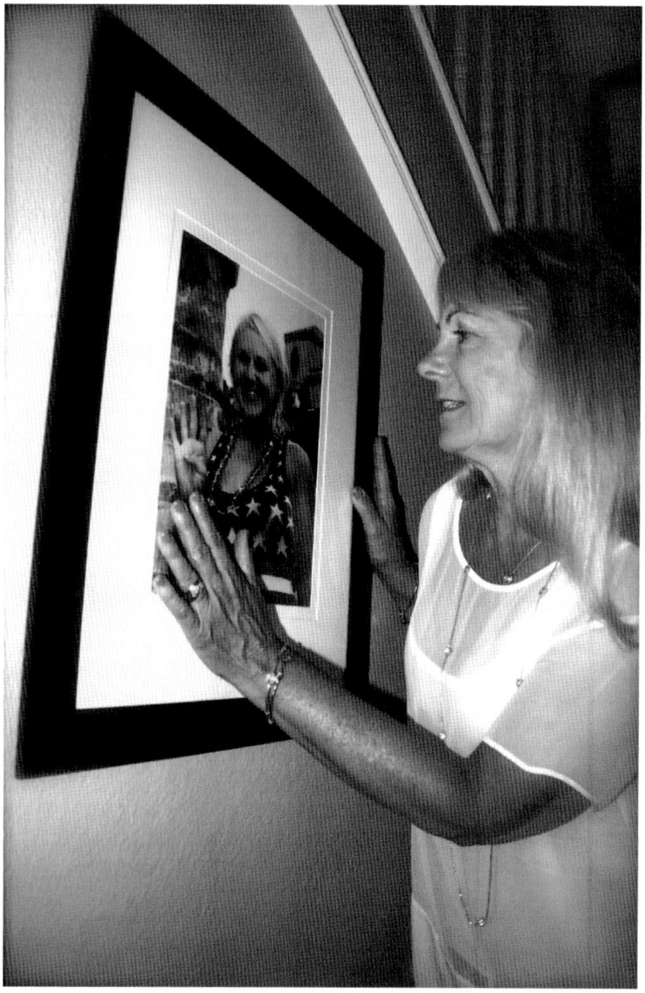

Kelly Blue

Kelly Blue Moorehouse was killed in 2013 on Goldenwest Street when a drunk driver, Tadashi Mizutani, 69, of Huntington Beach, collided with the motorcycle she was riding on. Taylor Rolfson, her boyfriend of eight years, was driving the bike. His legs were broken in the crash. Mizutani received one year in jail. This tragedy affected many people in Huntington Beach. Kelly was an outgoing, spirited young woman with many friends. She worked for nine years at the Sugar Shack Café downtown, where she was a favorite of many customers. Both of her parents were longtime teachers at Huntington Beach High School. Her father, Bill, retired a couple of years ago, and Karen retired in 2014. Karen, shown here with a photograph of her daughter, speaks movingly of Kelly: "For 39 years I've had the privilege of teaching kids. As I retire, I want to focus on the positive. No sentence can change what happened to my daughter. But the last thing I want to do today is give in to despair and misery. I want to celebrate all of the family and friends that came to court wearing blue for Kelly. Her friends have become my friends." As she prepares for this next chapter of her life, Karen says she does not want people to feel anger or rage toward the driver who took her daughter's life. "Two families were destroyed here. Not just mine but his too. What can we do today? We can make real, substantial changes. I would love to see a turn signal at that intersection where the accident happened. I think we need to talk about how to prevent these accidents. I think there should be Breathalyzers in every bar and in every car. That's what we can do as a community. We can focus and work together to create positive change."

The Ice Family

The Fourth of July is one of the busiest times of the year at one of the oldest businesses in town. In fact, Brewster's Ice is the oldest establishment owned by the original proprietors. Despite the rush, Mike Costello took time to describe the operation in between hauling blocks of ice off a delivery truck. He has worked here for 22 years. Costello is married to Ellen Brewster, whose dad started this cool operation in 1945. In this high-tech, gadget-obsessed era, Brewster's Ice may be the most refreshingly low-tech spot in California. The funky old blue-and-white rectangular building that houses it began life as an Army-issue meat locker on the beach during World War II, storing food used to feed soldiers at the gun encampments. After the Brewsters took it over in the mid-1940s, the building was moved to its current location. Today, it holds a small office, lots of ice, and that is about it. Mike explains that, twice a week, the ice truck arrives with big blocks of freshly cut ice. For Fourth of July week, it might be twice that. Over the years, Brewster's Ice has evolved as best it can, and Mike is fully aware that many young people today are oblivious to the fact that, years ago, an iceman would deliver blocks of the frozen stuff to families and businesses. That man was Virgil Brewster, who carved a reputation as one of the hardest-working merchants the city has ever known. He lugged 100-pound blocks of ice on his back through town, looking at the cardboard hexagonal measuring signs folks posted in their windows. The arrows might point at 20, 50, or 100 pounds, indicating how much ice they wanted that day. He took ice to the old Golden Bear, the Surf Theater, and most restaurants. If folks wanted ice, they called Brewster's, plain and simple. Today, newer businesses do the same thing.

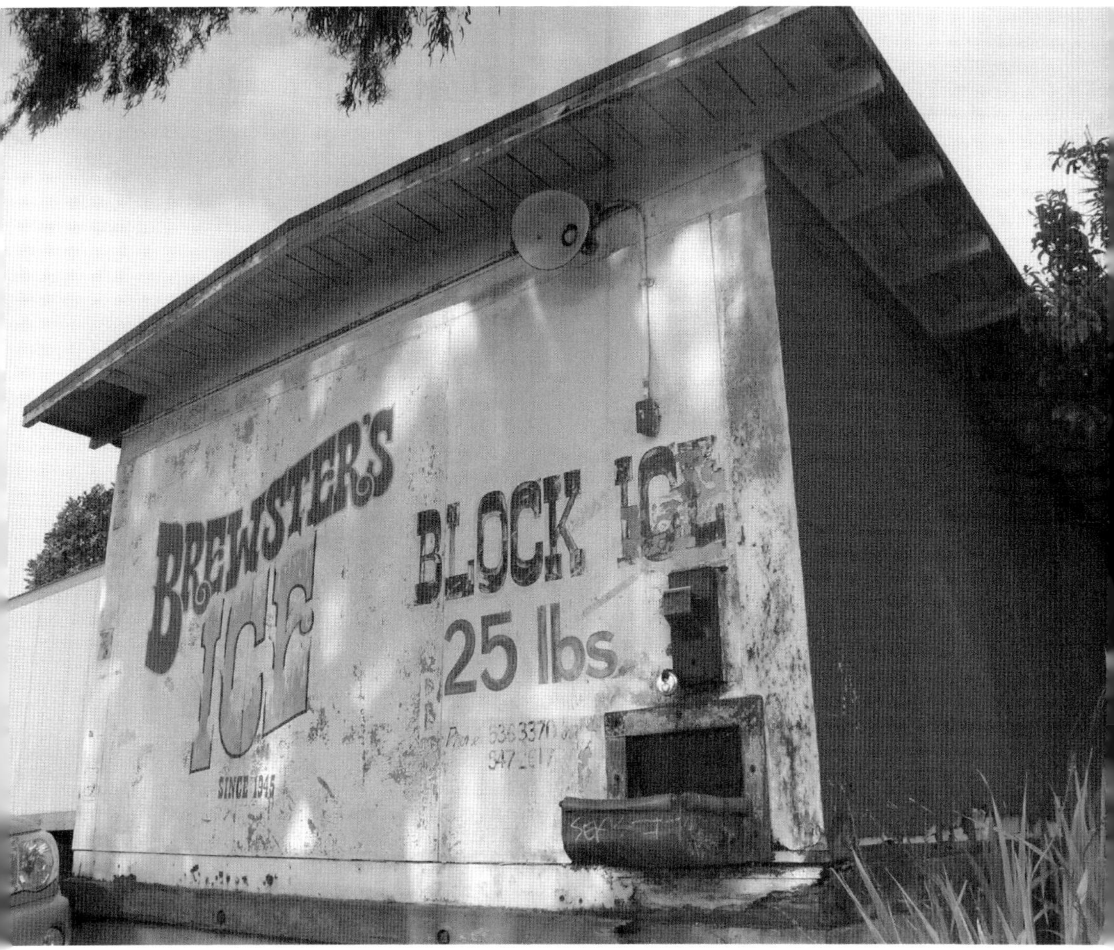

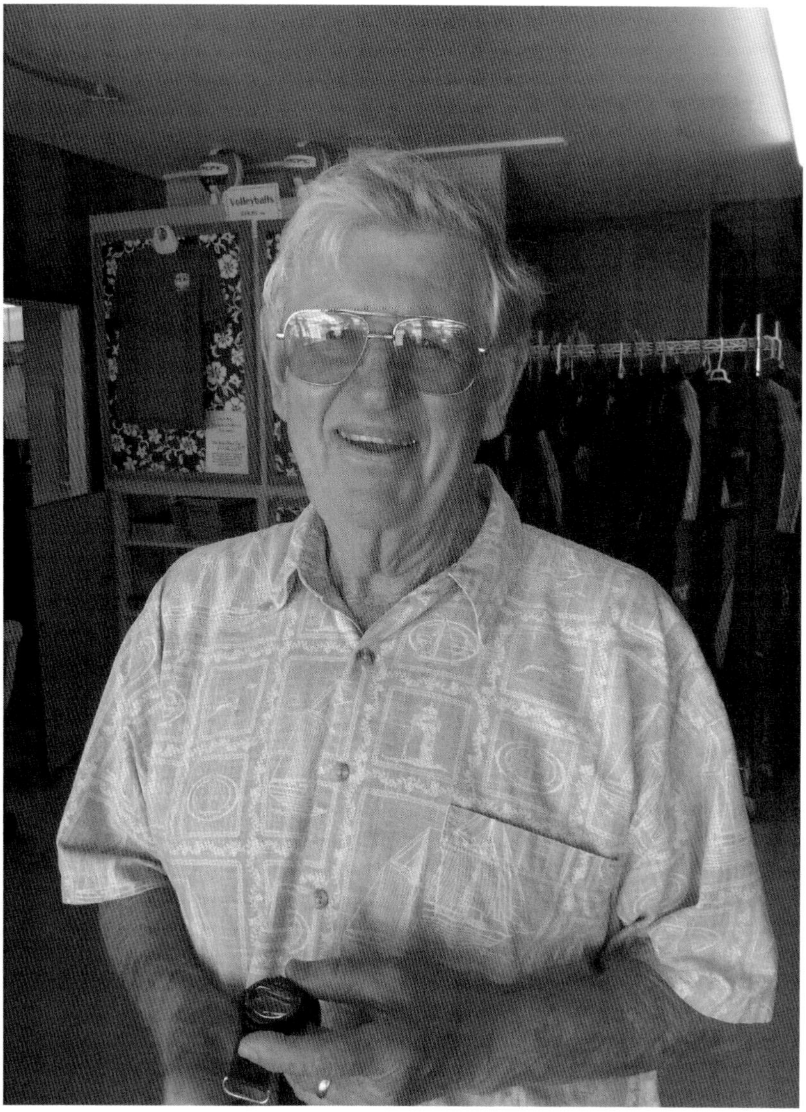

Cheese Strips (ABOVE AND OPPOSITE PAGE)
The Clapps represent four generations of beach concessions in Huntington Beach. It started when Dwight Clapp founded Dwight's more than 75 years ago—the original location is seen above opposite in the 1930s. After that, his son Jack founded a place called Jack's, and then his son David took over. As of this writing, Jack, who is in his late 70s, runs Dwight's, and David, who is in his 50s, runs Jack's. This amazing family legacy goes back to the 1930s, when Dwight petitioned the local city council, asking them if he could use part of an old lifeguard station to sell food. He was granted one door and one window to serve food, and that was all he needed. Dwight, along with his wife, Fae, sold the usual things people enjoyed at the beach, including hamburgers and french fries. But they also developed something that has become something of a local culinary legend: their famous cheese strips. The recipe is pretty basic: tortilla chips covered with a layer of fresh grated cheese and topped off with the Clapps' now-famous secret sauce. The sauce is a story in itself, a combination of chili powder, tomato, garlic, and vinegar. The flavorful concoction is now sold by the gallon at the concession stand. Dwight's is today the oldest active business in Huntington Beach, with over 80 years of service. It is a must-visit for locals and tourists alike.

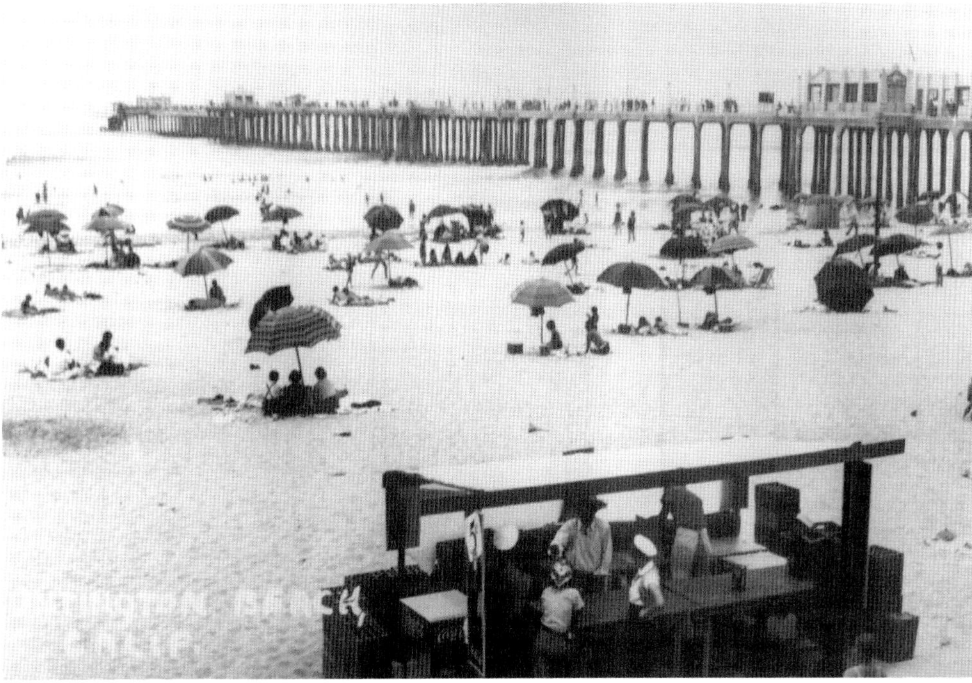

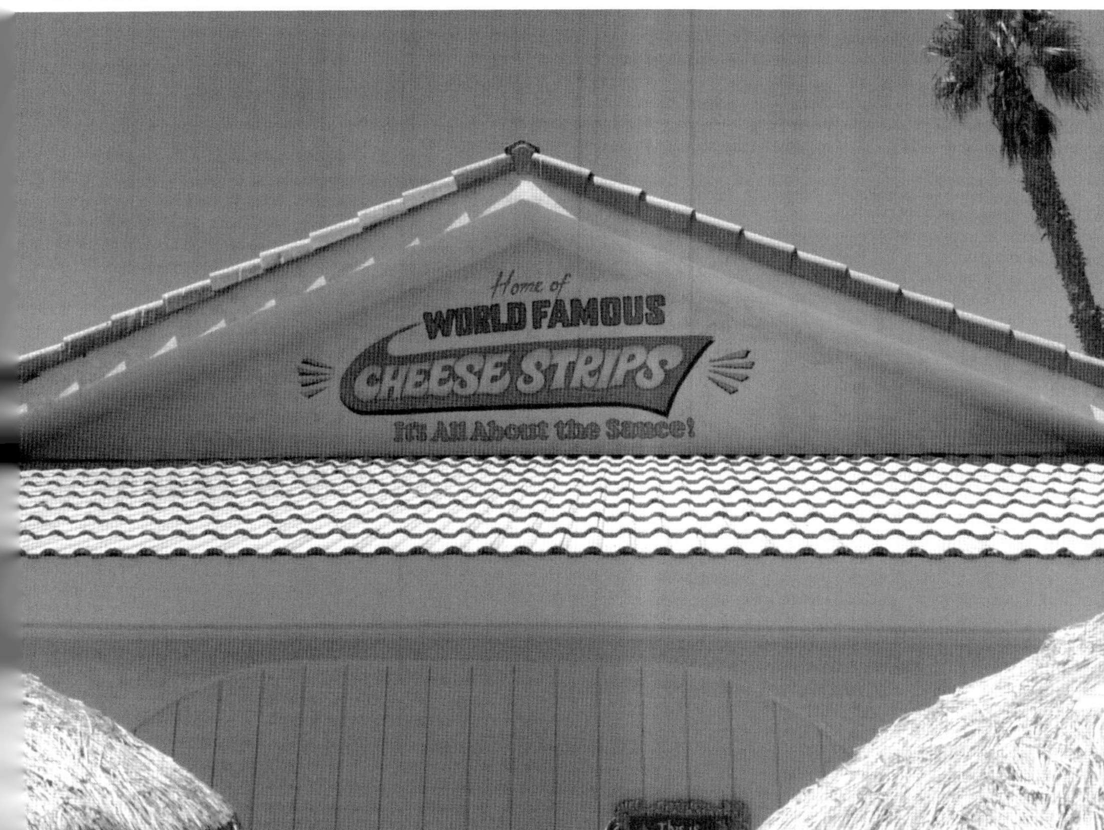
Home of
WORLD FAMOUS
CHEESE STRIPS
It's All About the Sauce!

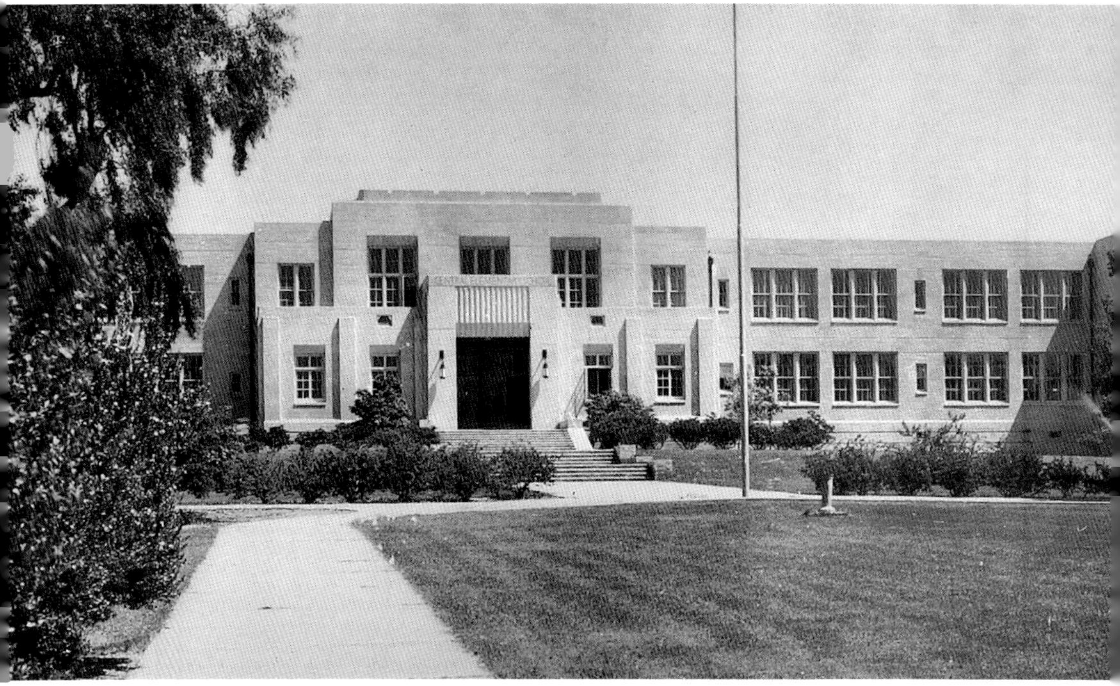

Haunted Middle School? (ABOVE AND OPPOSITE PAGE)
Harriet Ethel Dwyer's first teaching assignment in California was at Ocean View Elementary School in 1912. She taught there for nine years before moving to Central Elementary, then located on Orange Avenue between Fifth and Sixth Streets. It opened at a new facility, at Fourteenth Street and Palm Avenue, in 1923. By 1935, she had worked her way up to vice principal, and for the next 16 years, she greeted the students each morning on the second floor of the main building while seated at her desk at the end of the long hallway. But does Ethel Dwyer haunt the Huntington Beach middle school that today bears her name? For decades, rumors have persisted that the former student, librarian, and vice principal at Dwyer Middle School still makes her presence known, particularly in the boiler room, where few people ever set foot. Visiting the boiler room is like stepping back in time. In addition to the boilers and the 1930s metal rolling doors, there are the old, underground student locker rooms. It is no wonder the ghost stories persist. The cavernous, bunker-like basement still creaks and moans as students thunder down the hallways overhead. But haunted? The truth may never be known.

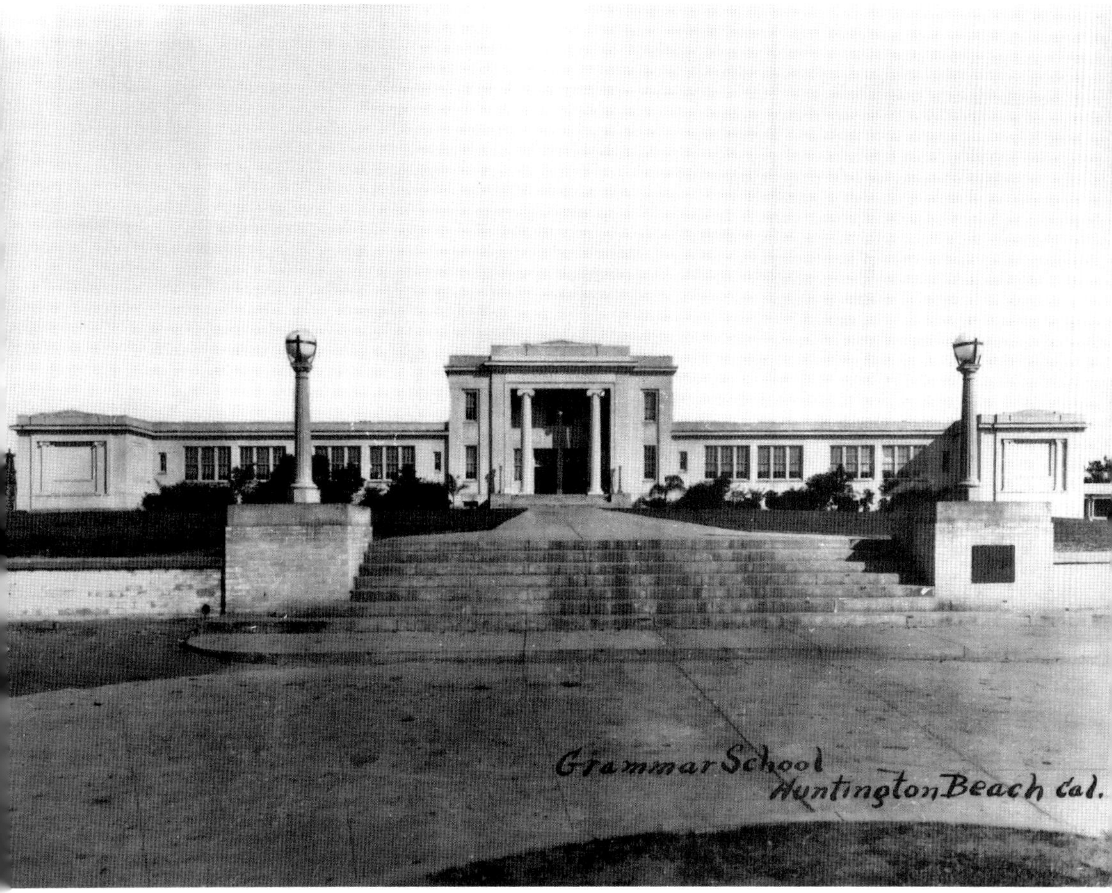
Grammar School
Huntington Beach Cal.

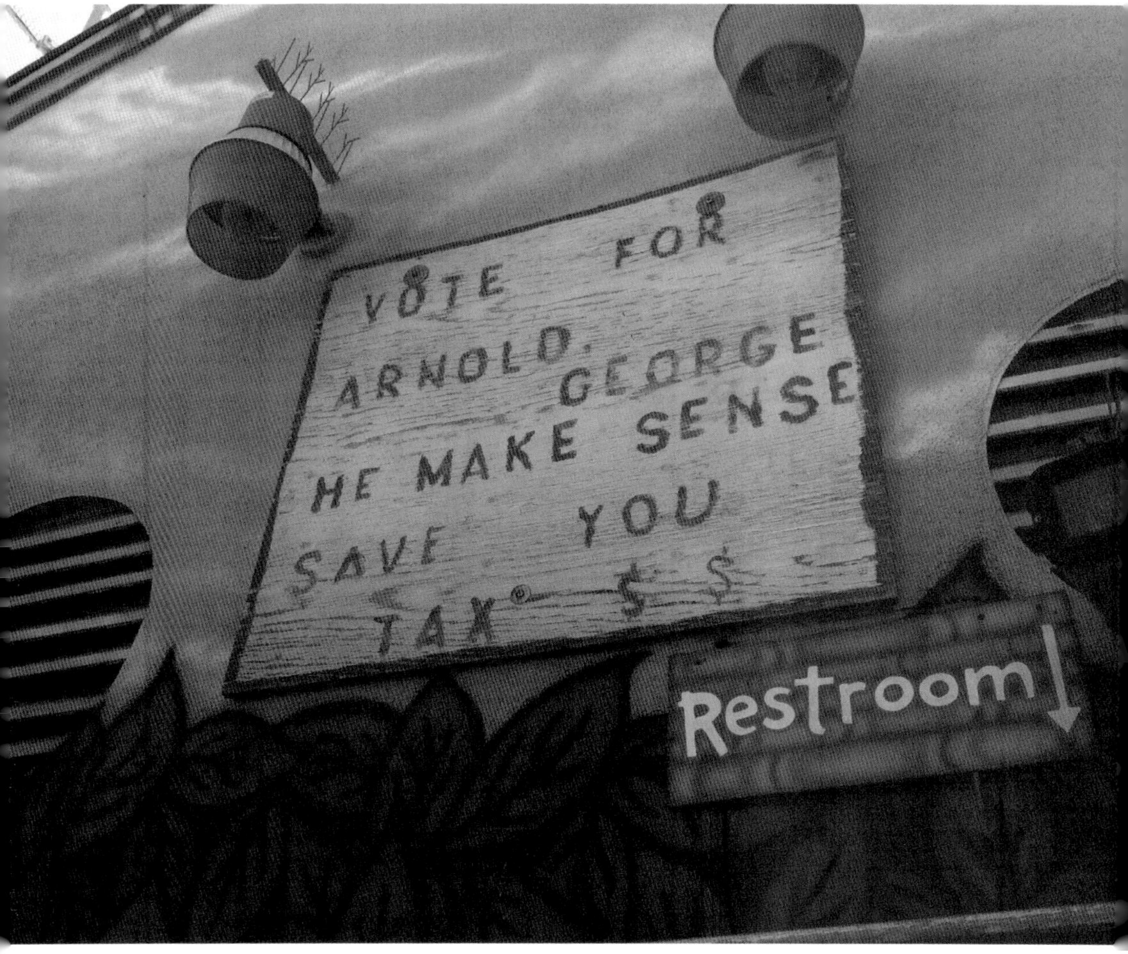

Man on the Inside

Many Huntington Beach locals remember George Arnold, a regular at the beach and at city hall. He may be best known as an ongoing but unsuccessful candidate for a seat on the city council, running six times from the 1960s to the early 1990s. Cranky, irascible, and a true local character, Arnold had a raspy voice, the result of having smoked many cigarettes. He was born in Huntington Beach in 1927. He never seemed to have a steady profession, but, through the years, people always saw him selling his campaign T-shirts from the back of his truck at the base of the Huntington Beach Pier. Over the years, Arnold had a variety of odd jobs, from working in the oil fields to doing handiwork. As time wore on, Arnold eventually got into trouble for selling his T-shirts near Main Street without a business license. However, the charges against him were typically dropped. After one arrest, he designed an entirely new campaign shirt, which featured him behind bars and the words "George Arnold for City Council. Your man on the inside." Arnold moved away in the late 1990s and passed away in Desert Hot Springs at age 73 in March 2002. A true local legend for his constant fight on behalf of the city he loved, Arnold is fondly remembered today by many, especially at the Sugar Shack Café on Main Street, where he often held court.

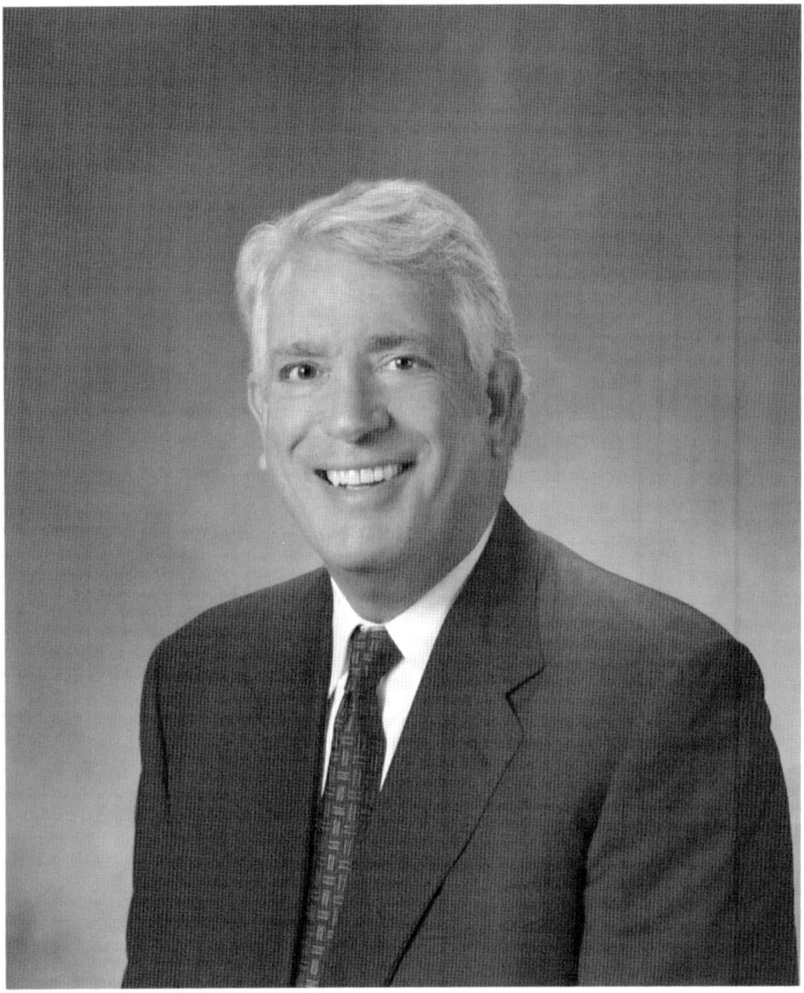

A True Civic Leader

A proud husband and grandfather, Steve Bone has also been a community leader for the better part of 30 years. As a partner with Robert Mayer and president of the Robert Mayer Corporation from 1986 to 2008, Bone developed Huntington Beach's Waterfront Beach Resort, a Hilton hotel, and the Hyatt Regency Resort and Spa. From 2008 until September 2013, Bone was the president of the Huntington Beach Marketing and Visitors Bureau. He was the founding chairman of the visitors bureau in 1989. During the last five years, Bone has been responsible for, or had a hand in, the following: a "Guide to a Sustainable Huntington Beach;" international marketing programs in England, Germany, and Australia; a new dining guide for the city; an innovative group meeting sales marketing program; a new film commission; national accreditation of the visitors bureau; a new information kiosk at the city's pier; funding for the newly refurbished International Surfing Museum; a new website; and a successful campaign to save the city's and state's beach bonfire rings. Bone's dedication to the Huntington Beach community can be seen in his past chairmanship of the chamber of commerce and his cochairmanship of the Huntington Beach Centennial Committee. Bone has been on the boards of many local organizations, including the Bolsa Chica Conservancy and the Huntington Beach Hospital. He has also been the recipient of the Orange County Visitors Association's Legacy Award, which honors a person whose accomplishments and dedication make Orange County the number-one destination in the country. An entire book could be written about Steve Bone. Hopefully, one day, it will be.

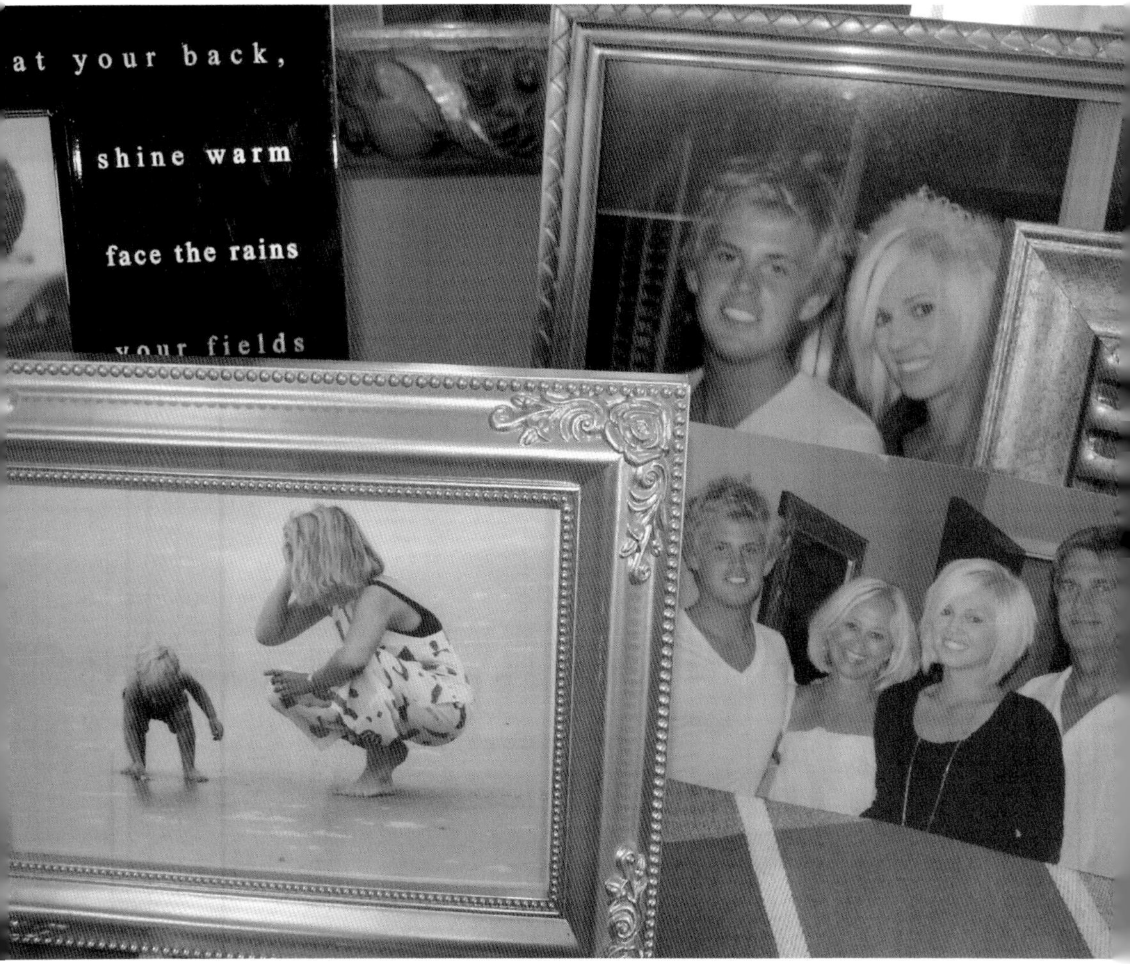

Dane Williams

Dane Williams, 23, was reported missing in late January 2008 while attending a trade show near the Gaslamp Quarter in San Diego. Several days later, his body was found in an alley in a downtrodden neighborhood about seven miles from where he was last seen. To try to describe the impact of this event on his mother, Valen, Dane's dad, Jim, and his sister, Hayley, not to mention Dane's many friends and associates, is simply not possible. It is beyond words. The young man was, by every account, good-natured, hard working, well raised, and a positive influence on virtually everyone he came in contact with. He came from a solid, tight-knit Huntington Beach family. At the time of his disappearance, he was probably trying to get back to his hotel room after a long day. But he did not make it. Hours later, his body, wrapped in an old blanket, was left in a nondescript alley. Valen described the tortured hours soon after learning Dane was missing, including the legal red tape to be maneuvered in order to review hotel security cameras, the reluctance of some store owners to let the family hang missing-person posters, then more red tape in trying to gain access to her son's cell phone records. "So many things should change to make it easier for people who go through this," she said. "We ask ourselves constantly, 'How much time was lost to red tape?' " Eventually, the murderer was arrested and convicted. He had drugged the young man before killing him. Each Christmas, the Williams family decorates a tree on Pacific Coast Highway in honor of Dane. They also hold a charity surfing event. And they keep his spirit alive.

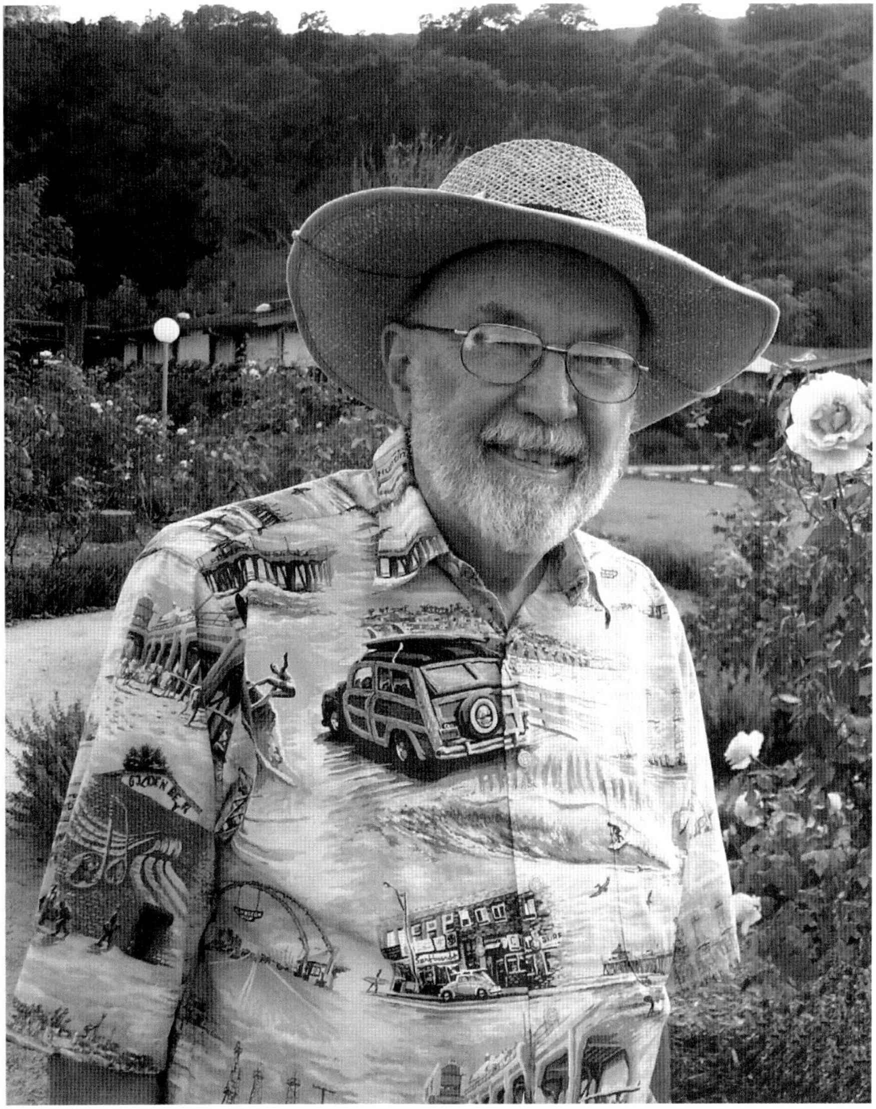

Scientist and Author

David Carlberg was born in Los Angeles, and he raised his fine family in Huntington Beach. Now a retired microbiologist, Carlberg has held positions in both the private sector and academia. He has been a chemist; an executive for a major pharmaceutical company; a research scientist in the aerospace industry, working in astrobiology and biological warfare detection; a consultant in the medical device, pharmaceutical, and motion picture industries; and a professor of microbiology at California State University, Long Beach. He is married to Margaret, and they have two sons, Howard and Marvin. David is the author of five books on microbial genetics, environmental and industrial microbiology, and local Huntington Beach history. Perhaps his most important book, at least for city residents, is *Bolsa Chica: Its History From Prehistoric Times to the Present, and What Citizen Involvement and Perseverance Can Achieve*. It focuses on the successful 30-year struggle by local citizens to prevent one of Southern California's last and largest coastal wetlands from being transformed into an immense marina/residential development. Residents are grateful to Carlberg and the many that have worked so hard to protect this precious piece of cultural and historic landscape.

Teacher in the Woods

In a glowing green meadow in the shadow of the El Capitan rock formation at Yosemite National Park, eighth-grade classmates from Mesa View Middle School gawk at a nearby hulking figure. At first, they are intimidated as he paws the air and gestures toward the sky. But they break into smiles when he approaches and playfully tousles a kid's hair. It is not a bear, but, rather, a lion of a man, science teacher Jay DuVal. For 35 years, he has led students on a pilgrimage to what he considers a sacred place—a hallowed teaching sanctuary.

The former Iowa farm boy has taught in Huntington Beach since 1963, starting at Mesa View in 1993. The five-day Yosemite trips started 35 years ago, when he and colleagues Rod Collier and Jim Henderson first dreamed up the idea (DuVal calls Collier the "father of the program"). One part General Patton, one part Pied Piper, DuVal trudges through the forests orating on Indian spirits, faith, hope, struggle, and sacrifice. He implores the kids to "open their hearts" so they may learn about themselves. He commands and demands discipline, respect, and decency. DuVal builds character by barking, teasing, complimenting, and comforting—sometimes all in one moment. He seems to know every leaf, bird, and bit of bark. He shares his stories, folklore, theories, and outrageous puns. And he exhibits ire if the kids stray from the course.

Photographer Ansel Adams said, "A true photograph need not be explained, nor can it be contained in words." When Adams once greeted DuVal and his students in a meadow, he could just as well have been describing this great (now retired) teacher.

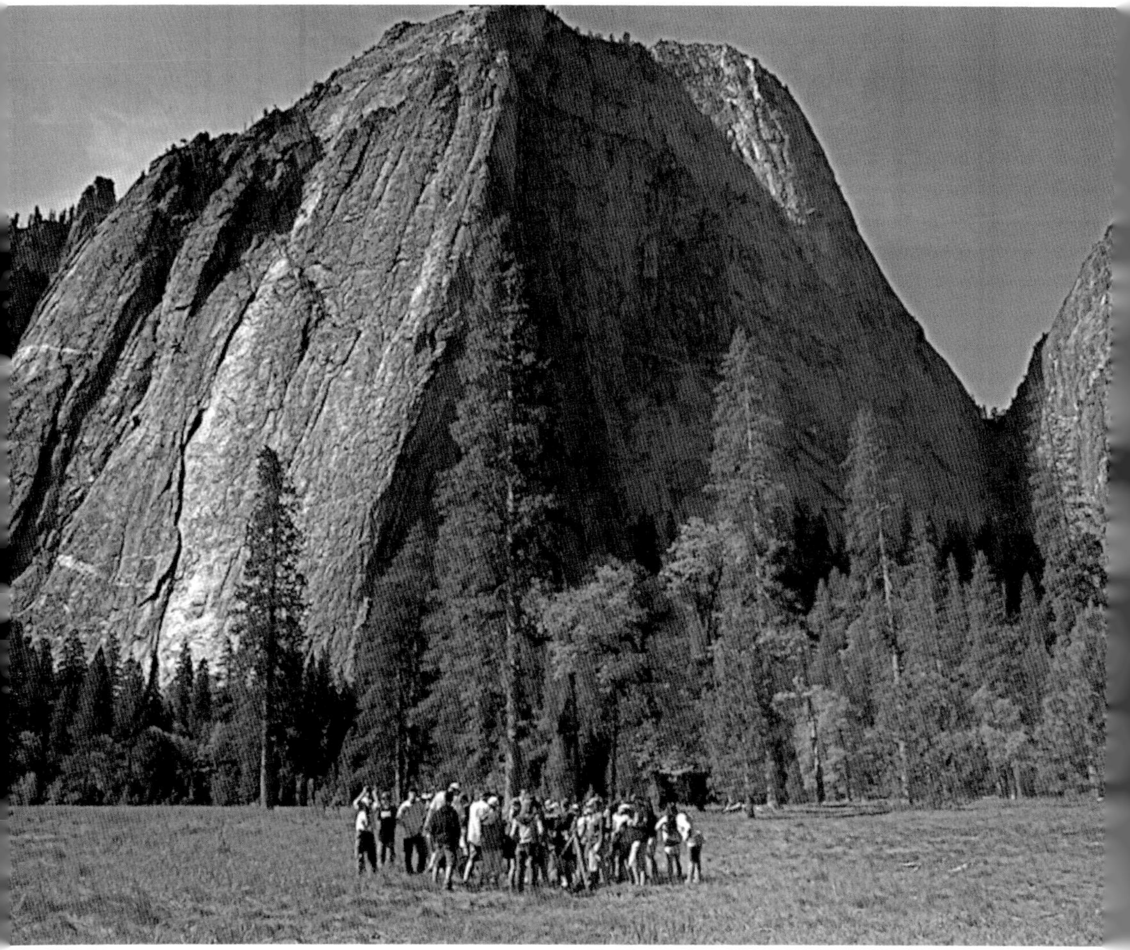

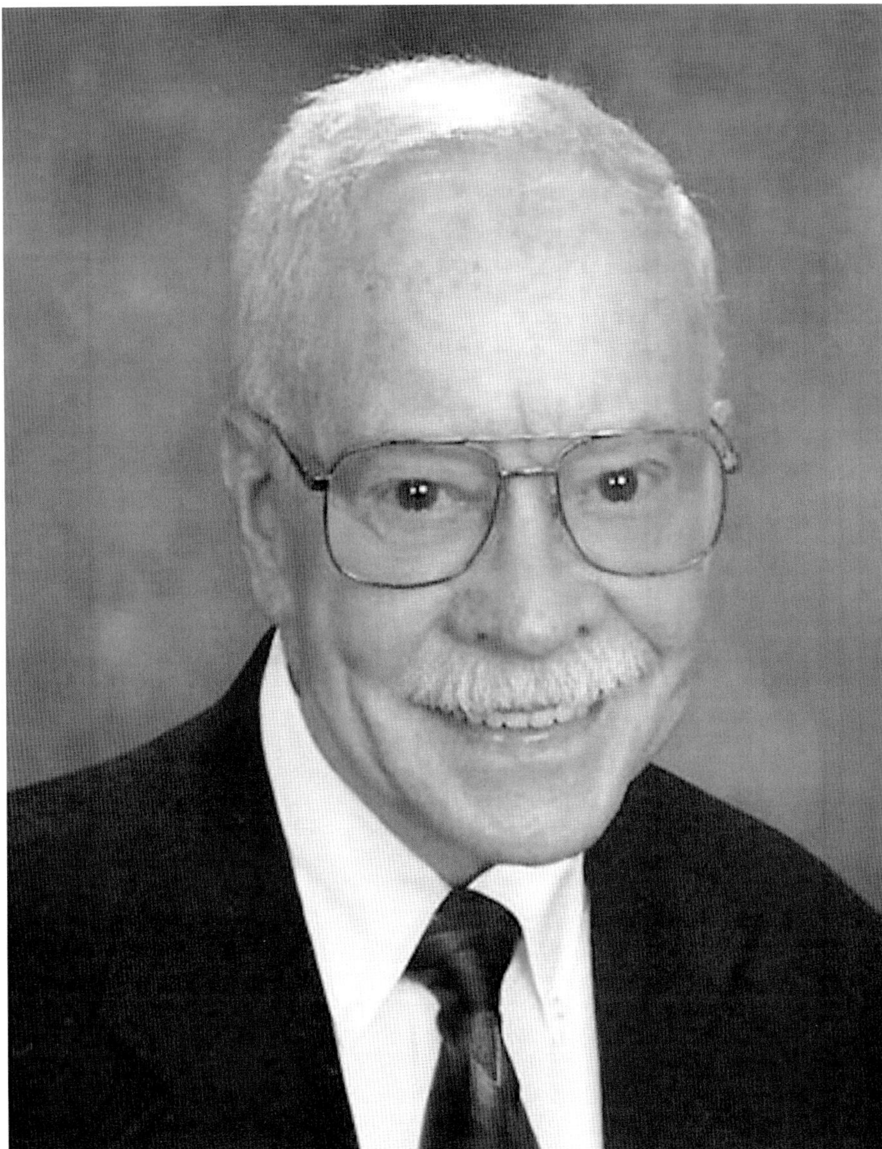

Parks Commissioner

Thomas J. Cooper was born and raised in Charleroi, Pennsylvania. He moved to Huntington Beach in 1962 and was an active member in his community for over 52 years. He earned his master's degree in chemistry at Iowa State University and his doctorate at the University of Southern California. Cooper worked at Cypress College for over 35 years as the dean of student activities, a counselor, and an articulation officer. He served on the Huntington Beach Parks and Recreation Commission for 19 years and played an integral part in the establishment of Huntington Beach Central Park. Tom Cooper hosted the local television program *Reflections of Former Mayors* for a number of years. He was also an active member in the CERT (Community Emergency Response Team) program for the city. Cooper was an active member of the Community of Christ Church, serving as a youth leader, financial officer, and pastor. He passed away in April 2014 at the age of 78 but left a lasting legacy in the city he loved. Today in Central Park, there is a bench dedicated in his honor.

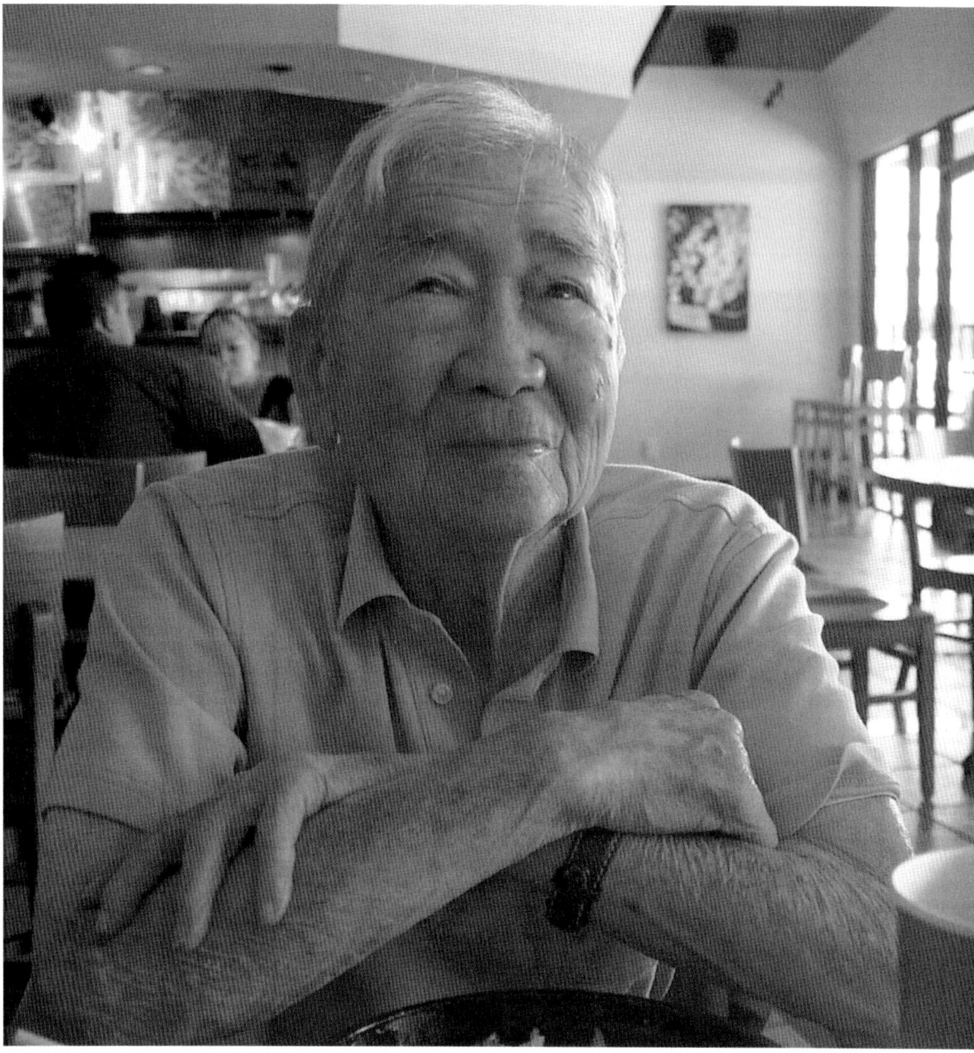

Man at the Airport (ABOVE AND OPPOSITE PAGE)

For years, he was one of the most familiar sights at the beloved Meadowlark Airport in Huntington Beach. Art Nerio's family was sent to an internment camp in Arkansas at the start of World War II. Nerio was a teenager then. When his family was released, they returned to the area. Thankfully, all of the property they owned in Orange County was still in their name. They lived where the Westminster Mall is located today. Before selling the property, Nerio recalls that one could see all the way up to the ocean from their backyard. His dad was keen on buying up lots of property back then, and this served the family well. His father bought the airport in 1947, and the Nerio family ran it through its most popular era, the 1960s through the late 1980s, when it closed. Many pilots can recall seeing Nerio pedal around on his bicycle, collecting the $3 landing fees from planes as they taxied to a stop. Now 89 years old, Nerio still lives near where the airport used to stand. His house is bursting with curios related to the airport, including civic plaques and scrapbooks filled with old newspaper clippings and yellowed photographs. The airport may be gone, but, thank goodness, Art Nerio is still here.

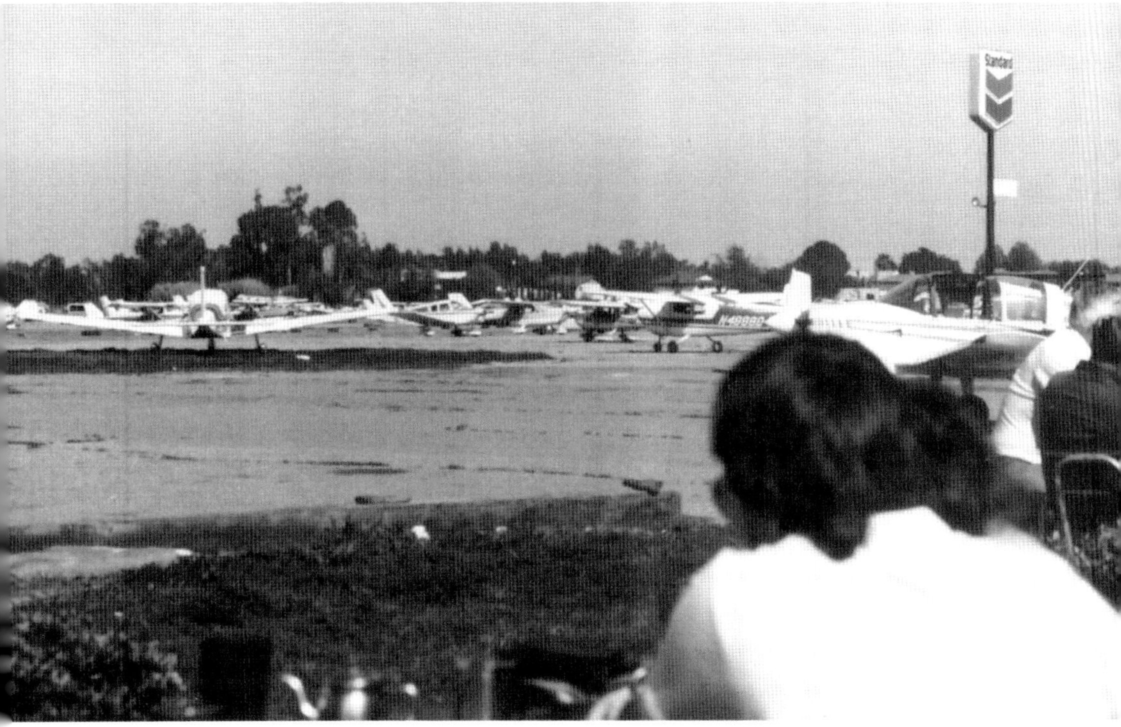
Standard

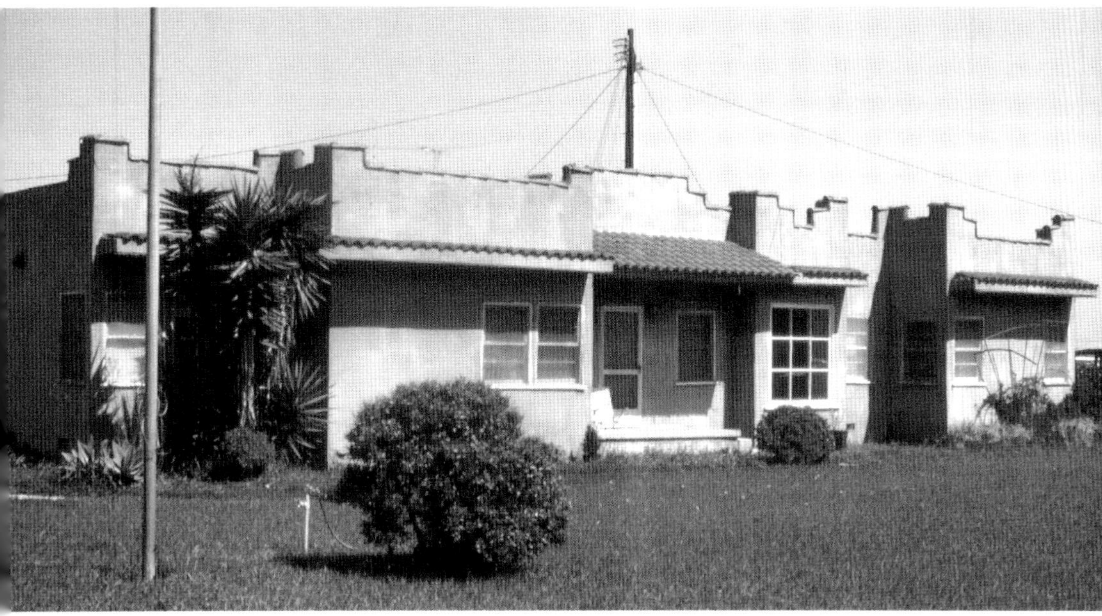

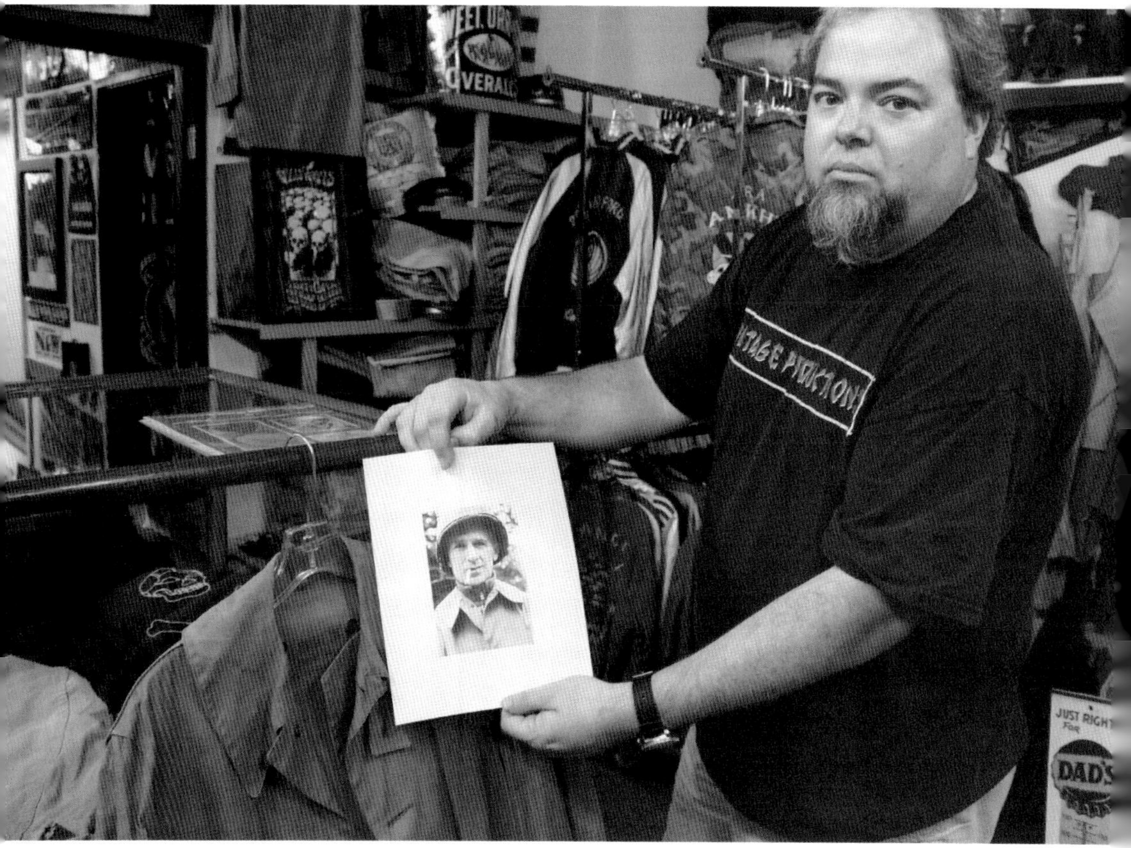

The Collector

In a nondescript warehouse tucked away off of Edinger Avenue near Gothard Street, there exists a mind-boggling, jaw-dropping, awe-inspiring collection. It is an emporium crammed with so many fascinating artifacts and dusty, musty, one-of-a-kind pieces of history, it is hard for the mind to process it all. Vintage Productions is the sort of place that makes visitors feel as if they have climbed into one of the great attics on the planet. Bob Chatt (pictured) is a renowned war-era memorabilia collector and dealer. With a self-effacing sense of the absurd, Chatt picks through his warehouse collection, calling out certain favorites. "See this flight jacket?" he asks, holding up a worn, frayed bomber jacket. "The patch on the pocket is from the Manhattan Project. The guy that wore this worked on the atom bomb. I'm a third-generation antiques seller. My grandfather dealt in guns, my dad dealt in Indian art. When I'd come home from school in the early 70s, the house would be full of just the most amazing Indian art known to man. If there was one rare blanket, there were a hundred of them. I have a photograph of me wearing Kit Carson's leather jacket." But traveling to hundreds of Indian and folk-art flea markets took its toll on the youngster. Within one room at Vintage Productions are clothing and artifacts from the Spanish-American War, World War I, World War II, the Vietnam War, and the Civil War, along with about 30,000 historic patches. In the next room are hundreds of vintage bowling shirts, baseball uniforms, and 1950s T-shirts. There are interesting hats, duffel bags, movie props, boots, peacoats, flags, matchbooks, figurines, belt buckles, signage, jewelry, and the oddest of all sorts of odds and ends. It is all right here in Huntington Beach.

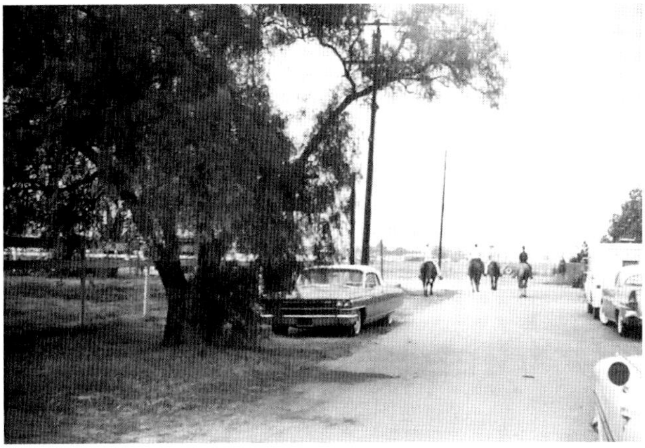

Old Pirate Lane

Every street in Huntington Beach should have a Gwendoline Runyard. She passed away in January 2014 at 90, a year after her husband, John. She left behind a remarkable trove of memories inspired by the neighborhood in which she lived. Runyard wrote in 1955: "During my search for a larger house for a larger family I found Old Pirate Lane. Here stood one old country type red farm house, with matching barn, positioned on this rarely traveled grass, gravel, and dirt track which led to the edge of a little airport. The house faced Graham Street." The farmhouse, built in 1906 by the Graham family (and no longer red), still stands, as does the house the Runyard family built in the 1950s and pretty much every other house originally constructed on this dead-end side street that does not run much beyond the length of a football field. But what a wonderful little world it represents—a peek back to simpler, uncluttered, more rugged Huntington Beach. Runyard, a poet and family archivist, published a small book some years ago named for her street. Her son John and this author once used it as a guide as they walked the neighborhood of his youth. The small paperback details the stories behind every house and each family that lived in those houses in both words and rare pictures.

John painted a fine picture, recalling the lush, thick, fragrant orange and eucalyptus groves, the agriculture, and the horses. His family, along with several others, kept horses in their backyards, along with goats, bunnies, chickens, pigs, and even a burro. In the early 1960s, John and his brothers would ride their horses to the beach, trotting down Warner Avenue before cutting across the wetlands and moseying to the sea. Can one imagine that today?

It is appropriate that this book close with one of Gwendoline Runyard's poems, "OPL—Then and Now":

Dapple shade of the pepper tree
Half-way down the Lane,
Was welcome in the Summer's sun.
'til sea winds blew cool again.
Eucalyptus trees in rows
Line some boundaries in the sun.
Grass struggles through the gravel path
In the road not yet begun.
Quiet. lies in the meadows here
Far from cities busy roar,
Enjoying the gift of the Spring rains,
Oblivious of what's in store.
For some day soon, the road will burst
With builders' trucks, and cranes,
Yet despite the construction's noise,
This rustic lane remains

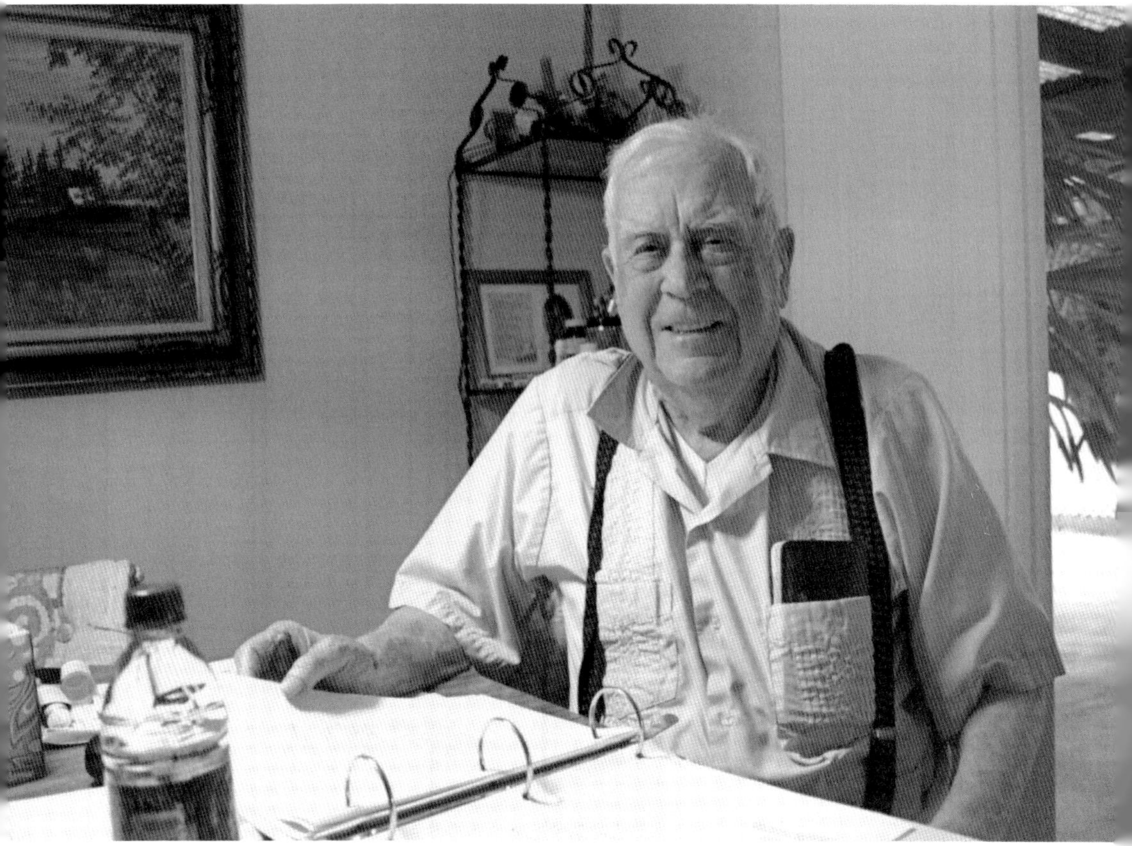

The Energy Man

"My father worked on the takeoff mechanism for the Wright brothers back in 1906. He was a blacksmith and when Wilbur Wright came into the shop he got right to it." Philip Hodgetts, 93, is at least as interesting as his dad. In his quiet kitchen, he explained that his father served in the honor guard for Pres. William Taft in addition to helping the famous flying brothers. This is even more interesting when one learns that Hodgetts himself was a design engineer on the space shuttle *Columbia*. The history of flight spans the lives of this father and son. Hodgetts is a man on a mission; a passionate alternative-energy advocate, he walks it like he talks it. He generates enough power through the solar panels on his roof that the energy company actually sends him a check every month for the amount he kicks back into the grid. All of his appliances are run this way, and he is so committed to teaching this country how to wean itself off of oil that he has written a book, *Solutions for Obtaining a Healthier Environment and a Wealthier Nation*. And sadly, the day the manuscript for the book you are reading right now was turned in, Philip Hodgetts passed away. So, in his honor, this book shall close with his story.

INDEX

LEGENDARY LOCALS

AN IMPRINT OF ARCADIA PUBLISHING

Find more books like this at
www.legendarylocals.com

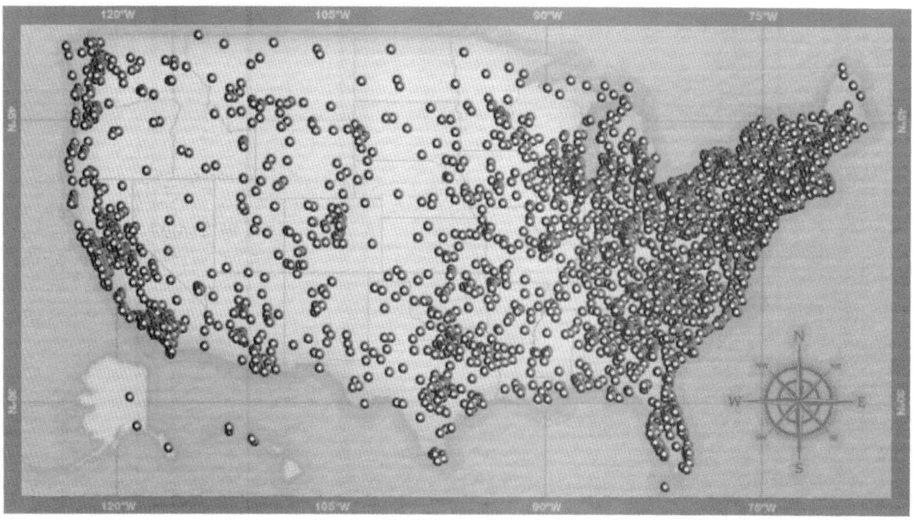

Discover more local and regional history books at
www.arcadiapublishing.com

Consistent with our mission to preserve history on a local level, this book was printed in South Carolina on American-made paper and manufactured entirely in the United States. Products carrying the accredited Forest Stewardship Council (FSC) label are printed on 100 percent FSC-certified paper.

MADE IN THE USA